THE HAND BEHIND THE INVISIBLE HAND

Dogmatic and Pragmatic Views
on Free Markets and the State
of Economic Theory

Karl Mittermaier

Foreword by
Isabella Mittermaier

BRISTOL
UNIVERSITY
PRESS

First published in Great Britain in 2020 by

Bristol University Press
University of Bristol
1-9 Old Park Hill
Bristol
BS2 8BB
UK
t: +44 (0)117 954 5940
e: bup-info@bristol.ac.uk

Details of international sales and distribution partners are available at bristoluniversitypress.co.uk

British Library Cataloguing in Publication Data
A catalogue record for this book is available from the British Library

ISBN 978-1-5292-0909-9 hardcover
ISBN 978-1-5292-0910-5 ePub
ISBN 978-1-5292-1579-3 OA PDF

Cover design: blu inc, Bristol
Front cover image: iStock/trendmakers

Bristol University Press uses environmentally responsible print partners

Printed in Great Britain by CPI Group (UK) Ltd, Croydon, CR0 4YY

For Isabella

Contents

Notes on Contributors

Karl Mittermaier (1938–2016) was a member of the Department of Economics at the University of the Witwatersrand from 1967 to 2001.

Daniel B. Klein is Professor of Economics and JIN Chair at the Mercatus Center at George Mason University, where he leads a programme in Adam Smith.

Rod O'Donnell is Professor of Economics in the Business School at the University of Technology Sydney, and a research affiliate in the History and Philosophy of Science Unit at Sydney University.

Christopher Torr is a member of the Department of Economics in the School of Economics and Finance at the University of the Witwatersrand.

Foreword

Isabella Mittermaier

This book was written by my husband, Karl Mittermaier, in one year. Every Sunday afternoon I would type, on a typewriter, what Karl had written on a foolscap pad the previous week. Karl would not set up the computer that he had purchased until he had completed this work. Karl submitted it as an occasional paper to Joubert Botha, who had asked him to present his views on the market order. Karl was then forty-eight years old and, as a result of the idiosyncrasies of academic life in South Africa at that time, had not yet obtained a PhD. Joubert Botha recommended that this occasional paper should be submitted as a doctoral thesis. Two highly respected North American economists agreed to examine the dissertation. The original title was 'The idea of market order in Adam Smith's "Wealth of Nations" and some of its later developments.' One of Karl's colleagues, Tony Marais, having heard Karl express his ideas, said, 'Oh, it is about the hand behind the invisible hand." Karl was awarded a PhD for this work and I thank Joubert Botha for his instigation more than thirty years ago.

Karl signed a contract for its publication, but he never proceeded therewith, not wanting to add a chapter on developments in Eastern Europe, where the transition was occurring from state-controlled economies to market economies. He thought that such an addition would have 'dated' the book. Karl was always the prescient type, as the reader can ascertain from the pages that follow.

Karl passed away in 2016. The head of the School of Economic and Business Sciences at Wits, Jannie Rossouw, encouraged the idea of publishing Karl's work, most of which Karl had never submitted for publication. I thank Jannie for getting the ball rolling. Michael Stettler and Christopher Torr took the manuscript from there, seeing it through to publication, and Giampaolo Garzarelli recommended Bristol University Press and made the necessary introductions. I thank them all for their contributions and their strong desire to see Karl's book published. I thank Paul Stevens of Bristol University Press for his belief in Karl's work, and Dan Klein, who volunteered to write a chapter on Karl as a classical liberal economist, which is included in the book. My thanks also go to Rod O'Donnell for writing an epilogue and to Christopher Torr for his chapter on the usefulness of the extended metaphor of 'the hand behind the invisible hand'. These three contributions help bridge the passage of time from when the book was written in 1986 to the present, showing that none of its novelty, import and force have been lost after 34 years.

Karl has written a synopsis of the aims of the book: 'To examine certain expositions of market order for the purpose of characterizing, formulating, and assessing what may be called dogmatic and pragmatic views on free markets: further to investigate the dual task economics has had of analysing ideals of economic order and the actual state of economic affairs, to consider the bearing of the distinction between free-market dogmatism and pragmatism on the present state of economic theory and to make proposals for bringing ideals of economic order more explicitly within the ambit of economic theory'.

Johannesburg
25 February 2020

Mittermaier's Modern Message

Christopher Torr

In an age of frequent upgrades and instant downloads, it is nice to come across a work of art containing an ancient line of thought and a modern message.

Karl Mittermaier submitted the final draft of his doctoral thesis to the University of the Witwatersrand in March 1987. A physical copy is housed in the Cullen Library of the university. He commenced the project over 30 years ago. Through the good offices of Bristol University Press, and in particular on account of the enthusiasm of the senior consulting editor, Paul Stevens, his thesis is at last being published, almost word for word, as it originally appeared. A special word of thanks is due to Giampaolo Garzarelli who provided the gateway to Bristol University Press.

The Hand Behind the Invisible Hand can be seen, in part, as an interpretation of Adam Smith's *An Inquiry into the Nature and Causes of the Wealth of Nations* (commonly referred to as *The Wealth of Nations*), which appeared in 1776.

Two hands appear in Mittermaier's title and at least one is invisible. Is the other also invisible? By considering answers to the question, Mittermaier classifies a stance on the free market as either dogmatic or pragmatic.

Within the first couple of pages of reading his work, it will become apparent that it is a work of great erudition. Nevertheless, the argument may at times come across as dense. It with this in mind that this chapter will attempt to identify the main message of the book, as reflected in the two hands of the title, one of which we immediately know to be invisible. Some preparatory remarks on the concept of an invisible hand are in order.

The concept of an invisible hand plays a vital role in Karl's analysis, even though Smith refers to it explicitly only twice in his two major books, once in *The Wealth of Nations*, and once in *The Theory of Moral Sentiments* (2005 [1759]). At a rough estimate, that means that Smith brings up the subject twice in the space of over 1,000 pages. The fact that a stone which the builder apparently neglects has become – at least in the hands of many of his interpreters – the head of the corner, is in itself an intriguing issue. This is not the place to address the issue – let us simply note that many scholars would agree with Otteson (2018, 48) when he remarks that the notion of the invisible hand 'is absolutely central to Smith's thought'. Others, however, are not convinced. The title of a book by as eminent a scholar as Warren Samuels (2011) – *Erasing the Invisible Hand: Essays on an Elusive and Misused Concept in Economics* – speaks for itself and indicates that, at the very least, opinion is divided on the matter. (See also Grampp (2000) and Kennedy (2009).)

While there is no generally agreed-upon definition of what is meant by an invisible hand, we shall employ the approach of Ullmann-Margalit (1978), which even Samuels (2011, 291) appears to regard as above reproach.

Suppose we identify an order in human affairs. On further investigation we ascertain that although the regularity came about as a result of human action, it did not arise from human deliberation. In other words, the order did not arise from human design. Under such conditions, says Ullmann-Margalit (1978, 263), we have an invisible hand explanation. She refers to this realm of things that results from human action but not from human design as a middle realm (1978, footnote 2) and cites Hayek (1966 and 1960) as her source. An example that comes most readily to the fore as an invisible hand explanation is the one associated with the creation of money (Ullmann-Margalit 1978, 264) or the emergence of language.

Ullmann-Margalit's approach accordingly relies on Hayek's identification of this middle realm to develop Smith's invisible hand argument. Hayek notes that if we confine our arguments to the natural and artificial realms confusion is bound to ensure: '… one would describe a social institution as "natural" because it had never been deliberately designed, while another would describe the same institution as "artificial" because it resulted from human action' (Hayek 1967, 130). Hayek is thus informing us that the framework of our analysis should include institutions that are 'The results of Human Action but not of Human Design'. Here Hayek (1967) is drawing attention to the work of another Adam, namely Adam Ferguson (1767, 90). (See Hayek 1967, 96; Langlois 1986, 241–7; Ullmann-Margalit 1997, 182.)

Immediately after introducing the concept of *spontaneous order*, Hayek (1967, 98–9) refers to Smith's notion of *an invisible hand* and the reader may not unreasonably be led to believe that Hayek prefers to use the more positive-sounding term *spontaneous order* than the more mystical-sounding *invisible hand*. Others, however, prefer to use another term. 'I prefer the term "unintended order" to the more familiar "spontaneous order" because the former conveys that the system of order was not anyone's intentional design without suggesting, as "spontaneous" might, that there is no way to account for the creation of the system' (Otteson 2002, 6; see also Otteson 2007, 21).

We have a means of identifying what an invisible hand is all about without necessarily using the terms *invisible* or *visible*. And should we find it more convenient to do so, we can associate an *invisible hand* argument with either a *spontaneous* (Hayek) or an *unintended* (Otteson) order.

Although Hayek generally gets the credit for introducing, or at least popularizing the notion of spontaneous order, Jacobs (1997–1998, 2000) argues that Michael Polanyi was employing the term prior to Hayek. (See Bladel 2005 for an opposing view.)

We have, therefore, Hayek's (1966, 1967) notion of spontaneous order being employed by Ullmann-Margalit (1978, 1997) in order to provide an invisible hand explanation along the lines of Smith (2007 [1776]). Let us call this the Hayek-Ullman-Margalit-Smith or HUMS approach. Although we shall not pursue the matter further, Ullmann-Margalit also points out that we can distinguish further between the *emergence* (or regularity) of such an order and the *endurance* of such an order.

Now let us make use of a modern-day example, namely the *Burning Man* event. It is an annual event lasting about a week and takes place in the Nevada Desert towards the end of August.

The following descriptions are taken from two articles in the *New York Times*, written by Laura Holson (30 August 2018) and Emily Badger (5 September 2019). We want to provide just enough detail of the proceedings in order to illustrate the point behind Mittermaier's question as to whether the hand behind the invisible hand is also invisible.

Burning Man had its origins in 1986 when the founder Larry Harvey set a wooden statue of a man alight on a beach in the San Francisco area. The procedure continued on an annual basis and the numbers attending grew. After four years, however, the concerns of fire authorities brought an end to the San Francisco part of the adventure. *Burning Man* subsequently moved to Black Rock Desert in Nevada.

The event lasts for a week – from the end of August to early September. A few days before it commences, the flat Black Rock Desert site is deserted. Recent attendance has been in the vicinity of 70,000. Coffee and ice can be bought on site, but purchases are otherwise not allowed. Those attending are expected to bring their own provisions and to provide gifts to others.

Picture it this way. Around the middle of August, in any particular year, the allotted site is empty. Within a couple of weeks thousands of people converge on what emerges as an instant city. A week or so later they are all gone.

One might expect conditions to be somewhat chaotic when some 70,000 people descend suddenly on an isolated part of a desert. In the early years of the exercise there were indeed signs that chaos could ensue, there being virtually no rules and no central authority. Guns and fireworks were in evidence. A fatal motorcycle accident occurred in 1996 and in another vehicle incident three people were seriously injured. The year 1996 appears thus as some sort of watershed when a decision was made to bring explicit rules into the proceedings. Streets were laid out. Fire prevention procedures materialized in the form of fire extinguishers. Explicit rules were applied. That coffee and ice can be purchased amounts to a rule.

Tens of thousands of human beings are 'doing their own thing' in the desert. In other words, human action is very much to the fore. If we leave out the organizers of the event, those who have descended on the scene are not intentionally at work designing any sort of order. Some sort of order has nevertheless emerged in this flat piece of earth, even if those flocking there had no thought of design in mind. In terms of the HUMS approach, we have the tinges of an invisible hand explanation.

Let us now apply Mittermaier's reasoning to the event. He would have us ask: Is the hand behind the invisible hand also invisible? Or is it visible?

In terms of the narrative sketched above, the answer would seem to be that from 1996 onwards, the hand behind the invisible hand was a visible one. The organizers had come to the conclusion that if the event were not to descend into chaos, some sort of planning or design was called for. Rules of behaviour were laid down, plans were made, streets were laid out.

The economist Paul Romer, who attended the 2019 event, was quoted in the *New York Times* as saying:

> I picture an economist showing up at Burning Man and saying: 'Oh, look! This is the miracle of the invisible hand. All of this stuff happens by self-interest, and it just magically appears.' And there's this huge amount of planning that actually is what's required beneath it to make the order emerge.

We can see, therefore, in Romer's remarks the idea behind Mittermaier's argument that we must investigate whether or not there is a hand behind the invisible hand and whether or not that hand is invisible. The order in the proceedings arises from the institutional setup – the set of rules enforced. Thousands of individuals are pursuing their own satisfactions, and institutional structures (street layout, fire prevention measures, moral codes etc) ensure that some sort of order prevails. The hand behind the invisible hand is visible.

An invisible hand process is at work if individual human action results in some sort of order that was not specifically designed by those individuals pursuing their own ends. But in order for the invisible hand to operate well, institutions need to be in place for otherwise the human action at play could result in chaos (no order at all). Mittermaier asks the question, does the institutional setup also emerge spontaneously via an invisible hand? As the 1996 watershed year specification makes clear, a decision was made to insist on arrangements deliberated upon with an idea to prevent chaos. In other words, in terms of Mittermaier's argument we could say that in the case of the *Burning Man* event, the hand behind the invisible hand is visible, which amounts to a pragmatic rather than a dogmatic stance on the emergence of the institutions involved.

We have thus an example in which the hand behind the invisible hand is visible, in line, therefore, with Mittermaier's presentation of the pragmatic view in which humans deliberately decide upon an institutional framework within which an invisible hand is supposed to operate. If, however, we were to argue that the appropriate institutional arrangements would have emerged of their own accord, in other words without such planning, Mittermaier would classify us among the ranks of the dogmatic free marketeers. For a dogmatic free marketeer, the hand behind the invisible hand is also invisible.

In his opening remarks Mittermaier (this volume, 25–6) has this to say on the type of issues involved:

> But since institutions vary so much from place to place and from period to period and since not all of them are conducive to an advantageous market order, the question arises how an arrangement of society which constitutes an invisible hand may come into being. Does it simply arise in the absence of meddling hands or does someone have to turn his hand to the task? Do the rules of conduct which give rise to a spontaneous order also arise spontaneously if governments do not interfere – or do governments or others have to bring them about deliberately? *There is a hand behind the invisible hand. The question is: Is that hand invisible too?*

It is intriguing to note that Mittermaier would have been putting the finishing touches to his thesis in the same year in which *Burning Man* originated (1986). He would have had no knowledge that a few friends had assembled in the San Francisco area around that time to set alight to a wooden man.

By way of an exercise let us imagine that the *Burning Man* event evolved differently. In particular, let us suppose that there was virtually no deliberate attempt to stamp any sort of design or planning on the proceedings. We saw that 1996 was the watershed year when procedures were adopted such as laying out the streets and introducing various forms of legislation such as forbidding firearms. Suppose that in spite of the lack of planning, some sort of order emerged, with the type of institutions necessary for the invisible hand to operate (at a different level) also emerging spontaneously, in other words, without being planned. If such were the case, Mittermaier's analysis would point to the fact that the hand behind the invisible hand can also be invisible. We would then have a situation in which the institutions necessary to ensure the persistence of *Burning Man* also emerged without design.

The HUMS invisible hand explanation does not explicitly indicate that the events under consideration involve markets and hence price signals. What the HUMS explanation does is to establish that the order emerging is one that has not been designed by the individuals involved in the action. In economics, the HUMS type of argument is typically applied to markets but as Hayek has indicated, it can also be applied to the emergence of language. Polanyi (1962) has employed it to indicate that individuals engaged in research can stumble upon an order that constitutes no part of their research agenda.

If the hand behind the invisible hand is also invisible, we have invisible hands operating, as it were, at different levels. The signalling device at the individual dimension (let's call this Level 1) will be the price system. If the hand behind the invisible hand is also invisible, then the HUMS explanation amounts to the claim that the system is spontaneously generating the kind of institutions (Level 2) necessary for the invisible hand to operate at Level 1. We would then have spontaneous or unintended order at Level 1 and Level 2.

Another way of examining the concept of an invisible hand is via Heilbroner's book entitled *The Making of Economic Society*, which is in its 13th edition and now appears under the authorship of Heilbroner and Milberg (2012).

Heilbroner and Milberg (2012, 6) make use of a three-part framework when they examine the making of an economic society, but they make no direct reference to Hayek's notion of a spontaneous order. Hayek is mentioned only once (in a footnote on page 63). When the authors refer on various occasions to notions of spontaneity, it is never with reference to the work of Hayek. They point out that there are three ways in which humankind has seen fit to solve production and distribution problems, and they call them *tradition, command* and the *market.*

Tradition is perhaps best understood by an example – see also Torr (1980). Writing of his experiences, Stefánsson (1913, 62–3 and 362) observes:

> I know now that the Eskimo [sic] temperament is that they never expect to find anything in any place where no one has found it before, so far as they know, and never having heard of any one catching fish in Smith Bay they had felt sure there would not be any. … This was a valuable lesson to me, and has on many occasions encouraged me to go into districts that the Eskimo considered devoid of game and in which I have usually found plenty.
>
> … Although Natkusiak reported that all winter the people of the Baillie Islands had caught no foxes, still he agreed with Ilavinirk in thinking that surely there must be plenty of them out at Cape Parry. Temperamentally it seems difficult for Eskimo to imagine that things can change. Natkusiak had found plenty of foxes on Cape Parry in January, 1910, and he could not see why there should not be plenty also in January, 1912.

The economic problem can also be dealt with by means of a command system in which plans are made by a central agency.

That there is such a term as market socialism should be enough to convince us that the command, tradition and market classifications should not be regarded as watertight compartments. A predominantly market-orientated economy can also contain elements of tradition. For example, the eldest son of a farmer might traditionally be the obvious person to take over the farm when the father retires.

To many, the concept of an invisible hand simply represents free market forces and the implication often drawn is that if only the government would stay out of the picture, an invisible hand (representing unfettered market forces) would ensure an optimal use of resources. Mittermaier's achievement is to show that invisible hand arguments do not exist *in vacuo.* He identifies invisible hand procedures at the level of individuals (Level 1), where the regularities being generated involve price signals. For the operation of an invisible hand at Level 1, institutions are required at Level 2. The analysis thus shifts to whether or not the institutions of Level 2 will emerge spontaneously or not. The argument that the requisite institutions will emerge spontaneously amounts to the dogmatic free market argument. The belief that the emergence of such institutions requires deliberate planning amounts to the pragmatic free market argument. The requisite institutions have to be created by the visible hand of government.

In Chapter 5, Mittermaier presents Murray Rothbard as a dogmatic free marketeer, whereas Henry Simons and Walter Eucken appear as pragmatic free marketeers. Mittermaier also spends some time considering Hayek's position. The younger Hayek comes across as someone with pragmatic views, whereas Hayek the elder appears to exhibit dogmatic free market views. In a somewhat different context, Hutchison (1981, Chapter 7) also distinguishes between what he terms Hayek I (views presented up to 1936) and Hayek II (views presented after 1937). Hutchison suggests that Hayek I is following the (a priori) philosophical views of Mises, whereas Hayek II comes across as a somebody enamoured of the views of Popper.

When any system is replaced by another, as in the Soviet system of command being replaced by a market system, the new system will require appropriate institutions. The dogmatic view on free markets is the view that such institutions would emerge of their own accord without the visible hand of government.

By the nature of their profession, economists are often asked to expound on the appropriate role of government. In my opinion *The Hand Behind the Invisible Hand* provides us with a platform to discuss one of the most pressing issues of our time, namely the appropriate role of government. At various times during the academic year, economics lecturers will be asked to expand on the role of government. It is not unusual then to find subsequent discussion being divided into two main groups, those of a free market persuasion arguing that the government is doing too much, while those of an interventionist persuasion argue that it is doing too little. I have found that raising the issue of whether or not the hand behind the invisible hand is also invisible gets an appreciative hearing from those who emerge as pragmatists and from those who emerge as dogmatists.

Mittermaier's approach provides a framework for discussion, whether one is in academia or not, or whether one leans to the left or to the right. Both the academic and non-academic community can at last benefit from having access to *The Hand Behind the Invisible Hand*.

Bristol University Press has done the economics fraternity a great favour by upgrading an essay written 33 years ago by a master craftsman. Through their foresight we are now able not only to hold a copy of a modern classic in our visible hands; we can also, should we wish to do so, download this modern classic instantaneously via some sort of invisible network.

I recall that I once approached Karl with a view to discussing a book by Paul Davidson on modern monetary theory, called *Money and the Real*

World. He asked to see the book, which I had brought with me. I recall him examining the title page. He shook his head – more with sadness than with surprise. 'Strange title,' he remarked with a sigh. Karl was wondering what kind of a thing Davidson's unreal world might be.

Don't think for one minute that if you were to discuss a modern economic issue with Karl that you could avoid a discussion of the economic lineage of your question. Don't imagine either that he would merely refer you to Marshall, whose *Principles of Economics* was published in 1890, or that he would stop at Ricardo's writings in the 1820s or even Adam Smith's *Wealth of Nations* of 1776. No – eventually you would find yourself being taken back to the Greeks, and in particular to Aristotle.

To get some idea of the pace of the proceedings, let us in closing trace the history behind Mittermaier (2018).

In the early 1990s Karl was encouraged by an ex-colleague, Jochen Runde, to submit a manuscript to the *Cambridge Journal of Economics*. I am not suggesting, of course, that Jochen stamped and sealed the envelope in which it was submitted, but I very much doubt that the manuscript would ever have reached Cambridge had it not been for Jochen's prompting.

From what I recall it was accepted for publication. The editor simply wanted Karl to correct or add a couple of technical things. Once again, I don't know if Karl couldn't be bothered by such technicalities or whether he didn't think it important enough. In any event, he never sent the final version back for publication. In these days of publish or perish, it is hard to imagine such a decision.

Karl is the only economist I ever met who put a manuscript into his bottom drawer after it had been accepted for publication. After Karl passed away, one of his colleagues, Michael Stettler, who had also been a student of his, played a key role in preparing the manuscript anew. With the kind permission of Isabella Mittermaier, and with the encouragement of Jochen, it was resubmitted.

The title of the paper originally presented to the *Cambridge Journal of Economics* in 1992 and subsequently published more than a quarter of a century later says it all. It is entitled 'Menger's Aristotelianism'.

I left the University of the Witwatersrand (Wits) in the late 1980s. In 2015, after having spent a decade away from academia, I returned to Wits in a part-time capacity and started wondering what had become of Karl's thesis and whether or not it had been published. So I started searching for *The Hand Behind the Invisible Hand* on the Internet and to my surprise I immediately came across publication details. It had been published, according to one of the references I found, on 1 November 1996. I even came across an ISBN number, and was informed that it consisted of 288 pages. I recall even seeing a revised edition specified, even though it had not been published. As we all know, fake news has been around for quite a while.

Karl is the only economist I have met who wrote an invisible book about the invisible hand. It is the only book that I have heard of that went into a revised edition without ever being published in the first instance.

Acknowledgements

I should like to thank Rod O'Donnell and Dan Klein for their most useful comments and suggestions on an earlier draft.

References

Bladel, J.P. (2005) *The Quarterly Journal of Austrian Economics* 8:4, 15–30.

Ferguson, A. (1767 [1782]) *An Essay on the History of Civil Society*, 5th edition. London: T. Cadell, published online by Liberty Fund, Inc.

Grampp, W.D. (2000) 'What Did Smith Mean by the Invisible Hand?' *Journal of Political Economy* 108:3, 441–65.

Hayek, F.A. (1960) *The Constitution of Liberty*. Chicago: Gateway Edition.

———. (1966) 'Lecture on a Master Mind: Dr. Bernard Mandeville'. *Proceedings of the British Academy* 52 (23 March 1966) 125–41.

———. (1967) 'The Results of Human Action but not of Human Design' in *Studies in Philosophy, Politics and Economics*. London: Routledge and Kegan Paul, 96–105.

Heilbroner, R.L. and Milberg, W. (2012) *The Making of Economic Society*, 13th edition. New York: Pearson.

Hutchison, T.W. (1981) The Politics and Philosophy of Economics. Marxians, Keynesians and Austrians. Oxford: Blackwell.

Jacobs, S. (1997–1998) 'Michael Polanyi and Spontaneous Order, 1941–51'. *Tradition and Discovery* 24:2, 111–27.

———. (1999) 'Michael Polanyi's Theory of Spontaneous Orders'. *Review of Austrian Economics* 11, 111–27.

———. (2000) 'Spontaneous Order: Michael Polanyi and Friedrich Hayek'. *Critical Review of International Social and Political Philosophy* 3:4, 49–67.

Kennedy, G. (2009) 'Adam Smith and the Invisible Hand: From Metaphor to Myth'. *Econ Journal Watch* 6:2, 239–63.

Langlois, R.N. (1986) 'Rationality, Institutions, and Explanation' in *Economics as a Process*. Edited by R.N. Langlois. Cambridge University Press, 1985.

Mittermaier, K.H.M. (2018) 'Menger's Aristotelianism'. *Cambridge Journal of Economics* 42:2, 577–94.

Otteson, J.R. (2002) *Adam Smith's Marketplace of Life*. Cambridge University Press.

———. (2007) 'Unintended Order Explanations in Adam Smith and the Scottish Enlightenment' in *Liberalism, Conservatism, and Hayek's Idea of Spontaneous Order*, pp 21–41. Edited by Louis Hunt and Peter McNamara. Basingstoke: Palgrave Macmillan.

———. (2018) *The Essential Adam Smith*. Canada: The Fraser Institute.

Polanyi, M. (1962) 'The Republic of Science'. *Minerva* I:1, 54–73.

Samuels, W.J. (2011) *Erasing the Invisible Hand: Essays on an Elusive and Misused Concept in Economics*. New York: Cambridge University Press.

Smith, A. (2005 [1759]) *The Theory of Moral Sentiments*. Edited by S.M. Soares. MetaLibri Digital Library.

———. (2007 [1776]) *An Inquiry into the Nature and Causes of the Wealth of Nations*. Edited by S.M. Soares. MetaLibri Digital Library.

Stefánsson, V. (1913) *My Life with the Eskimo*. London: Macmillan.

Torr, C.S.W. (1980) 'The Role of Information in Economic Analysis'. *South African Journal of Economics* 48:2, 115–31.

Ullmann-Margalit, E. (1978) 'Invisible-hand Explanations'. *Synthese* 39, 263–91.

———. (1997) 'The Invisible Hand and the Cunning of Reason'. *Social Research* 64:2, 181–98.

References to websites

Badger, E. 2019 https://www.nytimes.com/2019/09/05/upshot/paul-romer-burning-man-nobel-economist.html?utm_source=digg

Holson, L. 2018 https://www.nytimes.com/2018/08/30/style/burning-man-sex-tech.html?action=click&module=Intentional&pgtype=Article&action=click&module=RelatedLinks&pgtype=Article

THE HAND BEHIND
THE INVISIBLE HAND

*Dogmatic and Pragmatic Views on Free
Markets and the State of Economic Theory*

KARL MITTERMAIER

Contents

Author's Note

The expression 'the invisible hand' has become an aphorism for the idea that the pursuit of private ends by a large number of independent individuals leads to a situation that is beneficial to all. It is not clear whether, according to proponents of this idea, the beneficial guidance of the invisible hand may always be relied upon, provided only that man does not try to impose his own ideas upon the overall state of economic affairs, or whether the conditions under which the invisible hand may be expected to operate have to be created deliberately. In the first case, the social and economic institutions of a market economy would be in a sense natural whereas in the second case they would be an ideal of a possible form of social and economic organization, which, like and together with other ideals, one has to strive to realize as best one can. Though the matter may be seen in the end to be more complex, it may be said that those who incline to the former view hold a dogmatic and those who incline to the latter a pragmatic view on free markets. One of the aims of the study is to examine certain free-market arguments and to characterize, formulate and assess the dogmatic and pragmatic positions respectively. A working criterion for making the distinction is discussed in Chapter 2 and the two views are assessed in some detail in Chapter 9. The pragmatic position is particularly difficult to articulate, but it is suggested that it is the more tenable of the two.

In Chapters 3 and 4 an attempt is made to show that Adam Smith in his mature years most probably inclined to the pragmatic view. In Chapter 5 some modern developments of the idea of market order are discussed. The libertarian position as expounded by Rothbard and an analogy mentioned by Friedman are considered, but most of the section is devoted to a review of Hayek's position on these matters. Eucken's wholly pragmatic analysis, among others, provides a contrast but is discussed only after the pragmatic view has been characterized in Chapter 9. These developments of the idea of market order are relevant to the conduct of free-market policy, which would differ substantially according to whether dogmatic or pragmatic presuppositions served as its basis. However, the distinction between free-market dogmatism and pragmatism also has a bearing on the state of economic theory. The development of economic theory has been closely associated with the idea of market order and the concept of equilibrium was at least in part inspired by it. Moreover, economic theory was for a long time, at least in some cases, closely tied to the advocacy of free markets while at the same time it tried to describe the workings of actual economies. A further aim of the study is to examine the dual task economics has had of analysing ideals of economic order and the actual state of economic affairs. If there really were a natural economic order or certain exchange relations always established themselves spontaneously where individuals minded their own business, there would be that for equilibrium theory to describe. But a problem arises for economic theory if the premise underlying the pragmatic view of the nature of market order is correct. A theory of market order is then an analysis of an ideal which may serve as a guiding conception for policy but cannot be regarded as a description of the working of actual economies.

Chapter 6 is the first of three chapters concerned with the relation between the idea of market order and equilibrium theory. It tries to find the central idea of Smith's vision of an ideal market order and to show that it remains only as a remote presupposition in equilibrium theory. Chapter 7 deals with some aspects of the evolution of equilibrium theory. Considerations of commutative justice entered Smith's analysis of natural prices while allocative efficiency subject to commutative justice became the basis of Walras's general equilibrium theory. Walras apparently regarded the theory as a guiding conception for an *idéal social*, though he also appeared to think that it could describe actual markets. Pareto, however, saw general equilibrium as an analogue of celestial mechanics and tried to make of it a hypothesis for predicting actual economic events. This contrast in their understanding of the rationale of the theory is ascribed to their very different philosophical presuppositions. Chapter 8 argues that there is still some ambiguity as to whether general equilibrium theory is a guiding conception, an attenuated description of the 'market mechanism' or a hypothesis for making predictions. A sketch is given of an apparent drift of ideas (in which institutional considerations receded into the background) from ideals of market order to positive economics formulated in accordance with a certain perception of science.

The long Chapter 10 addresses itself to this perception of science and the obstacles it apparently puts in the way of treating ideals as objects of economic inquiry and makes certain proposals for bringing ideals into economic analysis. The idea of *Wertfreiheit* and the influence of the methods of physical science on mainstream economic theory are considered. Some linguistic analysis is used in the critique of the language of determination adopted by neoclassical economics under this influence. The 'subjectivism' of the Austrian school is considered, its extension to identifiable ideals (as one kind of institution) is proposed and the conceptual clarifications that would be needed are commented upon. A study of economic disorder is also proposed, in which problems such as unemployment and inflation would be analysed in terms of the incongruity of widely held ideals. For the purpose of illustrating the principles involved, an example of such a study is outlined. The final subsection deals with two rival premises on which, or rather on one or the other of which, thought about economic and social order appears to be based.

1.

Introduction

Adam Smith's *Wealth of Nations* is generally held to have set out the principles of a free-market economy. Its influence, especially during the 19th century, was perhaps strongest as a policy guide, as the authoritative work cited by those who wanted to make market order the dominant form of order in society. There is, however, some doubt about how Adam Smith conceived the nature of market order. He is commonly thought to have been an exponent of quite dogmatic laissez-faire views, according to which a natural order, a grand harmony of interests, establishes itself of its own accord under the guidance of the invisible hand, provided *only* that governments do not meddle in economic affairs. The text of the *Wealth of Nations* does not really bear out this interpretation, at least not unequivocally (Chapters 3 and 4 of the present study). Smith may also be interpreted to have held more pragmatic views. According to this interpretation, he had a vision of an ideal market order which, like other ideals, and together with other ideals, one has to strive to realize as far as one can. The distinction between these views on the nature of market order is the underlying theme of this study. It is reflected in rather different prescriptions for establishing market order. In one case little more is required than that interfering politicians and bureaucrats be rapped over the knuckles. Far more is required in the other case. The conditions under which the guidance of the invisible hand may be relied upon have to be deliberately created.

The division between rather more dogmatic and rather more pragmatic views on free markets has come to the fore in the development of the idea of market order since Smith's time. On the rather dogmatic side, one may consider the ideas of those who call themselves libertarians and, among the somewhat less dogmatic, the idea of spontaneous social and economic order, especially as it appears in Hayek's complex analysis of cultural evolution (Chapter 5). Among more pragmatic views on free markets there are at present, for example, those of James Buchanan and, some years ago, those of Walter Eucken, whose pragmatic analysis greatly influenced the economic policy of West Germany. The characterization of the pragmatic point of view is rather difficult and will be undertaken in the final assessment of the distinction between freemarket dogmatism and pragmatism (Chapter 9). Greater clarity on this issue would seem to be of some significance to the conduct of economic policy, especially in view of the recent revival of interest in market principles.

However, the influence of the *Wealth of Nations* was not confined to the area of economic policy. More than any other work, it helped to establish economics as a distinct discipline, and equilibrium, now the central concept of economic theory, was at least partly derived from the idea of market order. Smith freely intermingled his prescriptions of market order with the descriptions of institutions which make up the bulk of the book. Economic theory likewise was for long associated, at least in many cases, with the advocacy of free markets while at the same time it tried to describe the workings of actual economies. The history of economics seems to be as much the history of a prescription as the history of a description. This leads to a peculiar dilemma. One would not normally have occasion to advocate the adoption of market order if it were already there to be described. In other words, it is unlikely that the same theory of market order may be both a prescription for attaining an ideal order and the description of the actual state of economic affairs.

It is therefore of interest to ask how far equilibrium theory has really taken over Smith's analysis of market order (Chapter 6) and how an apparent prescription has been adapted to become, in many cases, an intended description (Chapters 7 and 8). It will be argued that some ambiguity remains. In this context the dogmatic–pragmatic divide again becomes important. Equilibrium theory may be regarded, analogously to the idea of natural order, as a model or analytical expression of the market mechanism in the natural state, with the prescriptive element removed in deference to the *Wertfreiheit* of science. But if the premise underlying the pragmatic view is correct, namely that market order is an ideal, equilibrium theory must be regarded as the analysis of an ideal of efficiency. Questions then arise about how ideals may be treated in a spirit of scientific disinterestedness, what the role of theory may be in this context and how the actual state of economic affairs may then be analysed. (Chapter 10.) These are the issues with which this study is concerned.

2.

Free-Market Dogmatism
and Pragmatism

After more than a century of retreat, the invisible hand seems to be showing signs of gaining ground again. Who would have believed 20 years ago that politicians who made a return to free-market principles and a reduction in the scope of government their main election plank would find favour among voters in a number of countries? Who would have believed that after some years in office, during which the success of their programme was not unequivocal, these politicians could still afford to persist in their intentions? The revival may be short-lived but for the time being at least there is evidence of a reawakening of free-market sentiment and of a readiness to 'leave to the market' what was previously left to the discretion of politicians and bureaucrats.

However, as may be expected of any broad-based movement, the present support for the free-market economy is probably based on a far-from-uniform set of principles. The supporters of free markets are able, as it were, to form a coalition because there is sufficient common ground. They share a dislike of discretionary powers entrusted to politicians and government administrators. They share a firm belief that free markets bring about a better coordination of economic activity than deliberate planning and detailed direction can achieve, that free markets leave individuals with strong incentives to act in a way that indirectly promotes an efficient use of resources and that free markets allow individuals a high degree of personal freedom, which is in itself worth striving for. But these shared tenets probably conceal a diversity of views on what kind of order market order is and correspondingly of how to gain the benefits of free enterprise in free markets.

The last chapter of Milton and Rose Friedman's *Free to Choose* is entitled 'The Tide is Turning'.[1] The tide of public opinion is turning against big government. They are probably correct that the present interest in freemarket principles is due to resentment of high taxes and of the deadening effects, especially on enterprise, of government control of the economy. Such resentment encourages a simple prescription for establishing and maintaining market order. Keep the government out of economic affairs and all else will fall into place of its own accord without the deliberate efforts of anyone. However, this is one area where a divergence of attitudes may become apparent. To some it may seem that the simple anti-government prescription is all that is needed while to others it may not be at all obvious that market order, as they understand it, would then come about automatically. We shall say that the former have a rather *dogmatic* view and the latter a more *pragmatic* view of the nature of market order.[2]

The pragmatist is likely to have misgivings, for instance, about the rather indulgent attitude of the dogmatist towards monopolies not enforced by government. 'The only viable definition of monopoly is a grant of privilege from the government.'[3] The pragmatist may appreciate how difficult it is to put one's finger on monopolistic practices and yet not be persuaded that they do not exist or are entirely benign. Clearly, to those who may be practising the elusive art, pronouncements to the effect that what they are doing cannot be done must be sweet music indeed. The pragmatist may have a picture of present conditions which is rather different from the dogmatist's. We live in an age not only of big government, but also of big business; an age of economic oligarchy in which the government is only one of the oligarchs, albeit the chief one. Oligarchs are apt to come into conflict and to make use of whatever weapons are at hand. The dogmatic view on government and the indulgent attitudes towards all forms of combination not sanctioned by government are likely to prove handy weapons for the lesser oligarchs, however unwittingly they use them. In confrontations reminiscent of those between king and regional potentates or between king and Church in an earlier era, the spokesmen for free markets may find themselves in the role of retainers or of a babbling priestly caste. They may always have to be mindful not to lose the support of the powerful. It is a position that the pragmatist may not relish at all.

The dogmatist, however, is likely to argue that governments make their edicts mandatory so that the law-abiding citizen has no choice but to obey and recalcitrants may be forced into compliance. The individual has no means of escape. It is otherwise with free associations and their rules, for the individual remains free to choose. Whatever he does, he does voluntarily and that is all that is needed for the operation of the invisible hand. The pragmatist, on the other hand, may feel that the difference between coercion by government and by others is merely a matter of degree. To him it may seem that organized government is simply the most convenient channel through which all manner of people force their will on others and, if a government does not oblige, they will find other ways of doing so. If every trade union, professional and trade association, agricultural union, cartel and so on is to be regarded as engaging in governing activity in so far as it tries to coerce, then the dogmatic anti-intervention prescription is by no means as simple as it may at first appear to be.

We need a criterion for telling the difference between these points of view. They do not differ, it should be noted, on the question of whether an order in economic affairs establishes itself spontaneously within the framework of a market economy. They differ on the question whether the framework itself establishes itself spontaneously in a society in which everyone minds his own business and leaves the overall order to look after itself. Let us derive a criterion accordingly.

Markets do not operate *in vacuo*. They constitute one part of the institutions of society. These institutions include not only a legal system laying down rights and obligations pertaining to property, contract and so on, but also a multiplicity of conventions, of established ways of doing things. We are educated on the basis of conventional standards, we seek conventional vocations or at least specialized tasks, we make use of conventional means of communication between buyers and sellers (markets), we use money, we may borrow under certain conditions, we adapt ourselves to conventional forms of government and so on into the minutest details of our lives. These institutions, as much as the physical environment, are the conditions and constraints under which we have to live. They set de facto 'rules of conduct', as Hayek calls them.

Social and economic institutions, as we well know, are not the same everywhere nor have they been the same for all time. What is more important, however, is that they are not always those which are thought to be necessary for markets to work to the best advantage, since otherwise it would never be necessary to press the case for free markets. (Forms of government are of course institutions.) There are certain arrangements of society, perhaps an indefinite number of possible ones, under which markets flourish. Because such an arrangement of society constrains individuals, it can take the place of the very visible hand of an authority with discretionary powers and constitute an invisible hand by which men and women are led to promote the general well-being though it was no part of their intentions to do so.

But since institutions vary so much from place to place and from period to period and since not all of them are conducive to an advantageous market order, the question arises how an arrangement of society which constitutes an invisible hand may come into being. Does it simply arise in the absence of meddling hands or does someone have to turn his hand to the task? Do the rules of conduct which give rise to a spontaneous order also arise spontaneously if governments do not interfere – or do governments or others have to bring them about deliberately? *There is a hand behind the invisible hand. The question is: Is that hand invisible too?*

The answer to this question, we shall say, shows whether a dogmatic or pragmatic view is held. 'Yes' indicates a dogmatic point of view. 'No' indicates a pragmatic point of view. This will be our criterion, at least until we consider the question in greater detail in Chapter 9.

There can be no doubt that the appeal of dogmatic views is strong because they seem to provide a firmer foundation than pragmatic ones. In both cases there is the obstacle that it is not really in anyone's private interest to promote free markets. Adam Smith was pessimistic about this:

> To expect, indeed, that the freedom of trade should ever be entirely restored in Great Britain, is as absurd as to expect that an Oceana or Utopia should ever be established in it. Not only the prejudices of the public, but what is much more unconquerable, the private interests of many individuals, irresistibly oppose it.[4]

But in the case of the pragmatic position, there is the additional problem to which Hayek constantly draws attention, namely that institutions would somehow have to be constructed. In this regard, Adam Ferguson, a contemporary and acquaintance of Smith, wrote:

> Men, in general, are sufficiently disposed to occupy themselves in forming projects and schemes; but he who would scheme and project for others, will find an opponent in every person who is disposed to scheme for himself. Like the winds that come we know not whence, and blow whethersoever they list, the forms of society are derived from an obscure and distant origin; they arise, long before the date of philosophy, from the instincts, not from the speculations of men. The crowd of mankind are directed in their establishments and measures, by the circumstances in which they are placed; and seldom are turned from their way, to follow the plan of any single projector.[5]

However, there is no choice between free-market dogmatism and pragmatism. It is not a matter of preference or values, nor of convenience or expedience. The question is in principle a factual one. We shall now consider what Adam Smith's standpoint on this question appears to have been.

3.

Adam Smith's Free-Market Credentials

The modern reader who is conversant with the way the case for free markets is usually put will find much in the *Wealth of Nations* with which he is familiar. He is shown how in diverse situations market institutions lead to favourable outcomes, how popular ideas turn out on a more comprehensive view of society to be fallacies or cases of special pleading, and so on. However, he will also find many remarks which would be met with raised eyebrows in certain free-market circles today.

Adam Smith was in favour of interest rate ceilings set a little above the lowest market rate so that 'the capital of the country' would be kept out of the hands of 'prodigals and projectors' who were prepared to pay a higher rate for it but who were quite likely to 'waste and destroy it'.[6] Consumer credit (to 'prodigals') means consumption of capital. But why would lenders who burn their fingers on over-optimistic 'projectors' not learn their lesson? A similar idea may have been behind his strictures on gold and silver mining ventures. These were lotteries in which 'the prizes are few and the blanks many' so that capital is usually lost. But so great is 'the absurd confidence which almost all men have in their own good fortune' that 'too great a share' of capital is apt to go into such ventures 'of its own accord'.[7] Perhaps all this was just a bit of prudishness. But what of his praise for the laws in the American colonies which discouraged engrossing of land by stipulating, on pain of confiscation, that a certain proportion of lands had to be improved and cultivated within a certain time?[8] Or what of his remark that roads cannot 'with any safety' be left to private enterprise? Since there is no obvious point at which roads, unlike canals, become impassable, the toll revenues would simply be pocketed while roads deteriorated.[9]

Smith's vision of the economy was hardly one of a harmonious market order, even where economic relations were far removed from the sphere of influence of government. Whenever people of the same trade meet they conspire against the public and contrive to raise prices.[10] They constantly combine not to raise wages. Sometimes they do so to lower wages and this they do 'with the utmost silence and secrecy, till the moment of execution'. The workers for their part combine to raise wages, complaining of high living costs and the high profits made 'by their work'. They do so with 'the loudest clamour' and sometimes with 'the most shocking violence and outrage'. This they do to bring about a quick decision. But the employers always have the advantage in such disputes. Being fewer, they find it easier to combine and they can live for long periods on their capital.[11] Still, employers 'complain much of the bad effects of high wages' in raising prices and lessening sales at home and abroad. But, said Smith: 'They say nothing concerning the bad effects of high profits. They are silent with regard to the pernicious effects of their own gains.'[12] As we shall see later, Smith held that the interests of merchants and manufacturers were simply opposed to those of the rest of society.

On the question of monopoly and competition, Smith followed a simple rule. Where the producers in an industry were many or widely dispersed, combination was unlikely. Where there were few or where they were gathered in one place, collusion was a strong presumption. One could say that he gave a new meaning to the old saying that safety lies in numbers. Since he used this rule even to justify price control, one may see that it is somewhat different from the rule that the only viable way of defining monopoly is as a grant of privilege by a government. Smith argued that it would be in the interests of a monopoly to destroy part of the wheat crop. But it was scarcely possible in the case of wheat because the growers were 'scattered through all the different corners of the country' and 'can never be collected into one place like a number of independent manufacturers'. (The 'never' we now know was too strong.) Since wheat was a staple, the value of the crop 'far exceeds what the capitals of a few private men are capable of purchasing'; the dealers at various levels were very numerous 'and their dispersed situation renders it altogether impossible for them to enter into any general combination'.[13] But where bakers have established an exclusive corporation, 'it may perhaps be proper to regulate the price of the first necessary of life'.[14] Two grocers in a particular town are better than one; 20 would make 'the chance of their combining together, in order to raise the price, just so much the less'.[15] Cattle farmers, being widely dispersed and 'separated from one another', could not combine to impose 'monopolies upon their fellow-citizens' nor to lift those imposed upon them by others. 'Manufacturers of all kinds, collected together in numerous bodies in all great cities, easily can.'[16] Smith extended his safety-in-numbers rule even to religious sects whose 'zeal must be altogether innocent where the society is divided into two or three hundred, or perhaps into as many thousand small sects, of which no one could be considerable enough to disturb the public tranquillity'.[17]

It was, however, the public tranquillity that he was concerned about and not the ideal or benefits of free thought. Smith's liberalism consisted of a great respect for the rule of law and for this a strong authority was needed. The following passage brings this out rather delightfully.

> That degree of liberty which approaches to licentiousness can be tolerated only in countries where the sovereign is secured by a well-regulated standing army. It is in such countries only, that the public safety does not require, that the sovereign should be trusted with any discretionary power, for suppressing even the impertinent wantonness of this licentious liberty.[18]

Smith also argued for state-subsidized education. In itself, this may not raise free-market eyebrows very much. But the way he presented the argument is surprising. What he said in the following passage could pass for Marx's immiseration thesis.

> In the progress of the division of labour, the employment of the far greater part of those who live by labour … comes to be confined to a few very simple operations, frequently to one or two. But the understandings of the greater part of men are necessarily formed by their ordinary employments. The man whose whole life is spent in performing a few simple operations … has no occasion to exert his understanding, or to exercise his invention in finding out expedients for removing difficulties which never occur. He naturally loses, therefore, the habit of such exertion, and generally becomes as stupid and ignorant as it is possible for a human creature to become. The torpor of his mind renders him, not only incapable of relishing or bearing a part in any rational conversation, but of conceiving any generous, noble, or tender sentiment, and consequently of forming any just judgement concerning many even of the ordinary duties of private life … His dexterity at his own particular trade seems, in this manner, to be acquired at the expence of his intellectual, social, and martial virtues. But in every improved and civilized society this is the state into which the labouring poor, that is, the great body of the people, must necessarily fall, unless government takes some pains to prevent it.[19]

This selection of Smith's remarks was not meant to create the impression that he had interventionist or even socialist leanings. But it does tell us something. Adam Smith certainly was no libertarian. Furthermore, he was quite prepared to let his opinions on the public interest be the judge of what constitutes a beneficial market order and apparently he did not regard this as presumptuous. He was not guided by the seemingly less questionable precept, more common among free-market proponents nowadays, that the market itself shows us what people consider worthwhile and is thus itself the means for discovering the public interest, provided only that choice is free and uninfluenced by governments. The question to which we must now turn is whether the precepts by which Smith *was* guided may reasonably be said to have been those with which he is so often credited.

4.

The Natural Order

4.1. Natural law

The belief that a provident invisible hand operates spontaneously in the absence of intervention – laissez-faire pure and simple – must rest on a notion of natural order. The notion is an ancient one, a part of natural law doctrine and one that, Schumpeter said, is 'beset with difficulties and an inexhaustible source of misunderstandings'.[20] What distinguishes all forms of natural law from the kind of theory in physics which may nowadays be called a law of nature is that natural law also lays down what is just and good, right and proper, may be obeyed or disobeyed and is therefore not inexorable law. Beyond that, however, there are many variants of natural law.

Sometimes the meaning is simply that certain institutions e.g. common law or statute law, while based on principles of expedience, are nevertheless natural in the sense of being adapted to human nature rather than to conditions in particular societies. The argument over this is whether it is sensible to speak of human nature, as, for instance, J.S. Mill thought it was, or whether human beings, apart from their physical features, have only cultural (institutional) characteristics, as was the view of the historical school in economics. Either view, however, is quite compatible with our conception of pragmatism. Dogmatic laissez-faire must be based on a belief in an underlying rational order with its own regulating forces which either take the place of or create the requisite institutions, but which are often rendered impotent by man's impairing designs. This is of course seldom spelt out as an intellectual conviction. In fact, it may perhaps best be regarded as a sentiment, namely the feeling that whatever is touched by the hand of man is somehow sullied. As such, it is still very much alive, even though it is not customary in our day to appeal to natural law. The sentiment finds expression in a great variety of ways: in marvelling reflections on 'Nature', as when the wonderful order of a beehive is extolled and implicitly compared to the messy state of affairs of human society; in the more extreme forms of environmentalism according to which all man-made structures are aesthetically offensive and never an improvement on what is found in 'Nature'; or in the preference for natural foods even though plants containing vile poisons grow quite freely without the cultivating hands of man.

There is a difficulty when natural law animated by this sentiment is brought into economics because economics deals in an essential way with what people do. The difficulty is resolved after a fashion by distinguishing between a sphere of people's immediate concerns, in which they are recognized to plan, scheme, act and try to exercise control, and a sphere of what in social matters corresponds to nature, namely an overall order in the relations between people which is indeed the joint outcome of individual actions but no one's immediate concern. In more advanced societies, among more civilized people, the first sphere begins to encroach on the second in so far as some people, especially those in government, make the overall order their immediate concern.

Something like this may be seen in the penchant of many 17th- and 18th-century writers for explaining basic, or natural, economic relations by considering imaginary primitive societies – man in his natural state, the noble savage and so on. In this respect, the European mind seems to have been peculiarly fascinated by the American Indian. This appears quite explicitly in John Locke's influential writings, for example in his discussion of property rights,[21] and perhaps even in Adam Smith's well-known beaver-and-deer example[22] illustrating the natural influence of labour-time on exchange ratios in an 'early and rude state of society' with few institutions.

A natural-law bias is seen in the opposition to Colbertist dirigisme by the Physiocrats, in their slogan *laissez-faire laissez-passer* and of course in the word *Physiocracy* itself, although they called themselves *les économistes*. The Physiocrats were natural-law fundamentalists. Lord Robbins records Quesnay's motto for the title page of a book on Physiocracy, which expresses in another way the sentiment that man's touch sullies: *Ex natura, jus, ordo, et leges. Ex homine, arbitrium, regimen, et coercitio.*[23] Robbins also quotes a conversation reputed to have taken place between Catherine the Great of Russia and Mercier de la Rivière. When Catherine asked on what basis laws should be made, the Physiocrat replied that the basis should be 'the nature of things and men'. The conversation continued inter alia: 'But when one wishes to make these laws what rules should be observed?' 'Madame, to give laws to mankind is God's prerogative'.

'To what then do you reduce the science of government?' 'To study the laws which God has so manifestly engraven in human society from the time of its creation. To seek to go beyond this would be a great mistake and a disastrous undertaking.' To this Catherine understandably replied: 'Sir, it has been a pleasure to meet you. I wish you good day.'[24]

4.2. Adam Smith and the natural order

Adam Smith praised physiocratic doctrine, 'with all its imperfections', as 'perhaps, the nearest approximation to the truth that has yet been published upon the subject of political economy'.[25] But he did so in a lukewarm and patronizing way. So where did he stand on the issue? The matter is complicated. Apparently he changed his mind or was simply inconsistent. In *The Theory of Moral Sentiments* of 1759, he did give an exposition of a harmonious order in nature with benevolent intentions towards mankind. It was natural law of the sort that was supposed to show on reflection that the status quo is really quite an excellent state of affairs. The invisible hand, which gets one mention in each of his two major works, here relates to the employment contract.

> The rich … consume little more than the poor, and in spite of their natural selfishness and rapacity … though the sole end which they propose from the labours of all the thousands whom they employ, be the gratification of their own vain and insatiable desires, they divide with the poor the produce of all their improvements. They are led by an invisible hand to make nearly the same distribution of the necessaries of life, which would have been made, had the earth been divided into equal portions among all its inhabitants, and thus without intending it, without knowing it, advance the interest of the society… When Providence divided the earth among a few lordly masters, it neither forgot nor abandoned those who seemed to have been left out in the partition.[26]

The *Wealth of Nations* may give one a similar impression. The terms *natural liberty* and *natural justice* keep coming up and there is a reference to 'the wisdom of nature'. There is also the following famous passage:

> All systems either of preference or of restraint, therefore, being thus completely taken away, the obvious and simple system of natural liberty establishes itself of its own accord.

> Every man, as long as he does not violate the laws of justice,
> is left perfectly free to pursue his own interest his own way,
> and to bring both his industry and capital into competition
> with those of any other man, or order of men. The sovereign
> is completely discharged from a duty, in the attempting to
> perform which he must always be exposed to innumerable
> delusions and for the proper performance of which no human
> wisdom or knowledge could ever be sufficient; the duty of
> superintending the industry of private people, and of directing
> it towards the employment most suitable to the interest of
> the society. According to the system of natural liberty, the
> sovereign has only three duties to attend to ...[27]

Anyone who knows only this passage from the *Wealth of Nations* will
hardly doubt on which side of the pragmatic–dogmatic divide Smith is
to be found. Dugald Stewart mentions a manuscript drawn up by Smith
in 1755, before the *Moral Sentiments*, in which the idea apparently already
found strong expression.[28] However, we have seen that as an older man
Smith also made statements of quite a different tenor (Chapter 3). Perhaps
in the 21 years it took to bring his ideas on natural liberty to publication,
Smith's views changed somewhat, so that we find remnants of an earlier
attitude side by side with a later more critical attitude. Moreover, contrary
to what is often thought, the idea expressed in the passage was not novel
at the time; it was becoming quite fashionable.[29]

The bulk of the book, however, is about something else. It consists
of a fairly detailed examination of a variety of social and economic
institutions.[30] There is the often quoted evidence, recorded by Stewart,
of John Millar, who was one of Smith's students and later his friend
and Glasgow academic, that the substance of the *Wealth of Nations* came
from the fourth part of Smith's lectures in which 'he considered the
political institutions relating to commerce, to finances, to ecclesiastical
and military establishments'.[31] It is in these considerations of specific
issues and in his proposals, published at the age of 52, that Adam Smith
revealed attitudes which are simply not at one with the harmonious order
extolled in the earlier work published at the age of 35. Jacob Viner, who
addressed himself to this question, came to the conclusion 'that on the
points at which they come into contact there is a substantial measure of
irreconcilable divergence between the *Theory of Moral Sentiments* and the
Wealth of Nations, with respect to the character of the natural order'. The
later book, he said, 'could not have remained, as it has, a living book
were it not that in its methods of analysis, its basic assumptions, and its
conclusions it abandoned the absolutism, the rigidity, the romanticism

which characterize the earlier book'. He went so far as to say that Smith 'recognized that the economic order, when left to its natural course, was marked by serious conflicts between private interests and the interests of the general public'.[32]

4.3. Evidence of Smith's attitude

To present evidence of this is not easy because it is scattered all over the book. In accordance with our question about the hand behind the invisible hand, we want to see how Adam Smith dealt with cases of institutions that evidently arose quite naturally, i.e. without being designed. Did he associate them with the principle which, in one place, he expressed in terms of the invisible hand, or did he have other uses for them or, at least, see them in a different light? Such questions will concern us below.

4.3.1. Undesirable consequences of natural liberty

Smith's statement that the system of natural liberty establishes itself of its own accord when all preference and restraint by government is removed may be regarded as a tautology. What is not so obvious is whether natural liberty, like the invisible hand, brings private interests into line with the public interest (especially when the latter remains undefined). In several cases Smith considered the possible consequences of natural liberty undesirable.

One case arises in connection with the well-known 'conspiracy' passage. 'People of the same trade seldom meet together, even for merriment and diversion, but the conversation ends in a conspiracy against the public, or in some contrivance to raise prices.' Such meetings, he said, could not be prevented by any law consistent with liberty and justice, but at least, to make it more difficult for people of the same trade to find each other, they should not be required to enter their names and addresses in public registers, nor allowed to levy themselves for poor, sick and widow funds.[33] It was quite clear to him, as apparently it is not to some of his modern followers, that the 'wretched spirit of monopoly' and the 'corporation spirit' taught people 'by voluntary associations and agreements, to prevent that free competition which they cannot prohibit by bye-laws'.[34] We have already seen that Smith said employers combine to keep wages down. He called this collusion tacit, constant and uniform and related these qualities to a subtle form of non-government coercion. Violations were most unpopular 'and a sort of reproach to a master among his neighbours and equals'. He added that such collusion was 'the natural state of things which nobody ever hears of'.[35]

Another case arises in connection with his proposals for paper money (issued by any bank in his day). He wanted banknotes to be restricted to denominations of £5 or higher and their immediate and unconditional convertibility into gold or silver ensured by law. To restrain bankers from issuing certain promissory notes even though others may be quite willing to accept them was, he said, 'a manifest violation of that natural liberty' which the law should normally uphold. 'But those exertions of the natural liberty of a few individuals, which might endanger the security of the whole society, are, and ought to be, restrained by the laws of all governments.' The obligation to erect party walls to prevent the spread of fire, he went on, was a violation of natural liberty of the same kind.[36] The restriction was intended to limit notes mainly to the circulation among dealers as opposed to that between dealers and consumers.[37] Dealers, apparently, were more likely than the general public to be in a position to judge the soundness of banks and to refuse notes issued by unsound banks, especially since sums of £5 or more were then fairly large.

Smith also had reservations about the joint-stock limited-liability company, which he considered 'reasonable' only when its operations could be reduced to a routine and when an amount of capital was required which was beyond the means of single individuals.[38] His uneasiness was due to the difficulty of attuning private interests to the objectives of a company. The employees of the East India Company, for instance, abused the powers vested in them in order to reach a financial position that would enable them to resign and forget about the company.[39] The directors frequently bought the qualifying stock so that they could disburse lucrative appointments among their friends.[40] Directors and officials therefore had an interest in keeping the company going but not in attaining its objectives. In other words, the guidance of the invisible hand is absent within companies. Hence the insistence on routine operations. A simple set of rules can be enforced.

Perhaps Smith was still groping to articulate his apprehensions about these institutions. Even today it is still debatable whether they are really compatible with a market order. It is important in our context that this is so despite the fact that they may be said to have evolved quite naturally, at least in so far as banking and company legislation has merely codified what had evolved on its own. The institution which in the event has come to perform one of the functions Smith meant for his proposal on banknotes is the general opinion that a large bank cannot be allowed to fail because of the disruption this would create. It relieves almost all of us of the difficult task of ascertaining the soundness of banks. But it does not perform the other function Smith had in mind because it also relieves us of the opportunity of being led by an invisible hand to promote investment in sound projects though we intend only our own financial security. (The present international debt crisis is evidence of that.) The more or less free (natural) development since Smith's time of banking and the international monetary system has of course also raised the bigger questions whether effective control of money supply is possible at all within the present institutional set-up and whether a beneficial market order is possible without a firm monetary constraint. In his tract *A Positive Program for Laissez Faire*, Henry Simons, the main founder of the Chicago School, advocated, simply and without qualification, the abolition of private fractional-reserve banking. He argued that the state had been remiss in so far as it had not maintained the kind of institutions which make it possible to avoid political adjudication and control of relative prices. The required reforms included that of banking and an 'outright dismantling of our gigantic corporations'.[41] One may also recall how Schumpeter described and foresaw the effects of the spontaneous evolution of financial assets and of large companies on the institution of property.

> The capitalist process, by substituting a mere parcel of shares for the walls of and the machines in a factory, takes the life out of the idea of property ... Dematerialized, defunctionalized and absentee ownership does not impress and call forth moral allegiance as the vital form of property did. Eventually there will be *nobody* left who really cares to stand for it – nobody within and nobody without the precincts of the big concerns.[42]

4.3.2. A process of social interaction

Adam Smith was of the familiar persuasion that the conduct of people is shaped by their circumstances and by 'the system'. After describing the unscrupulous conduct and corruption of East India Company officials, for example, he said he did not mean 'to throw any odious imputation upon the general character' of these people. He meant to censure the system of company government. The officials 'acted as their situation naturally directed, and they who have clamoured the loudest against them would, probably, not have acted better themselves'.[43]

This was characteristic of his approach. He typically reached his conclusions by considering how people would act (a) according to what he thought were the interests of various parties and (b) within the constraints imposed by the physical situation and the institutional arrangements of society. But this was not the full extent of the method. Institutions for the most part are established ways of doing things. It is therefore likely that in time some of the action within constraints becomes itself an established way of doing things, i.e. a part of the institutional constraint. By following up this line of thought, one arrives at a conception of a process of social interaction. It is quite normal as historical analysis and, with notably different emphases, it is akin to the analysis of market process by the modern Austrians.[44] Smith used the method constantly and it seemed to present no problem to him.

It does, however, raise enormous problems for a mind attuned to thinking in terms of long-run equilibrium. With that habit of mind, the inclination is to compress the process, to take an interest only in what it leads to. But what kind of society is it in which all the institutional and other adjustments have taken place? Is that the natural order? Is it perhaps the fabled state of communism at the end of the dialectic process? There was no natural order of this kind in Smith's analysis. The process of social interaction was endless. The habit of looking for ultimates seized economists after Smith's time. Ricardo gave it prominence, Marx extended its range, and Keynes deprecated it.

We may illustrate the difference made by this habit of mind by considering the curious way Smith explained why the French sugar colonies were more productive than the English ones and were thus able to finance themselves out of savings. French colonial government, he said, was more arbitrary, i.e. more autocratic. Hence, officials who also acted as magistrates were independent of local notables who were also the major slave owners. Hence, magistrates were free to let 'common humanity' dispose them to give some protection to slaves. Hence, the masters treated slaves with a modicum of respect and less resentful slaves were more effective workers.[45] That arguments of this kind may be made up to explain almost anything is beside the point. What is significant is that he was prepared to argue in this way at all. The mode of thought of many of his followers might have inclined him to reject the argument simply on the grounds that, were the reasoning correct in the French case, market forces would long previously have induced English colonists to treat their slaves with more respect, if not actually to petition for more despotic government.

The habit of thinking in terms of long-run equilibrium very often leads to a disregard of institutions or to their relegation to the status of market imperfections. Smith, however, was immersed in institutional analysis and the natural order could scarcely play an ontal role in that.

4.3.3. The natural order as a heuristic fiction

If the above is correct, the question arises why Smith made the references to a natural order which he undoubtedly did make. Such references were highly fashionable in the 18th century and usually conjured up visions of primitive societies. As early as 1756, Smith remarked that the 'life of a savage, when we take a distant view of it' seems to be one either of indolence or of great adventure and both qualities 'render the description of it agreeable to the imagination'.[46] In the *Wealth of Nations* the natural order seems to serve as a heuristic fiction, a foil against which to see the historical process. Man in a state of 'perfect liberty' became like man in his natural state, a creature driven by instinct and individual preference, in contrast to whose doings one was enabled to appreciate the role institutions play in actual events. We still use such a method today. When we speak, say, of factor price distortion, we have in mind prices in some equilibrium state from which the actual factor prices are distorted by the conditions to which we want to draw attention.

The heuristic fiction may be seen in Smith's well-known remarks about labour-time and exchange ratios. 'In that early and rude state of society which precedes both the accumulation of stock and the appropriation of land, the proportion between the quantities of labour necessary for acquiring different objects seems to be the only circumstance which can afford any rule for exchanging them for one another.'[47] Thus, if it usually takes twice as long to kill a beaver as it does to kill a deer, one beaver should naturally exchange for or be worth two deer. Furthermore, in 'this state of things, the whole produce of labour belongs to the labourer'. But as 'soon as stock has accumulated in the hands of particular persons' and as 'soon as the land of any country has all become private property' the situation is far more complex.[48] There are also three places early in the book where Smith discusses what we would nowadays describe as the determination of equilibrium market prices where factor mobility is perfect. Smith added the proviso: 'This at least would be the case in a society where things were left to follow their natural course, where there was perfect liberty.'[49]

One may also see the heuristic fiction at work in the task Smith set himself in Book III. Because necessities take precedence over luxuries and because of the charms of country life (he had very romantic ideas on this), one would expect, he thought, that the capital of a growing society would be directed first to agriculture, then to manufacturing and only then to foreign trade.[50] That everywhere in Europe the actual course of events had been almost the reverse of this, he said when giving advance notice of Book III, was 'contrary to the order of nature and of reason'.

He would therefore explain the 'interests, prejudices, laws and customs which have given occasion to it'.[51] 'Had human institutions, therefore, never disturbed the natural course of things' the progress of towns would have followed in proportion to the improvement of agriculture.[52] Among the offending institutions were primogeniture and entails (prescribed rules of succession to and prohibitions on the sale of estates). They retarded the development of small proprietorship, drove up land prices and thus kept enterprising and profit-conscious merchants and manufacturers from making farming a business. The origin of these institutions, according to Smith, went back to the days after the break-up of the Roman empire and was understandable as part of a *modus vivendi* in barbarous and disorderly times. But the conditions which had made them reasonable had passed. Because of institutional inertia, they were still influencing economic affairs centuries later.[53]

4.3.4. The stationary state

There was of course the idea in classical political economy, following Smith, that economies naturally tended to an ultimate stationary state – the idea which earned the subject the tag of the dismal science. The stationary state was not a happy prospect. Smith introduced it to lend colour to his thesis that wages rise in an expanding economy. A stationary economy, however opulent, has unemployment, low wages and low profits, with most of the product presumably going to rentiers, while craftsmen run about the streets 'begging employment'. China was his example of a country of vast riches which had long been stationary, in which apparently nothing had changed since Marco Polo's visit 500 years earlier. With a pungent pen, he portrayed a state of affairs in which the friendly Providence he wrote about as a younger man seemed indeed to have abandoned those left out of the original partition of resources. In the vicinity of Canton, thousands of families live in houseboats and 'are eager to fish up the nastiest garbage thrown overboard from any European ship. Any carion, the carcase of a dead dog or cat, for example, though half putrid and stinking, is as welcome to them as the most wholesome food to the people of other countries.' The grim picture had other aspects, such as the people who earned their living by performing the service of drowning unwanted children 'like puppies' every night.[54]

But in Smith's rendition this unfortunate state of affairs was not the natural order, nor the ultimate state towards which all economies inevitably tended. He stressed that it was all a matter of 'laws and institutions'. China had developed as far as its laws and institutions would permit;

with others it might have been different.[55] When the stationary state was later introduced into the corn-law debate, its function was to assist in the agitation for the repeal of a law.

4.4. Adam Smith's pragmatism

After quoting at length the passage in which Smith discussed the influence of laws and institutions in China and elsewhere, James Buchanan ascribed to him the following opinions:

> The well-being of a society is a function of its basic laws and institutions; these are variable and subject to explicit modification; there is nothing sacrosanct about those laws and institutions that emerge in what may be called the natural process of social evolution; and, finally, the basic laws and institutions must be (or should be) equally available to all persons and groups within a society.[56]

Though he seems to read rather a lot into one passage, Buchanan does here articulate what appears to have been Adam Smith's standpoint throughout the book. That standpoint, it may be seen, is far removed from a dogmatic belief in natural law. By our criterion (page 26 above), it is a pragmatic position.

Lord Robbins held that liberal theories of economic policy have two philosophical origins – the natural law tradition and the utilitarian tradition. He considered English classical political economy to have been almost wholly within the utilitarian tradition.[57] The founders of English political economy he took to be the Scotsmen David Hume, whose utilitarian disposition is well known, and Adam Smith, 'who so frequently uses the terminology of the *Naturrecht*, but whose arguments are so consistently utilitarian in character'.[58] He pointed out that the difference was noticed as early as 1814 by the first editor of the *Wealth of Nations*, who remarked about the Physiocrats that they seemed to deduce the free-trade doctrine 'from the principles rather of abstract right, than of general expediency'.[59] In summing up the classical economists' utilitarian conception of market order, Robbins said, among other things:

> Thus, so far from the system of economic freedom being something which will certainly come into being if things are just left to take their course, it can only come into being ... if a conscious effort is made to create the highly artificial

environment which is necessary if it is to function properly. The invisible hand … is not the hand of some god or some natural agency independent of human effort … Not only the good society, but the market itself is an artifact.[60]

The utilitarian position on liberal economic policy which Robbins described is quite clearly a pragmatic position by our criterion.

One cannot say with certainty how Adam Smith reached his conclusions nor can one expect to come to a definitive judgement in a few pages when, after all, volumes have been written on the subject. However, the interpretations by Viner, Robbins and Buchanan, as also our own analysis, do at least show that those who advocate a dogmatic reliance on the natural order in economic affairs cannot find unequivocal and unqualified support in the mature writings of Adam Smith. As a younger man, Smith was perhaps taken with the idea of the natural order. In the *Wealth of Nations* he continued on occasion to use its terminology and he appears to have made it serve as an expository device, sometimes in the guise, as he called it, of the original state of things. But this was probably no more than a matter of style. The substantive issue is whether Smith really believed that in societies in which everyone minded his own business and left the overall order to look after itself there always emerged the kind of institutions which gave rise to an economic order beneficial to all. When all his discussion of specific questions is taken into account, it seems very unlikely that he did believe this. Judged by the criterion we have been applying, Adam Smith appears therefore to have held predominantly pragmatic views.

From a pragmatic point of view a beneficial market order is a possible order that may be realized by conscious effort and according to some set of values or at least some ordering principle. From the same point of view it appears that dogmatists mistake this possibility for a natural order frustrated almost always by mankind's misguided machinations.

5.

Spontaneous Order

5.1. Exogenous and endogenous values

The principles by which order may be recognized are probably unlimited in number. Disorder (or randomness) according to every conceivable principle would be very difficult to define. The interesting question, therefore, is not whether economic affairs constitute one or other order but whether they constitute a beneficial or desirable order. The answer will of course depend on some set of values, usually the analyst's own values. The values which an analyst brings to bear on his analysis we may call exogenous values. At the end of Chapter 3 we noted that Adam Smith certainly did consider the economic order in the light of his own opinions on the public interest. But exogenous values carry with them the implication that the analyst knows what is good for others and this is not only presumptuous but also offends against the ideal that scientific discourse should be *wertfrei*, i.e. neutral with respect to values. It may seem that one may avoid these strictures by relying purely on the other values which enter any consideration of economic affairs and which we may call endogenous, namely the values which people in the system under consideration reveal by their actions. Scientific neutrality may be maintained, it may seem, if the course of events is recognized as the arbiter of what is desirable.

At times, however, it may be quite difficult to carry through an analysis based purely on endogenous values. With regard to desirability, only one conclusion then seems possible, namely that whatever happens in the sphere of human relations reflects on balance the wishes and the values of the people involved. So, for instance, when an interventionist government that invests itself with coercive powers appears on the scene, one should, on the basis of the revealed preferences, regard this state of affairs as a desirable order. When the intention is to advocate free markets, such a conclusion is unwelcome. One cannot in any case advocate anything unless one is committed to some values. While, therefore, analysis of economic order may nominally be based on endogenous values only, exogenous values are usually introduced implicitly in the distinction between action which freely reflects individual values and action which does not. Since action is never completely free even in completely free markets – *vide* the discipline of the market – the distinction becomes one between acceptable and unacceptable forms of duress. By implication, acceptable and unacceptable kinds of institutions are also distinguished. In this way, implicit exogenous values lead to a contrast between natural or spontaneous order and contrived or constructed order.

When the economic order is considered in this light, as it is in much recent discussion, there is no longer any presumption that there is a unique order in the nature of things but rather that cases of spontaneous order arise as the joint and *unintended* consequence of the pursuit of individual interests. Nor need one ask whether the natural is desirable because the natural or spontaneous is so conceived now that it always is desirable according to the exogenous values. To avoid confusion between this kind of order and the natural order already considered, we shall refer to it as spontaneous order. The expression is used by Hayek, who is the foremost thinker in this field.

A writer on spontaneous order holds pragmatic views to the extent that he realizes that his own values, or at least some exogenous values, enter his analysis. The more he realizes this, the more apparent it will be to him that the institutions necessary for his version of spontaneous order cannot be expected to arise on their own but would have to be developed deliberately. This has been our criterion all along.

5.2. Libertarian order

Murray Rothbard is a libertarian spokesman – in Buchanan's opinion he best exemplifies the libertarian anarchists or property-rights anarchists.[61] In a fairly recent book, Rothbard actually says that the free-market economy forms a kind of natural order.[62] There is also a natural-law tone in his injunction that 'the libertarian must fashion his standard by means of reason and cannot simply adopt existing legal custom'.[63] Reason, it seems, is not merely the principle of sound thought but also something which may be a substitute for legal custom and for institutions in general. In this, as we shall see, Rothbard and Hayek are at opposite poles. In contrast with the full-blooded institutions recognized by Hayek, the libertarian order makes a very scanty allowance for institutions. The legal foundation consists of natural property rights which imply complete freedom of contract and include, in the Lockean mould, ownership of the self.[64] There are other entities which some might call institutions, but which are perhaps better called business schemes available to anyone who wishes to use them. So, presumably, one may choose whether to communicate by letter or by telephone, whether to participate in time-sharing schemes, whether to use a credit card and so on. Libertarian man appears to be driven very largely by instinct and individual preference since he appears to have no cultural characteristics other than the very strong one of being a libertarian. This conception of man is of course not unique. In so far as micro-economics of the general-equilibrium variety presupposes any kind of human beings, it seems to be this kind.

Rothbard, however, takes this conception of man in society to its logical conclusion and argues that 'a truly free market is totally incompatible with the existence of a State'.[65] The truly free market or libertarian order, like the ultimate state of communism, operates without government. But, while in the latter the State withers away because law enforcement becomes unnecessary, in the libertarian order the State disappears because law enforcement and judicial services are taken over by private enterprise. Business firms offer the public, on a competitive basis, business schemes whereby these erstwhile state functions are performed. Individuals may avail themselves, at a price, of the opportunity of taking out service contracts, rather as in the 'real world' people take out service contracts for the maintenance of television sets, and they presumably patronize the police-hire and judge-hire firms which seem to give them the best deal.[66]

In this way Rothbard argues that the ultimate form of market order is based purely on voluntarism. As long as property rights are respected, no one is ever coerced. It follows that whatever anyone does is something he has freely chosen to do and could have refrained from doing. While people may not always know beforehand what in the event they are going to like, there is no reason to suppose that anyone else knows better. Armed with this bit of easy logic, one may criticize all manner of actual conditions and then wonder how anyone could be so obtuse as not to see how nice the libertarian order would be for everyone.

Indeed, it is not the logic of the libertarian proposition that is dubious but the institutional assumption that it needs. Our final remarks on this have to be left to a later chapter. However, it is not difficult to see that libertarian rules of conduct would have to be ingrained very deeply if the game were to be played in the libertarian way. One does not have to be very cynical to believe that mercenary police forces would be hired to perpetrate the extortion they are meant to prevent and that salesmen of rival firms would soon be knocking at the victim's door to offer sweet revenge. Rothbard says free-enterprise judiciaries would compete on the basis of 'a reputation for efficiency and probity'.[67] But it is not probity that the customer would always want and rent-a-judge firms would surely find it more profitable to gain a reputation for sticking to the maxim that the customer, or the highest bidder, is always right. Rothbard considers such possibilities, but discounts them. There will always be some criminals. He adds, perhaps too strongly but not entirely without foundation, that a society without a government apparatus would at least have no 'regular, legalized channel for crime and aggression'.[68]

However, he probably underestimates what the libertarian order would require. He says, for instance, that libertarians should not 'balk at changing a few clauses of the common law' and that the resultant code would be applied by 'free-market judges, who would all pledge themselves to follow it'.[69] But what of the person who does not want the common law changed or wants to hire himself out as a judge but chooses not to make the pledge because he thinks he knows a better law. One need hardly wonder what would happen to the principle of voluntarism then. Rothbard himself dedicates the book in which he sets all this out to 'Libertarians of the Future, who Shall Overcome'.

As an exercise in singling out one aspect of society, as *homo oeconomicus* was meant to single out one aspect of man, or as an exercise in showing the kind of society implied by much of our micro-economics, a great deal can be said for the libertarian order. Sometimes it seems that this is what Rothbard has in mind but he does not say so. He makes it clear that he does consider a free-enterprise police and judiciary to be quite feasible. That means he can envisage a society in which people play the game very closely by the libertarian rules. There must be many who, when they try to do the same, manage to see only that state of affairs about which Hobbes said that in it life would be nasty, brutish and short.[70]

Rothbard's point is not to advocate free-enterprise police and judiciaries but to advocate the abolition of all forms of government as a prerequisite for truly free markets, for a purely voluntaristic economic order, the exact form of which would depend on endogenous values. He envisages that without government some form of law enforcement service would be offered spontaneously in the market, like everything else, in response to demand. Its exact form would depend on the endogenous values. The difficulties of a long-run institutional equilibrium have already been noted. But that is not all. The only properly called institution (in the present context) that libertarian order seems to require is a great respect for absolute and all-embracing property rights. Such respect would set the libertarian rules of conduct. If Rothbard thinks that this institution would also arise spontaneously or naturally, that this is reason, then it appears that he is not aware of the extent to which libertarian values, a vision of the good society, i.e. exogenous values, enter the libertarian order.

5.3. The language analogy

Friedman has remarked that economic activity is not the only area of human life where the invisible-hand idea finds application. He mentions language as another area where a complex and sophisticated structure has arisen spontaneously. He compares a spontaneous economic order with what he calls the well-defined order of a language. Both have developed out of the voluntary interaction of individuals and are constantly evolving further. Neither has been planned by a central authority.[71]

This analogy is interesting and complex. It may be understood in several ways. Language is orderly in the sense that speech is not a random jumble of sounds (and *mutatis mutandis* in the case of written texts). The economy is orderly in the sense that the goods and services that are produced are not a random jumble of physical objects and movements. There are forms of order in human activities without which we could not refer to speech or production. It appears that Friedman had this order in activities in mind. But he also refers to language as a complex structure and that introduces another way of understanding the analogy.

Language does not consist in the activity of speaking. When we ordinarily refer to English, French, German and so on as languages, we are referring to certain sets of rules which certain sets of people observe when they engage in the activities of speaking, reading, writing and so on. The syntax, semantics and idiom of a language – let us call them grammar for short – make up a set of rules. Grammar is then one instance of those rules of conduct which we have called institutions. It is because people follow rules of conduct, as well as such other rules as are commonly called reason, that there is an order in human activities. Let us return to the analogy. Since it is proper to compare like with like, we really have two ways of understanding the analogy or two comparisons – Friedman got them rather mixed up – namely (a) between the activities of speaking, reading, writing and so on and economic activities and (b) between language or grammar and economic institutions, i.e. a comparison of activities and a comparison of the rules which at least partly govern activities.

The latter is quite a telling analogy. The ideal of a market economy may be expressed in terms of it. The grammar of a language (a system of market institutions, i.e. rules of conduct) is reflected in the way people use and understand words (conduct their economic activity). In this sense it is in the minds of people and only partially and imperfectly written down in grammar books and dictionaries (statute books). It prescribes *how* things should be said (done) and not *what* should be said (done). When we think of treatises on novel and intricate ideas, of poetry, speeches and commands, of mundane description and amiable chatter, all of which observe the rules of grammar, we may see that grammar is not unduly restrictive. Analogously, the rules of conduct we call market institutions leave the individual ample freedom to do his own thing and venture into the unknown future in his own way. Institutions do not prevent novelty, they allow freedom within the law.

Friedman, however, draws attention to the spontaneous evolution of a language and associates this with the invisible hand. The analogy is quite clear. By their efforts to make themselves understood, countless individuals are led to promote the development of language though they intend to serve only their immediate purposes. However, it is here that the analogy may lead us badly astray. The invisible hand has become an aphorism for the principles of free enterprise in free markets, and in the case of market order we have certain criteria for speaking of an order at all. Friedman, one may presume, would expect a market order to be such that markets clear or that resources are optimally allocated. If this expectation is not met, economic activities, according to this criterion, are to some extent out of order, in disorder or in disequilibrium. We do not have corresponding criteria for a language – or so it seems. We may have a vague notion that one language is somehow better than another as a medium for communication or as a vehicle for scientific, artistic, emotive or convivial expression. But can we be more definite than that when language is so fundamental to us that it itself sets the limits of what we think there is to be said?

To say, therefore, that language evolves spontaneously through the guidance of the invisible hand is to say no more than that whenever and wherever people have lived together they have found some way of talking to each other. By analogy, we may say that whenever and wherever people have lived in communities, some or other social and economic institutions have evolved more or less spontaneously. No doubt this is so. But where is the basis for associating this spontaneity with a market order (the invisible hand)? Is the mere fact that people got along, that they managed to survive, a sufficient criterion for the order associated with the invisible hand? The claims made for that order surely are stronger than that.

This is a mistake easily made with regard to spontaneous order. Spontaneity, however conceived, comes to be regarded as desirable. But such generalization from market order is unwarranted. A desirable market order, the order of the invisible hand, is a spontaneous order in activities which depends upon and derives its desirable features from certain rules of conduct which at least implicitly have been made to accord with certain exogenous values. Rules of conduct, such as grammar and economic institutions, undoubtedly also evolve spontaneously, but their evolution does not normally depend on yet further rules of conduct from which they may derive desirable features more or less by definition. One may presume that there is no limit to the variety of institutions that may evolve spontaneously. But there is no guarantee that the order in activities arising from just any spontaneously evolved set of institutions would accord with anyone's vision of the good society.

5.4. Hayek and cultural evolution

The language analogy was probably no more than a stray thought in Friedman's book. It was worth consideration because it took us into Hayek's complex realm of thought. The expression *spontaneous order* is used by Hayek, and the analysis of institutions as rules of conduct is also his.[72]

5.4.1. Rules of conduct and spontaneous order

It is time for a closer look at rules of conduct. It would be interesting if, for instance, the institutions of a modern monetary system were set out in terms of rules of conduct. Hayek does not appear to have done anything as explicit as that. Rules of conduct are in fact quite difficult to deal with. Hayek alludes to the distinction made by the philosopher Gilbert Ryle between *knowing how* and *knowing that*.[73] Rules of conduct are cases of knowing how. People know *how* to follow an intricate grammar when they speak but may not be able to state *that* their grammatical rules are such and such – in less erudite societies, they may not even understand what is required of them when asked to articulate the rules of their grammar. Again, people may know how to conduct themselves in business negotiations, at cocktail parties or at funerals without being able to write a manual on the subject. As know-how, skills or practices, rules of conduct remain largely unarticulated; they are cases of what Polanyi has called tacit knowledge.[74]

The tacit dimension also extends to perception. A person knows how to recognize each of possibly a large number of friends and acquaintances, or how to tell the difference between a Persian cat and a Pekinese dog, without necessarily being able to get very far in stating what the distinguishing characteristics are. Hayek accounts in particular for our ability to see each other's intentions and emotions along such lines and for the fact that people with a common cultural background are able to understand each other better than outsiders.[75] Very significantly (as we shall see) for his outlook on economic order, Hayek sees reasoning, the rules of rational thought, in the same light.[76]

For Hayek it is a matter of great importance that rules of conduct are a knowing-how which is seldom spelt out as a knowing-that and of which people may even be quite unaware. The implication is that rules of conduct are not devised and adopted deliberately. Hayek argues that these rules, i.e. the institutions of society, are neither natural in the sense of being independent of human action nor constructed in the sense of being reasoned out and adopted to serve particular purposes. There is, he says, a 'middle category' comprising the *unintended consequences of human action* among which an order may form itself that no one intended.[77] The spontaneous evolution of cultural order, conceived as a phenomenon distinct both from nature and from human design, is central to Hayek's thought. He credits Mandeville[78] and after him Hume, Ferguson and Smith with having given the idea its first explicit recognition in modern thought, considers the *invisible hand* a good name for it and says that it became 'the great discovery of classical political economy' and the basis of our understanding of economic life.[79] He favours Adam Ferguson's expression of the idea, viz (the continuation after the quotation on page 26 above): 'Every step and every movement of the multitude, even in what are termed enlightened ages, are made with equal blindness to the future; and nations stumble upon establishments, which are indeed the result of human action, but not the execution of any human design.'[80] For example, though nobody, according to the usual conjecture, ever invented a medium of exchange or a language, such institutions nevertheless evolved as the unintended consequence of countless individual efforts to effect exchanges or to communicate.

But there is more to cultural evolution, as Hayek explains it. When a society stumbles upon institutions, i.e. rules of conduct, which within the environment and circumstances of that society are particularly advantageous, the members of that society prosper and increase in numbers. People of other societies without such rules of conduct are either driven out or, far more likely, begin more or less unwittingly to imitate and to learn these rules. In this way, those institutions spread which are fittest, both in the sense that they allow societies to cope with physical constraints efficiently and in the sense that they combine well with other existing institutions. Cultural evolution thus tends to bring about a spontaneous institutional order.[81] Cultural selection differs from biological natural selection in so far as it does not depend upon a genetic mechanism. Rather, acquired characteristics are passed on and, in fact, are acquired by the ever-increasing numbers who are assimilated into a culture. Like natural selection, however, cultural selection, though it may be understood, does not allow prediction of the course of evolution in the future – and it certainly does not follow a predetermined course to an ultimate natural state.[82]

We may let Hayek's own words express the conception of man to which all this leads.

> Man is as much a rule-following animal as a purpose-seeking one. And he is successful not because he knows why he ought to observe the rules which he does observe, or is even capable of stating all these rules in words, but because his thinking and acting are governed by rules which have by a process of selection been evolved in the society in which he lives, and which are thus the product of the experience of generations.[83]

5.4.2. Constructivism

Hayek's preoccupation with cultural evolution leads him to his pet aversion, the idea which he despises and never seems to tire of condemning as the bane of social life and, lately, as the fatal conceit, namely that man may, by applying his reason, reorganize his society to create a desirable economic and social order. One may derive the names under which he denounces this idea by turning any one of the words *Cartesian*, *rationalist* or *constructivist* into a noun used either by itself or qualified by one or both of the other two.[84]

His argument may be summed up as follows. The spontaneous order brought about by the impersonal process of cultural selection is an adaptation to millions upon millions of particular factors and specific circumstances. The signalling function of prices in a market situation ensures that all the particular adaptations are integrated into a general adaptation, a coherent order, even though no one person knows or could know all the details which are thus taken into account. It is the fatal conceit of planners that they could know enough to improve on such an order. Hayek extends the argument. He speaks of the 'concurrent evolution of mind and society' or of 'mind and culture'.[85] The significance of this is that the 'mind does not so much make rules as consist of rules of action'.[86] Tradition, moral standards and reason are on an equal footing, the products of the same process. 'It was when these learnt rules, involving classifications of different kinds of objects, began to include a sort of model of the environment … that what we call reason appeared' and 'man has certainly more often learnt to do the right thing without comprehending why it was the right thing, and he still is often served better by custom than by understanding'.[87] Hayek contrasts this view, which recognizes the limitations of human reasoning, with the view, which he seems rather strangely to ascribe wholly to Descartes, that reason stands outside history and ideally should be invoked to justify all our beliefs and endeavours.

> The errors of constructivist rationalism are closely connected with Cartesian dualism, that is with the conception of an independently existing mind substance which stands outside the cosmos of nature and which enabled man, endowed with such a mind from the beginning, to design the institutions of society and culture among which he lives. The fact is, of course, that this mind is an adaptation to the natural and social surroundings in which man lives and that it has developed in constant interaction with the institutions which determine the structure of society … The conception of an already fully developed mind designing the institutions which made life in society possible is contrary to all we know about the evolution of man.[88]

The 'errors of constructivist rationalism' are the basis of Hayek's criticism of socialist attempts to create new societies. When he speaks of constructivism, he has in mind mainly intellectual socialists and proponents of the welfare state. The inclination to rely on administrative decisions, the belief in treating each case on its merits, and the disdain of general rules are the chief targets of his criticism. In this regard he quotes Keynes, who said of himself and his friends in their younger days that they did not feel themselves bound to obey general rules or to conform to customary morals, conventions and traditional wisdom, that they claimed the right and considered themselves qualified to treat each case on its merits and that he (Keynes) had always remained, in the strictest sense of the term, an immoralist.[89]

5.4.3. Hayek and free-market pragmatism

More to the point here, however, is whether Hayek's strictures also apply to what we have called free-market pragmatism. Though it seems that they must, the answer is in fact not straightforward. Formally at least, he makes allowance for a pragmatic view but in spirit he is probably opposed to it.

Let us look at the thoroughly pragmatic sentiment expressed by Buchanan and Tullock at the end of their joint book.[90] 'With the philosophers of the Enlightenment we share the faith that man can rationally organize his own society, that existing organization can always be perfected, and that nothing in the social order should remain exempt from rational, critical and intelligent discussion.' One may safely say that Hayek does not share that faith and that he would dislike the Cartesian overtones in the passage. But he does not reject the substance of the idea provided that the organization of society is not effected by 'specific commands' but rather by modifying 'general rules' so that one would 'influence only the general character and not the detail of the resulting order'.[91] We may grasp Hayek's meaning better if we recall the distinction made in connection with the language analogy between an order in activities and the rules or institutions on which it rests (page 47 above). His strictures on constructivism apply to efforts to arrange an order in activities directly by specific commands and not, at least in some parts of his writings, to efforts to improve rules. Carrying the language analogy to somewhat absurd lengths, we might say that a language academy may well try to change some parts of grammar and the usage of a language, i.e. to try to prescribe *how* people should speak. It would be quite another matter if it tried to lay down by specific commands *what* each one of a multitude of people had to say every day. The latter, in terms of the analogy, is what central planning taken to its logical conclusion tries to do and what is attempted to the extent that the details of economic activity are controlled by specific commands.

However, let us look at Hayek's own words:

> Although undoubtedly an order originally formed itself spontaneously because the individuals followed rules which had not been deliberately made but had arisen spontaneously, people gradually learned to improve those rules; and it is at least conceivable that the formation of a spontaneous order relies entirely on rules that were deliberately made.[92]

> What the general argument against 'interference' thus amounts to is that, although we can endeavour to improve a spontaneous order by revising the general rules on which it rests … we cannot improve the results by specific commands that deprive its members of the possibility of using their knowledge for their purposes.[93]

Again, the classical economists applied the term *interference* or *intervention* only to specific commands which

> unlike the rules of just conduct, do not serve merely the formation of a spontaneous order but aim at particular results … They would not have applied it to the establishment or improvement of those generic rules which are required for the functioning of the market order and which they explicitly presupposed in their analysis.[94]

On the evidence of such passages, Hayek's views do not differ fundamentally from those of notable free-market pragmatists such as Henry Simons and Walter Eucken. Simons, as we have seen (page 37 above), urged that government should create the kind of institutions which make it possible to avoid political control of relative prices and presumably of the size and composition of output, production methods and so on. Eucken, whose followers at Freiburg University are now Hayek's colleagues, concluded a short book with the words: 'State planning of forms – Yes; state planning and control of the economic process – No! The essential thing is to recognize the difference between form and process, and to act accordingly.'[95] Eucken dwelt on the question: 'How can modern industrialized economy and society be organized in a humane and efficient way?'[96] For this, telling the difference between form and process, between what is general and what is particular – the solution to what he called the Great Antinomy of economics[97] – is most important. Hayek, as we have seen, rests the case against intervention on the same distinction.

However, what Hayek's analysis brings out more clearly than those of others is that most of the intricate web of institutionalized rules, at least in societies with which we are familiar, has evolved spontaneously so that deliberately made rules can at most modify what already exists. He speaks of the 'stratification of rules of conduct'.[98] In the course of cultural evolution, as he sees it, there has been a 'super-imposition' of 'layers of rules' from the moral and other rules which he thinks developed in the clan or tribe and to which in his opinion modern socialists appeal,[99] to the various rules which made the open society possible and finally to the 'thin layer of rules, deliberately adopted or modified to serve known purposes'.[100] Conflicts may arise between such layers of rules of conduct, as between 'social justice' and economic freedom in modern western societies.

In so far as Hayek would countenance at all what we have called a pragmatic programme, it would have to take into account on the one hand the existing institutions, which would require some way of articulating tacitly known rules, and on the other some vision of a desirable and feasible order. On the latter, Hayek says after noting that *Utopia* has become a bad word:

> But an ideal picture of a society which may not be wholly achievable, or a guiding conception of the overall order to be aimed at, is nevertheless not only the indispensable precondition of any rational policy, but also the chief contribution that science can make to the solution of the problems of practical policy.[101]

5.4.4. Discovery and the ethics of success

There is, however, another side to Hayek, a side which has been coming to the forefront in recent years.[102] It appears that he has come to regard the results of cultural selection as so far superior to anything man could reason out that any thought of deliberately deviating from tradition, if it went beyond 'humbly tinkering' with the order, would be a dangerous folly. In contrast to the expression of faith in Enlightenment ideas by Buchanan and Tullock, Hayek says: 'If the Enlightenment has discovered that the role assigned to human reason in intelligent construction had been too small in the past, we are discovering that the task which our age is assigning to the rational construction of new institutions is far too big.'[103] His main contention in a lecture delivered in 1983 was 'that traditional morals may in some respects provide a surer guide to human action than rational knowledge'.[104] Anyone, therefore, who wished to show that Hayek's views are really dogmatic by our criterion (page 26 above) would not have too much difficulty in doing so.

The issue is bedevilled, however, by an apparent conflict of intentions. Hayek quite obviously wants to advocate free enterprise in free markets and the institutions associated with it but he also wants to maintain a scientific detachment, to honour the *Wertfreiheit* of science. There is undoubtedly much that dispassionate science can do, as the Hayek of 1973 said (in the quote at the end of the previous section), in providing a guiding conception for policy. But the basis of any guiding conception and of any sincere economic or social policy is some value-laden vision of the good society and about the relative merits of competing visions, it is widely accepted, science can say nothing. Hayek, as we shall see, has come to the conclusion that there is something science can say on the question. An unkind critic, however, might suggest that scientific detachment is being pressed into service as a dogmatic advocate of free markets.

Hayek's standpoint may perhaps be dubbed the ethics of success. He appears to have arrived at it along the following route. His discussion of free markets has long focussed on the use of knowledge in society – his papers of 1937 and 1945 on the subject are deservedly famous.[105] Knowledge of local conditions, of very particular circumstances, is widely dispersed and no one person could comprehend and process it all. But the market order harnesses all this knowledge for the benefit of all. He then extended the argument to the gaining of knowledge. Competition, he says, is a discovery procedure.[106] Micro-economic theory, in dealing with the allocation of *given* resources through competition, is missing the essential point. We need competition in order to find out what people really want and consequently what are and what are not resources and how scarce they are. If this were already known or 'given', competition would not be indispensable since a socialist computer might do as well.

Bearing in mind the distinction made in Section 5.1, we may say that, in the respects mentioned, Hayek's analysis is based on the unobtrusive exogenous value that endogenous values should hold sway. In other words, it is a good thing to have an economic order in which individuals have at least a good chance of getting part of what they want. This is also the basis of the libertarian voluntaristic order, but, as Hayek rightly points out, it is by no means all there is to the market order.[107] It also needs certain rules of moral conduct. Such rules do not serve individual preferences or the satisfaction of individual desires; in Hayek's view their function is to restrain and temper the pursuit of individual pleasures.[108] Since individuals may be expected to have preferences and desires whatever the form of economic order may be, it is in fact the way these are tempered by moral rules which distinguishes economic systems from one another. In this way Hayek seems to have been led to a long preoccupation with the rules of moral conduct required by the market order, by which he means such rules as uphold the family, private property, inheritance, the obligations of free contract and so on.

But there are many, often conflicting, moral rules. Is there any way of showing that those which uphold the market order are somehow superior to others which uphold, for example, communes based on fellowship, sharing, mutual love and collective activities? Moral rules tell us what is good and proper. How then do we decide which of all the moral rules are the good and proper ones? Hayek claims to have an answer of sorts. Cultural selection – the survival of the fittest institutions – demonstrates to us which moral rules are the fittest.[109] We may decide the question by the ethics of group success, where success is indicated by 'the proliferation of the group' – a criterion, Hayek says, used also by Adam Smith. Those morals prevail which uphold an economic order capable of sustaining a large population and thus of giving a group of people an advantage in the competition among groups. Cultural selection is therefore also a discovery procedure, but a very peculiar one since discoveries are not necessarily recognized. A group becomes dependent 'for the very survival of its increased numbers' on the observance of practices 'whose beneficial assistance to the survival of men' individuals do not perceive, which they generally 'cannot rationally justify', which may conflict with their 'intellectual insight' and which may often be maintained by religious sanction.[110]

If the ethics of success is really compatible with scientific detachment, as Hayek seems to think, it surely calls for veneration of whatever prevails. But Hayek uses it only to argue that one should 'revere and care for', and above all that one should not question, the family, private property and other pillars of the market order which are often under attack from socialists. Here he seems to be on weak ground. It is at least debatable whether the ethics of success support him in his contentions. The areas of the world with the most proliferating populations are not all noted for their respect for private property and free markets. Apart from some recent stirrings of doubtful permanence, the market economy has not made great strides in this century while socialism and the welfare state have. One must presume that the author of *The Road to Serfdom* also did not always think that the continued survival of the market order was beyond question.

To make his argument stick, Hayek introduces various subsidiary considerations. Areas on the periphery of the market economy have such burgeoning populations because they profit from their contact with the market economy. The present experiments in collective ownership will not see out a century.[111] But his main resource is an implicit distinction between sound cultural evolution and constructivist folly. Marx, for instance, constructed new morals to serve old instincts. Freud destroyed indispensable values by scientific error.[112] Neither is treated as an episode in cultural evolution. One is left with the impression that a wholesome market order would evolve spontaneously if only people could be stopped from thinking, especially about the economic order.

> The exclusive reliance on rational insight as sufficient ground for human action is a grave intellectual error to which those secondhand dealers in ideas who regard themselves as intellectuals seem to be particularly prone. One might almost define them as those who are not intelligent enough to recognize the limits of reason and who in consequence deprive us of the only guide that has enabled us to produce order by structures based on more information than any human agency can use.[113]

Critics, even constructive critics, are told that they are too stupid to question the market order, that they are constitutionally incapable of doing so.

Even if this were quite true, would it be a politic defence of free markets? Would it not be better to bring one's (exogenous) values into the open, to endeavour to make their implications understood and to induce people to try them, to have a taste of them? It is not a formula that guarantees success, but neither is it likely that Hayek's insight into the limitations of rational insight will be very persuasive in a world in which so many are marching for their causes.

However, the conflict between scientific decorum and a value-laden field of interest runs deep in economics. Equilibrium theory, that other descendant of the invisible hand, also has its roots in a guiding conception for policy, and that, however embarrassing it may be for some economists, necessarily carries with it a vision of the good society.

6.

Producers and Predators

Frank Hahn has remarked that Adam Smith 'started us off on the road to answering' the question why a social arrangement of decentralized decision making does not lead to chaos. General equilibrium theory, as stated by Arrow and Debreu, he went on, 'is near the end of that road'.[114] To what extent has equilibrium theory in general really developed and refined the idea of economic order Smith had in mind? The answer is of interest to us. It would not only throw more light on Smith's position apropos free-market pragmatism and dogmatism, but more importantly would show whether those who, for the purposes of a pragmatic programme, may be looking to equilibrium theory as a guiding conception for policy are really availing themselves of the full extent of the original conception.

As usual, however, there is no straightforward answer. Equilibrium theory had at least its beginning in the idea of an efficient allocation of resources – the non-occurrence of chaos narrowly conceived – and that idea is certainly to be found in the *Wealth of Nations*. But allocative efficiency was not the only kind of order Smith was concerned with. One may also find evidence in Smith's work of the other, though possibly related, kinds of order we have come across: the voluntaristic order and the order whose strongest features Hayek saw as discovery and the dissemination of information. But there is stronger evidence of yet a further kind of order which is presupposed for the other kinds and may be regarded as the basis of the invisible-hand argument. Though the principles it involves are all too familiar, it has become such a remote presupposition in equilibrium theory that one may easily lose sight of the part it plays in the overall market order. Some introductory explanation is therefore required.

6.1. Predatory activity

Frédéric Bastiat wrote in one of his essays: 'There are only two ways of obtaining the means essential to the preservation, the adornment, and the improvement of life: *production* and *plunder*.' He added: 'What keeps the social order from improving … is the constant endeavour of its members to live and to prosper at one another's expense.'[115] Marx of course said as much (at about the same time); it was his constant theme. But it is good to hear a proto-libertarian say it because it would be a pity to presume that Marxists have a copyright on the whole idea, rather than simply on its application in their analysis of class struggle and the exploitation of workers by capitalists. As Bastiat also remarked, 'one is compelled to recognize that *plunder* is practised in this world on too vast a scale, that it is too much a part of all great human events, for any social science – political economy least of all – to be able to ignore it'.[116] We shall try to show that the idea also informed and ran through the invisible-hand argument.

The plunder in question here is of course not the kind of pillaging that goes with blood and fire. That kind of plunder is easy to recognize. The problem with plunder in the required sense is that it is very difficult to recognize. Where people specialize, the rule is to live by production and exchange and it is in the institutional set-up of an exchange economy that opportunities arise for some people, let us call them predators, to live and prosper at the expense of others.

The immediate and visible effects of such predatory activities differ of course from those of violent plunder but the long-term economic effect is the same, namely impoverishment. Let us look at this more closely. Let us imagine the unruly conditions in Europe after the breakdown of the Pax Romana. (Historical accuracy is unimportant.) An earnest husbandman labours on the land for the sustenance of his household while marauding bands of pillagers prowl nearby. At harvest time the marauders swoop down and take the crop. When the following year, or perhaps the year thereafter, another band of marauders does the same, the husbandman is likely to surmise that production is a rather foolish business. But there is a way out. Unlike animal predators and their prey, man can change sides. As ever more producers become predators there is less and less to plunder and everyone, producer and predator alike, becomes poorer. If the economic definition of productive activity at the time excludes predatory activity, the product actually diminishes until eventually feudal arrangements bring about a change in the economic order.

In a civilized and sophisticated society, the would-be predator has to take whatever opportunities the institutions of his society allow him to find. But once opportunities are found, the changing of sides has the same effect. In inflationary times, for instance, institutions of borrowing and lending, and especially those which make the money supply ever expandable, create opportunities for running into debt and prospering by capital gains while others do the work which produces the actual goods. As ever more people become borrowers, a situation arises which is perhaps too familiar to need elaboration. Again, arrangements intended to alleviate hardship create the opportunity in the modern welfare state for democratic institutions and prevailing notions of social justice and human rights to be exploited for the purpose of living at the expense of others.

6.2. The liberal order of the invisible hand

In the *Wealth of Nations*, Smith treats monopoly in its many and varied forms as a predatory activity. This may be seen in the way he expresses himself. One does not *have* a monopoly. One *imposes* a monopoly *upon one's fellow-citizens* or *obtains* a monopoly *against one's countrymen*. A few paragraphs before the invisible-hand expression occurs, he says that many sorts of British manufacturers have obtained 'a monopoly against their countrymen'. Some paragraphs after the expression occurs, he says that country gentlemen and farmers, usually 'the least subject to the wretched spirit of monopoly', demanded the monopoly of wheat and meat in the home market in imitation of merchants and manufacturers, who, by their combinations, 'were disposed to oppress them'.[117] Wool-combers, he says elsewhere, by 'combining not to take apprentices', reduced woollen manufacture 'into a sort of slavery to themselves'.[118] He speaks of laws 'which the clamour of our merchants and manufacturers has extorted from the legislature, for the support of their own absurd and oppressive monopolies'; such laws 'may be said to be all written in blood'.[119] Restrictions on competition enable dealers 'by raising their profits above what they naturally would be, to levy, for their own benefit, an absurd tax upon the rest of their fellow-citizens'.[120] Townspeople, because they find it easy to combine (see page 28 above), get a greater share of the 'whole annual produce of the labour of the society' than they would otherwise.[121] In China 'the oppression of the poor' establishes 'the monopoly of the rich'.[122]

The allocative effects of monopoly are also mentioned. The monopoly of the colony trade, for instance, changed the 'quality and shape' of some British manufactures, reduced the overall size of the manufacturing industry and, by raising mercantile profits, discouraged the improvement of land.[123]

It is in this context that the order of the invisible hand has to be understood. It is an economic order which excludes both the oppression and the distortion of monopoly. In other words, it is an order in which effort is not dissipated in predatory activity, i.e. in attempts to take from one another, but rather is directed at using resources as effectively as those most immediately concerned with them judge that they can be used.

The actual invisible-hand expression was used very much as an aside. Smith had said that on more or less equal profitability every individual prefers to employ his capital in domestic rather than foreign industry and that he 'endeavours as much as he can' so to direct that industry that its product may be of the greatest value. In doing so, he promotes the public interest though he intends only his own security and gain,

> and he is in this, as in many other cases, led by an invisible hand to promote an end which was no part of his intention. Nor is it always the worse for the society that it was no part of it. By pursuing his own interest he frequently promotes that of the society more effectually than when he really intends to promote it.[124]

In itself, the passage is not about allocative efficiency though that is dealt with in the next paragraph, where Smith says that every individual 'in his local situation' is better able to judge than a distant statesman in which industry his capital is likely to be most productively employed. The context has often been taken to show that the invisible hand refers to a natural harmony of human interests, as it did in *The Theory of Moral Sentiments* (see page 33 above). The interests of the owners of capital in security and ease of supervision (and therefore in domestic investment) just fit in with the interests of workers in having employment. But this is not Smith's general argument and he does not mention other coincidences of this nature. The general form of the argument is set out five paragraphs earlier:

> Every individual is continually exerting himself to find out the most advantageous employment for whatever capital he can command. It is his own advantage, indeed, and not that of the society, which he has in view. But the study of his own advantage naturally, or rather necessarily leads him to prefer that employment which is most advantageous to the society.[125]

The necessity mentioned in the last sentence is not self-evident. One has to gather from the context what Smith meant. In another place he explained that by advantage to society he understood the increase of the value of the annual produce of land and labour[126] and that is in line with the general conclusion of his inquiry into the nature of the wealth of nations. He started the paragraph in which the invisible-hand expression appears with the national accounting identity of value of product and national income – he called the latter the revenue of society – and then, after the linking word *therefore*, said that every individual in trying to maximize the value of what he produces necessarily labours to maximize the revenue of society. Far from being about a grand harmony of interests, the invisible-hand argument is seemingly quite trivial. The product/revenue of society is the aggregate of what individuals produce. Where all are striving to produce more, all are striving to increase the product/revenue of society and that is by definition advantageous to society or in the public interest.

But the argument does not seem so trivial when one considers that it appears in a chapter on tariff protection and import control and that Smith's criticism of mercantilism was directed against monopoly in all its forms. If the study of his own advantage leads a manufacturer continually to exert himself and to endeavour as much as he can to raise the price (value?) of his product *by* imposing a monopoly upon his fellow citizens, the argument becomes quite misleading. To Smith's way of thinking, monopoly may raise the price but not the value of the product. When, as nowadays, the distinction between price and value is not made, Smith's argument makes good sense only if everyone in some sense creates a product; if there are no zero-sum games; if the gain of one is not the loss of another; in short, if there is no predatory activity.

If Smith's analysis had been quite novel, he would presumably have expressed himself more explicitly. But it was not really novel. J.R. Commons mentions a number of cases heard in the early years of the 17th century in which the English common-law courts extended the economic meaning of *commonwealth*, a meaning later taken up by Puritan clerics. Wealth acquired by industry and frugality is an addition to the common wealth, whereas wealth acquired by monopoly, i.e. by exclusive rights to trade or manufacture, is an extraction from the common wealth, so that the commonwealth (which then also had the meaning of public welfare) is the sum total of private wealth acquired by industry and frugality.[127] Smith's term *the revenue of society* is simply the increment (before consumption) of the commonwealth in this sense. The association of monopoly with plunder was common among political economists. Ricardo, for example, countering a point apparently made by Lauderdale, said that in the case of a hypothetical monopoly of water the gain of the monopolist would be exactly equal to the loss of those who would be obliged to give other commodities for the water which beforehand they had for nothing.[128] J.S. Mill, though sympathetic towards socialist writers, chided them for their declamations against competition. 'They forget that wherever competition is not, monopoly is; and that monopoly, in all its forms, is the taxation of the industrious for the support of indolence, if not of plunder.'[129]

One should remember that Smith and the classical school thought and wrote in the tradition of classical liberalism (if that term may be used to distinguish their outlook from what is called liberalism nowadays, especially in America). Classical liberalism has always been based on individualist values, prominent among which is a high esteem of self-reliance and the incentives and responsibilities that go with it. The isolated individual and his household, as they appear in conjecture, measure up to individualist values in full. The liberal ideal is to combine the virtues of the isolated individual with the advantages of social cooperation. The ideal requires that social cooperation really is cooperation among individuals, that, for example, no one loses his status as a free individual and becomes merely the means to the well-being of others. It is not so easy to define freedom in such a way that the freedom of one person cannot interfere with the freedom of another. The perennial problem of classical liberalism is how to draw the thin line between freedom and power over others.

The *Wealth of Nations* opens with a consideration of the division of labour, the most general aspect of social cooperation. It is within the logic of classical liberalism that it should go on to develop a guiding conception for liberal policy because the division of labour raises not only the problem of coordination, but also that of how to draw the line between economic freedom and economic power over others. The order of the invisible hand is that guiding conception, albeit a very broad one.

6.3. Merchants and manufacturers versus the rest

If there really were a natural harmony of all individual interests, there would be no predatory activity, no problem of defining freedom and, one may presume, no need for a liberal policy. Perhaps Smith did entertain a notion of such harmony in the *Moral Sentiments* but the later work is so much an argument for liberal economic policy that those who think the same natural-law notion is to be found there have somehow to qualify it. According to the most usual qualification, Smith had come to see that the folly of those in government may disturb the harmony of individual interests.

While government certainly does enter Smith's argument, it is not the root of the problem to be solved by liberal policy. The fundamental problem is quite simply that there is *not* a harmony of all interests; that, as Viner pointed out (see page 34 above, the economic order when left to itself is marked by conflicts between private interests and the public interest. Smith mentions many cases of conflicts between private interests, as, for instance, a trade-off between profits and wages[130] or the situation in mature economies (as opposed to colonies) where 'rent and profit eat up wages, and the two superior orders of people oppress the inferior one'.[131] But wage earners, landlords and the rulers of a country all have an interest in making the total product as large as possible and Smith always equates that with public interest. In his perception, however, those who live by profits find themselves in a different position. They do not gain from general prosperity. According to Smith, the rate of profit is low in rich countries, high in poor countries and 'highest in the countries which are going fastest to ruin'.[132]

> The interest of the dealers, however, in any particular branch of trade or manufactures, is always in some respects different from, and even opposite to, that of the public. To widen the market and to narrow the competition, is always the interest of the dealers. To widen the market may frequently be agreeable enough to the interest of the public; but to narrow the competition must always be against it ...[133]

This conflict, for example, placed the East India Company in a quandary when it ruled India. A sovereign normally stands to benefit from the prosperity of his subjects. He therefore has an interest in export prices being as high and import prices as low as possible. As merchants, the East India Company had an interest in exactly the opposite. 'As sovereigns, their interest is exactly the same with that of the country which they govern. As merchants, their interest is directly opposite to that interest.'[134]

Smith has often been represented as a spokesman for capitalists or for business, as we would say now. Certainly he did recognize fully that the prosperity of the rest of society depended in a large measure on the initiative taken by entrepreneurs.

> It is the stock that is employed for the sake of profit, which puts into motion the greater part of the useful labour of every society. The plans and projects of the employers of stock regulate and direct all the most important operations of labour, and profit is the end proposed by all those plans and projects.[135]

Still, he was a strange kind of spokesman for he reserved the only invective in the book for merchants and manufacturers. The problem was how the initiative of such people could be prevented from flowing into predatory activity. The solution, he apparently thought, lay in the common law as conceived in classical liberalism and as it had been developed to some extent under the influence of classical liberalism. This is the force of the phrase 'as long as he does not violate the laws of justice' in the famous passage quoted on page 34 above.

At this point government enters the argument. It is responsible for a firm administration of justice but in fact frequently administers the predatory moves which merchants and manufacturers make on their countrymen. Smith saw the government of his day as composed of nobles and bumbling country gentlemen who understood little about economic affairs and who were no match for quick-witted merchants and manufacturers who not only did understand economic affairs, but also knew exactly what was in their interests and had a persuasive and insistent way of presenting their interests as the public interest. It was this which evoked Smith's eloquent invective, as in the following passages taken from a variety of contexts.

Merchants and manufacturers argued their case 'with all the passionate confidence of interested falsehood'.[136] It was addressed to parliaments, to nobles and country gentlemen 'by those who were supposed to understand trade, to those who were conscious to themselves that they knew nothing of the matter'.[137] The spirit of monopoly invented and propagated a doctrine

> and they who first taught it were by no means such fools as they who believed it. In every country it always is and must be the interest of the great body of the people to buy whatever they want of those who sell it cheapest. The proposition is so very manifest, that it seems ridiculous to take any pains to prove it; nor could it ever have been called in question, had not the interested sophistry of merchants and manufacturers confounded the common sense of mankind. Their interest is, in this respect, directly opposite to that of the great body of the people.[138]

Smith's advice was:

> The proposal of any new law or regulation of commerce which comes from this order, ought always to be listened to with great precaution, and ought never to be adopted till after having been long and carefully examined, not only with the most scrupulous, but with the most suspicious attention. It comes from an order of men, whose interest is never exactly

the same with that of the public, who have generally an interest to deceive and even to oppress the public, and who accordingly have, upon many occasions, both deceived and oppressed it.[139]

But the member of parliament who heeds this advice would have a difficult time. If he opposes the monopolists

and still more if he has authority enough to be able to thwart them, neither the most acknowledged probity, nor the highest rank, nor the greatest public services, can protect him from the most infamous abuse and detraction, from personal insults, nor sometimes from real danger, arising from the insolent outrage of furious and disappointed monopolists.[140]

Smith wistfully visualized a legislature whose deliberations were directed 'not by the clamorous importunity of partial interests, but by an extensive view of the general good'.[141] His thought is familiar enough but surely not that of a person who believes in a natural harmony of interests. It is hard to see how such a belief can be ascribed to him when he made explicit statements about opposed interests. Yet this is a common perception of Smith. One of the contributors to the 1974 edition of the *Encyclopaedia Britannica*, for instance, speaks of 'Smith's doctrine of laissez-faire, based upon a profound belief (borrowed from the French Physiocrats) in the natural harmony of individual wills ...'.[142] That is wide of the mark in every respect. Smith's view of merchants and manufacturers is alone enough to lay the ghost of his dogmatic belief in a harmonious natural order.

However, we are also concerned with another question, namely whether general equilibrium theory really captures in a more rigorous form what Smith was writing about. The answer, it now appears, must be a qualified No. General equilibrium theory presupposes the liberal institutions which Smith advocated and for this reason it is not *about* them. It took up only Smith's intimations of allocative efficiency and has so developed that it is no longer clear whether even that is what it is principally about. It is most usually regarded as a model which, if it were perfected, would somehow represent the actual state of affairs in a market economy or, at least, be useful as a hypothesis for making predictions. There is a gulf between that and a guiding conception for policy, not a difference of degree but of kind. We shall now look at this more closely.

From Guiding Conception to Hypothesis

7.1. Productive contributions

It is a fair question whether in a society with an extensive division of labour there can be a practicable way of telling predators from producers. To be able to distinguish between in effect taking the wherewithal of life away from others and actually creating it, one would have to be able to say who produced what or, at least, which were the productive factors and how much each of them contributed to the total product. Opinions no doubt differ on whether economic theory has accomplished much in this regard.

Some economists, usually of socialist inclination, simply deny that it is possible to disentangle the product of social cooperation for the purpose of attributing it to individuals. Since they cannot then say who is producing and who is merely taking, they usually maintain that the distribution of income is settled entirely by predatory activity. Edward Nell's position, for instance, is that 'in an interdependent system there is no way of isolating any one particular productive contribution'. He rejects the neoclassical idea of the market as an 'orderly shopping centre' where people 'get what they pay for and pay for what they get' and instead favours what he calls the Classical-Marxian perception according to which 'the marketplace is the arena for the exercise of economic power, the battlefield in which the division of the spoils between classes and subclasses is settled'.[143] Everyone, it appears, is a freebooter or, rather, a member of one or other pack of prowling predators.

The marginal productivity theory, which Nell and his friends at Cambridge and elsewhere reject, is of course supposed to show productive contributions at the margin, at least in principle. But, quite apart from the reswitching issue and technical limitations such as the need for variable techniques and the requirements of the product exhaustion theorem, marginal productivity theory is of little use for distinguishing between predatory and productive activities. It is formulated for cases in which it is taken for granted that we know which are productive activities. For the distinction in question, however, the definition of production is the crucial issue. We have an intuitive understanding of production but have not found it easy to translate that into a workable definition. For instance, the working definition for the national accounts, involving such things as values added and imputations for non-market services and goods, seems yet to fall short of the intuitive understanding. The profits of a firm with, say, a state-enforced monopoly of an essential agricultural input are taken as a measure of the owners' productive contribution. Likewise, the productive contributions of tax lawyers and tax accountants are reckoned at the not-inconsiderable amounts they get for protecting what may be predatory gains from the predatory hands of a voting majority. This seems not to accord with the intuitive understanding of production. The emotive meaning of production does not conjure up a vision of someone labouring to find tax loopholes which others are labouring to close; nor of someone working hard at lobbying and at getting in with the right people. Emotive meanings are not irrelevant. If economists deliberately ignore them, their subject may lose much of its significance.

Many people of course have pondered at one time or another over the meaning of production. Many of them through the ages came to the conclusion that *price* times quantity is an inadequate measure or indication of product, that somehow it should be *value* times quantity. The venerable distinction between value and price has disappeared from modern mainstream economics and perhaps the loss is not too great since it did not really resolve the issue. Nevertheless, the distinction had something to do with the genesis not only of the labour theory of value, but also of general equilibrium theory.

7.2. Natural prices

In Adam Smith's analysis, productive contributions are indicated by value produced so that monopolistic practices are shown up by divergences between value and price (though not every such divergence indicates a monopolistic practice). The distinction between value and price is first dealt with in Chapters V and VII of Book I of the *Wealth of Nations*.

Chapter V on real and nominal prices, or prices in labour and in money, contains the material which, together with the opening remarks of Chapter VI, has led some commentators to ascribe a labour theory of value to Smith. The leading thought of the chapter is rather similar to that behind the comparisons one occasionally sees of the cost of living in various countries. A table is drawn up showing how long it would take in various countries for people in a few selected occupations to earn enough to buy a certain assortment of basic commodities. Such a comparison is regarded as more telling than one based on prices and exchange rates or on prices and earnings. Similarly, Smith says that the real price of a commodity, what it really costs to one who wants it, is the 'toil and trouble of acquiring it'. What a commodity is worth (i.e. its value) to one who has it is the toil and trouble it saves him, since having it makes its acquisition unnecessary. In exchange, people bear in mind the toil-and-trouble value of commodities. Hence real prices are a better basis than nominal prices in gold and silver (of which the values fluctuate) for comparisons involving different times and different places. Toil and trouble is the measure of value, though labour-time, as he makes plain in the fourth paragraph, is a very imperfect indication of toil and trouble.

The opening remarks of Chapter VI have a rather different purpose. The chapter shows that prices resolve themselves into factor earnings. The opening remarks simply make the point that in a primitive setting, where land is not owned and capital has not been accumulated, labour is the only factor of production and prices resolve themselves purely into labour earnings. It is a bit of heuristics that Smith often used. (See Section 4.3.3. A part of these opening remarks is quoted on page 39 above.) Schumpeter's comments to the effect that Smith floundered badly and was thoroughly confused in these two chapters, though not entirely without foundation, yet seem rather unfair.[144]

Chapter VII on natural and market prices, together with some elaborations in Chapter X, explains the distinction between value and price in the form in which it is most frequently used in the rest of the book. It is a short but interesting chapter. It sets out a general equilibrium conception in an admirably concise way, though of course without any of the technicalities which have come into the subject since then. A natural or ordinary price – Mill's necessary and Marshall's normal price – is a cost price and, as Smith puts it at one place in the chapter, 'the price of free competition'. Its basis is an imaginary though not altogether impossible state of perfect liberty. ('This at least would be the case where there was perfect liberty.') In this state a person has a perfectly free choice of occupation and is able to change his occupation as often as he pleases. Owners of capital enjoy the same freedom of choice and of movement in the use of their capital. Where industries are long established and well known, labour and capital are forever moving about, seeking the most advantageous employments. In this way a tendency to uniform natural rates of wages and profit is established. Though rent is a residual, landowners also seek the most advantageous uses for their land. There is therefore also a natural rate of rent which, however, varies with the location and the fitness of the land for various uses. The natural price of a commodity is that price which just covers the earnings at their natural rates of the labour, capital and land involved in producing the commodity and in bringing it to market. When a commodity is sold at its natural price, it is 'sold precisely for what it is worth'.

But it is not necessarily sold at its natural price. The actual prices of commodities are market prices. They are established by demand and supply and are forever varying with changes in demand and with accidental circumstances affecting supply. Samuel Hollander argues that Smith's treatment of market prices is far closer to modern demand and supply analysis than is commonly supposed.[145] When market and natural prices diverge, wages, profits and rents, or any one or two of them, are either above or below their natural rates. Factor mobility then comes into play and, if unimpeded, brings about a situation in which the quantity of labour, capital and land employed in various industries 'suits itself in this manner to the effectual demand'.

Natural rates of factor earnings and therefore natural prices may themselves change with economic expansion or contraction, changing affluence and economic development in general. This would be the case where technology changes or a resource becomes scarcer as incomes rise. However, Smith did not, at least in Book I Chapter VII, allow for factor substitution. In our parlance, he assumed fixed factor proportions, though it was very likely an assumption by default. Furthermore, Smith did not formally connect factor earnings with 'effectual demand'. Perhaps he took the connection for granted, as he did the need for reciprocity in international trade. But he showed no awareness of the problems later economists were to see in the circular flow.

Smith used the general-equilibrium idea as a backbone for his discussion of a great welter of detail in the rest of Book I; more specifically as a heuristic device (see Section 4.3.3) to bring out the significance of circumstances which make actual situations deviate from the general equilibrium case. These include the frequent changes beyond human control in the supply of agricultural goods, which make the prices of these goods fluctuate much more than those of manufactured goods, which vary only with changes in demand; or the influence of continuity of employment, risk and the cost of training on earnings. Above all, however, he used it to deal with monopolistic practices. The last quarter of Chapter VII and more than half of Chapter X are devoted to the topic and it is brought up repeatedly in the substantial middle section of the *Wealth of Nations*, where Smith pursues his argument against mercantilist policies.

Interpreted very freely, monopolistic practices enable certain parties to impede the mobility of capital and of labour and even to restrict the uses of land and thereby to raise their own earnings above the natural rate and to depress those of their suppliers and sometimes of their employees (e.g. by long apprenticeships) below the natural rates. The predator in a market setting creates for himself the opportunity of concluding transactions in which he receives more than the value of his product and pays others less than the value of their product. The time, the effort and the ingenuity devoted to creating such opportunities is incompatible with the liberal order of the invisible hand (see Section 6.2).

It would be incorrect to say that Smith introduced natural prices expressly to deal with monopolistic practices. The notion of natural or ordinary prices, without or with only an inkling of general equilibrium, had then been current for some centuries[146] and Smith would have been expected to say something about them in a comprehensive book on political economy. Scholastic moralists had used the notion to distinguish between fair and extortionate prices. Their purpose had been to provide a moral guide. Smith articulated the analytical basis and then used it as a heuristic and explanatory device. One of its most important functions was to serve as a guiding conception for liberal economic policy, which was but one remove from the moral guide of the Scholastics. The emphasis changed and in so far as attempts were made to analyse the conditions for allocative efficiency, general-equilibrium theory became a guide to efficiency. It is still sometimes seen in this light. More often, however, it is seen in quite a different light. Smith's heuristics were taken up in a different way and developed into what is intended to be either an instrument for prediction or at least a hypothesis which is supposed somehow to reflect the actual state of economic affairs, rather than a state of affairs that some people would like to see or, if they are free-market pragmatists, that they would like as far as possible to create.

7.3. Walras: equilibrium as guiding conception

Francis Hutcheson, who was one of Adam Smith's teachers, is credited with having been the original author of what became something of a utilitarian slogan, namely that actions and institutions should be judged by whether they procure the greatest happiness of the greatest numbers. It was not Smith, however, but Walras who brought a version of Hutcheson's criterion into his economic analysis. Walras had set himself the task of investigating the claims made for free competition[147] and for this purpose he used utility maximization rather as though it were the greatest-happiness principle. He did so not because he was a particularly ardent utilitarian but, according to Jaffé, because his father had tried unsuccessfully for many years to develop a theory of value based on scarcity and because a colleague at Lausanne, a professor of mechanics, had shown him how to handle utility maximization with derivatives (the equi-marginal principle) after he (Walras) had more or less completed his theory of interrelated markets.[148]

Where Smith had argued that a liberal economic order would allow the revenue of society, i.e. national income, to be as great as any laws and institutions could allow it to be, Walras argued that free competition would bring about such a composition and quantity of output as would give the greatest possible satisfaction of wants. Apart from this difference and of course the mathematical exposition, Walras's analysis of general equilibrium prices was not very unlike Smith's analysis of natural prices.[149] The essential point about free competition when production is taken into account was factor mobility, and utility maximization occurred under the double condition that there is an equilibrium price for each product and that this price is equal to the cost of the services employed in making the product.[150] Above all, however, Walras's general equilibrium theory was of the same genre as Smith's argument in so far as the ultimate role Walras had in mind for it was that of an ideal or a guiding conception for policy. It was Pareto who made general equilibrium into a rather different sort of thing. Though he did not alter the basic format of Walras's theory, he treated it purely as a hypothesis about the workings of *actual* market economies, as opposed to a conception of an *ideal* market economy.

In Lesson 22 of his *Elements*, Walras interrupted the exposition of his model to reflect on what he had been doing. He had studied 'the nature, causes and consequences of free competition'. For this 'it did not matter whether or not we observed it in the real world, since, strictly speaking, it was sufficient that we should be able to form a conception of it'. The study of such a conception had shown that the consequences of free competition 'may be summed up as the attainment, within certain limits, of maximum utility. Hence free competition becomes a principle or a rule of practical significance, so that it only remains to extend the detailed application of this rule to agriculture, industry and trade.'[151]

In answer to an imaginary critic, he said he had not 'attempted to predict decisions made under conditions of perfect freedom' but only to express in mathematics the effects of such decisions once made. Nor would he be put off by the imaginary critic's remonstration about market imperfections:

> … nevertheless, the equations we have developed do show freedom of production to be the superior general rule. Freedom procures, within certain limits, the maximum of utility; and, since the factors which interfere with freedom are obstacles to the attainment of this maximum, they should, without exception, be eliminated as completely as possible.[152]

He conceded that this had been said all along by the advocates of laissez-faire. What he had done, he claimed, was to prove the argument scientifically. As a result its applicability had become clear. He then mentioned its inapplicability to cases of public goods and natural monopolies and to arguments about 'distributive justice'.

Walras had socialist leanings but had been persuaded to consider whether free markets did not hold out greater promise than socialist schemes. He was prepared to consider a programme of free-market pragmatism and thought he had proved its case in the manner of the utilitarian greatest-happiness principle by showing that individual utilities were maximized. The soundness of his argument is open to question. He had shown that individual utilities were maximized subject to the constraints of a market economy. They could also be shown to be maximized subject to other constraints, say, to those of a centrally planned economy. One would have to show that the maxima in the one case are greater than in the others. Since this would involve interpersonal comparisons of utility and since utility as a quantity is dubious in any case, it does not seem likely that the argument would succeed.[153] The soundness of Walras's argument did not become an issue because utility maximization soon came to be regarded purely as the driving force in actual economies, or rather as a representation of it that allows one to say something about the relations between various prices and quantities in market economies as they are actually found in the world. Since no comparison is involved in this, the theory in this form is not open to the objections outlined above. In this form, however, the theory has also lost its status as a 'rule of practical significance', as Walras called it (see the quotation two paragraphs above). What is important in the present context is that Walras did think, perhaps mistakenly, that his theory had practical significance.

Walras's remarks in Lesson 22 were not a momentary aberration. They conform to his lengthy introductory remarks stretching over four chapters in Part I of the *Elements*. There he had said that economics encompasses a natural science, a moral science and an art. Adam Smith's view of political economy as the science of the statesman or legislator he called incomplete. Statesmen and legislators are concerned with attaining desirable objectives (as Smith had said) and such endeavours Walras called an art. The art of the statesman presupposes a pure science and 'the distinguishing characteristic of a science is the complete indifference to consequences, good or bad, with which it carries on the pursuit of pure truth'. Smith's definition of political economy was therefore incomplete.[154]

On the other hand, J.B. Say's definition of political economy was 'inaccurate and inferior to Adam Smith's'. According to it, political economy was entirely a natural science which showed 'the ways in which wealth is produced, distributed and consumed', as though this took place 'if not spontaneously, at least in a manner somehow independent of the will of man'. This definition had been pleasing to those who dogmatically rejected every proposal for reform simply on the grounds that it was not natural. The point of view had been taken over by Say from the Physiocrats. But it was mistaken because the explanation of production, distribution and consumption was not 'a sequel to the natural history of bees':

> Man is a creature endowed with reason and freedom, and possessed of a capacity for initiative and progress. In the production and distribution of wealth, and generally in all matters pertaining to social organization, man has the choice between better and worse and tends more and more to choose the better part ... The superiority of later forms of organization over the earlier forms lies not in their greater naturalness ... but rather in their closer conformity with material well-being and justice. The proof of such conformity is the only justification for adhering to a policy of *laisser-faire, laisser-passer*.[155]

The pure science which the art of the statesman presupposes should provide this proof. One should understand how Walras conceived pure and mathematical sciences such as his general equilibrium theory. He revealed himself to be what philosophers call a rationalist. This is important because it made of the original version of general equilibrium theory something rather different from what it became after Pareto, who was a positivist and decidedly unsympathetic towards Walras's rationalism. The mathematical method, Walras explained, is a rational method and the sciences based on it go beyond experience as soon as they have drawn their type concepts from it. 'From real-type concepts, these sciences abstract ideal-type concepts which they define, and then on the basis of these definitions they construct *a priori* the whole framework of their theorems and proofs. After that they go back to experience not to confirm but to apply their conclusions.' This is how geometry deals with triangles, circles and so on, and reality confirms its definitions and demonstrations only approximately, and 'yet reality admits of a very wide and fruitful application of these propositions'.

> Following the same procedure, the pure theory of economics ought to take over from experience certain type concepts, like those of exchange, demand, market, capital, income, productive services and products. From these … [it should] … define ideal-type concepts in terms of which it carries on its reasoning. The return to reality should not take place until the science is completed and then only with a view to practical applications.

In other words, pure economics could investigate the concept of a market economy even though there may be nothing in the world which may strictly speaking be called a market economy and the conclusions of pure economics, like those of geometry, need not be tested.[156]

Walras regretted 'the absence of philosophy among French economists which offsets and nullifies' their intellectual qualities of 'clarity and precision'.[157]

7.4. Pareto: equilibrium as hypothesis

Writing of Walras and Pareto, Schumpeter said:

> Their common ground was confined to pure theory and specifically to Walras' equations of equilibrium. But in every other respect they were as different as two men can be, and even their companionship in arms in the fight for mathematical economics and Pareto's obligation to Walras in the matter of the Lausanne professorship did not prevent their deep-seated mutual dislike from asserting itself or even from spilling over in conversation with third persons. While their pure theories are cast in the same mould, their systems of thought taken as wholes and their visions of the social process are not. And all those economists who are not disposed to neglect a man's philosophy and practical recommendations completely …

will, for this reason alone, consider the Paretian structure to be something completely different from that of Walras.[158]

Although the word *Walrasian* is nowadays applied quite generally to an important segment of neoclassical economics, the word *Paretian* would be more accurate as a description of the most usual form of this kind of economics. That the Walrasian and Paretian 'structures' are 'completely different' and stem from quite different 'systems of thought taken as wholes' is a matter which is not easy either to set out or to comprehend. Nevertheless, some indication of the difference will be attempted in this section.

There was first of all Pareto's disdain of Walras's preoccupation with social policy and with economics as not only a pure science, but also an art and a moral science. As Schumpeter again puts it:

> Walras presented his immortal theory in the garb of a political philosophy that is extra-scientific in nature and, moreover, not to everyone's taste. I am afraid that there is no better way of conveying what that philosophy was than to call it the philosophy of petty-bourgeois radicalism. He felt called upon to preach an *idéal social* that hails from the semi-socialist French writers of the first half of the nineteenth century or, as we may say with equal justice, from utilitarianism.[159]

Schumpeter was merely unsympathetic towards such an outlook; Pareto held it in utter contempt. The man who spoke of *ophelimity* to avoid the possible moral connotations of *utility* simply despised any talk of welfare or the common good. That Pareto became (once more in Schumpeter's words) 'the patron saint of the "New Welfare Economics" … [and] … came to render a service to a cause with which he was – or would be – completely out of sympathy is not without its humor'.[160]

However, this difference of temperament was only one manifestation of a much more deep-seated discord. Walras and Pareto were separated by the ancient philosophical divide between realism and nominalism, in their case between Walras's rationalism and Pareto's positivism. One cannot avoid touching on the often abstruse and difficult ideas involved in this schism if one is to understand how the general equilibrium analysis of Walras and even of Smith has become something very different in this century despite maintaining a resemblance in its outer form.

What is important in our context is that realists, in the sense in which they are contrasted with nominalists, are committed to the view that significant scientific conclusions may be drawn from what others would call conceptual analysis and realists regard as investigations of rational forms, i.e. of the nature of something and of the logical implications of an idea (e.g. the nature and logical implications of free competition, in the case of Walras). In fact, the realist position is that exact science, as opposed to empirical description, takes the form of investigations into rational forms and therefore shows not only *that* such and such is the case, but also *why* it is what it is. That the realist point of view was dominant until fairly recently even in the English-speaking world (which in a way was the cradle of empiricism) may be seen from the entries for 'Empirical' in the *Oxford English Dictionary*. Three of the four entries indicate that whatever is said to be empirical is based on or guided by mere experience or observation without scientific theory or scientific knowledge.

Nominalists, on the other hand, are committed to the view that the words which make up theories or hypotheses are mere names and are of no significance unless they are tied, rather like labels, to objects and events in the world, or, as it became in positivism, unless hypotheses are tested. On this view, conceptual analysis by itself cannot possibly lead to significant scientific conclusions. Since welfare, for example, is not really sufficiently visible for having a label tied to it, nominalists would tend to regard it as a non-scientific term or mere word and any disquisition on it as more or less meaningless.

We have already seen that Walras conceived pure economics, of which his general equilibrium analysis was an example, along rationalist and therefore realist lines. Pure economics goes beyond experience as soon as it has framed its definitions, constructs its theories a priori and returns to experience not to test but only to apply theories, as is done in geometry. Moreover, one could investigate the nature of free competition even if one had no experience of it as long as one could form a conception of it. In paragraph 16 of the *Elements* Walras even hailed the realist position as a truth long established by Platonic philosophy. At the end of the preface to the fourth edition he remarked that no one could say that it had taken unduly long for economics to become a rational as well as an empirical science since it had taken longer in astronomy and mechanics. He took pride in counting himself among those who had had a hand in bringing economics to maturity so rapidly.

Pareto made his nominalism quite clear in his published replies to two letters by Benedetto Croce, particularly in the second reply.[161] The issue under discussion was how to state the problems of pure economics. Croce had criticized Pareto's analogy between the 'tiny slice of economics' called pure economics and mechanics. In his first reply Pareto put the matter as follows:

The movements of celestial bodies were a real puzzle. A tremendous number of facts were available but one did not know how to relate them. A hypothesis was made – and mark you, my illustrious friend, that I call it a hypothesis – and only by this means were all those facts related. But, how does it happen that one body attracts another? We do not know but it does not matter. We work on this assumption meanwhile, and the facts are exactly as the theory predicts them … Let us do the same with that tiny slice of economics. Let us try out a hypothesis.[162]

The general problem to be solved, he put as follows: 'given certain individuals, who have certain tastes revealed by their choice, and who encounter obstacles in satisfying their tastes, predict the phenomena which will occur in that society'.[163] A little further on, Pareto remarked: 'I am only easy-going about the names of things. If you attack me on relations between things I will no longer give way and I will accept battle. What alone matters is the objective relationship, whilst the means of expressing it is of secondary importance.'[164]

In his reply to Croce's second letter, Pareto expressed his nominalism and positivism more explicitly. At the outset he told Croce: 'As to the manner of defining the limits of a science, our disagreement can be traced back to that famous clash between the nominalists and the realists.' He went on: 'I am the most nominalist of nominalists. For me the only objective cases are concrete cases. Their classifications are man-made and are therefore arbitrary …'[165] The contrast with Walras, who had taken his cue from 'philosophie platonicienne', could hardly be greater.

While Walras had investigated the *nature* of free competition, Pareto eschewed any such thing:

For my part, with due modesty, I only study facts and concrete cases and try to find out what regularities and analogies they present … Let others concern themselves with the *nature*, with the *essence* of 'value'. I am interested only in seeing whether I can discover which *regularities* are presented by prices.[166]

Where Walras had held up mechanics as an exemplar of 'science rationnelle' for economics to follow, Pareto saw it as a positivist achievement which economics should emulate:

Astronomers know nothing about the nature of universal gravitation … if astronomers had wasted their time …

investigating the nature of universal gravitation, astronomy would still be in its infancy. Luckily they carried on. They simply admitted the hypothesis that celestial bodies move *as if* forces were applied to them ... and thus astronomers created celestial mechanics which is a splendid achievement of human science.

Now political economy, which for too long has refused to follow that path, is at last showing signs of intending to do so, and I am among those who intend to follow it most strictly and decidedly.[167]

Walras said pure economics went beyond experience and needed no testing. Pareto told the realist Croce:

We experimentalists ... leave the concrete, which we are always looking at lovingly, only with reluctance and when forced by necessity. When we follow your path we do so only *hypothetically*. We accept hypotheses not for any intrinsic value they may have but only in so far as they yield deductions which are in harmony with the facts ... If the deductions do not agree with the facts, Madam Hypothesis can go to blazes.[168]

Finally, Pareto summarized his standpoint:

I look for a theory which may include and present economic facts. For my part, I know only the system of equations of pure economics as being capable of attaining that end, just in the same way that the system of equations of celestial mechanics explains and represents the movement of celestial bodies. I have no other reason for accepting the theories of pure economics ... Naturally I would drop them if somebody found something better.[169]

The reader will recognize in these extensive extracts from Pareto's letters to Croce an exposition of the ideal of positive economics which a majority of present-day economists seem to share. The ideal is, however, not shared by all economists nor, it seems, honoured in practice by the majority all of the time. The question is bedevilled by the similarity in the words *positive* and *positivist*. The former has been used in economics since the time of John Neville Keynes as an antonym of *normative* and has also come to be used in the place of *positivist*, which has a meaning of non-normative in the specific sense of a certain nominalist attitude to scientific procedure, namely the one Pareto articulated so lucidly. The expression *positive economics* appears, for instance, in the title of Friedman's well-known article on the subject as also in the title of a well-known textbook.[170] In both cases the expression quite clearly is meant to convey that the kind of economics in question is not only non-normative but also positivist. Understood in this way, positive economics is not at all the same thing as Walras's pure economics. The latter may have been positive in so far as it was prior to and independent of normative considerations,[171] but it was not positivist and nominalist, i.e. it differed from positive economics on the question of whether conceptual analysis by itself is a worthwhile scientific activity.

That this is in fact a big difference may be seen most clearly when economics is meant to guide policy, i.e. when normative considerations do come into play. Except in cases where it is meant to preserve the status quo, economic policy is intended to bring about a desirable situation which does not as yet exist but is only projected, imagined or conceived – which in fact may be said not only of economic policy but of human endeavours in general. Conceptual analysis such as Smith's and Walras's analysis of free competition may serve policy by providing and analysing that merely conceived situation which guides policy. Further analysis may be intended to show to what extent actual situations may be made to conform to the conceived situation, such as when an examination of what the participants in Walrasian *tâtonnement* markets would have to know leads to the conclusion that it is not really feasible to create such markets. This is how thinking has guided action presumably for all time. But positive economics cannot serve policy in this way. Positivist hypotheses gain significance only in so far as they conform to the already existing situation in the sense of yielding fairly accurate predictions deductively. When theory serves as a guiding conception, the world is to be made to conform to theory; as positivist hypothesis, theory is to be made to conform to the world and then theory can serve policy only in so far as it helps in the search for something unchanging in the existing situation which may be exploited for policy purposes.

By way of illustration, one may consider an updated version of Pareto's statement of the general problem he wanted (positive) economics to be able to solve (page 80 above). Here is what Lucas would like economists to be able to do:

> Our task as I see it ... is to write a FORTRAN program that will accept specific economic policy rules as 'input' and will generate as 'output' statistics describing the operating characteristics of time series we care about, which are predicted

to result from these policies. For example, one would like to know what average rate of unemployment would have prevailed since World War II in the United States had M1 grown at 4 percent per year during this period, other policies being as they were.[172]

When Smith recommended the dismantling of mercantilist policies and when Walras recommended what amounted to a programme of free-market pragmatism, their recommendations were based on analyses of the *concept* of free competition. The projected policy recommendations of those who pursue positive economics are based on the hope of finding stable coefficients by means of which economic affairs may be predicted and manipulated.

8.

The Ambiguity of Equilibrium Theory

8.1. Prescription and description

'Political oeconomy, considered as a branch of the science of a statesman or legislator, proposes two distinct objects': to enable 'the people' to provide themselves with a plentiful subsistence and to provide the state with sufficient revenue for public services.[173] This is the gist of the remark by Adam Smith, which Walras regarded as an incomplete but not incorrect definition of political economy (page 76 above). Smith clearly implied that political economy may be considered also in other ways. He did not suggest any alternatives but presumably one of the alternatives is that it may be considered as some kind of description and explanation of the economic relationships that actually prevail. Economics is perhaps more commonly regarded in this way nowadays but in the past its association with the art of a statesman was very close and equilibrium theory and its antecedents in particular were closely tied to the advocacy of economic liberalism and even to the ethical question of what constitutes a fair price. The history of economics is not only, nor even mainly, the history of a description but the history of a prescription.

Since prescription that is not preceded by some description is hardly to be taken seriously, the mixed character of our legacy is not remarkable in itself. It would appear, however, to be a source of ambiguity in equilibrium theory and that ambiguity is of importance to the question whether equilibrium theory may serve as a guiding conception for free-market pragmatism. We have already become acquainted with the background of the ambiguity. We shall now look into the issue more directly.

85

Mises was wont to say that human action is the attempt to substitute a more satisfactory state of affairs for a less satisfactory state. One imagines conditions which suit one better and one expects to be able to turn the actual situation into the imagined one.[174] The execution of policy prescriptions is also human action and involves an imagined more desirable situation and some knowledge of the actual situation, though for policy purposes this knowledge need relate only to the possibilities of transforming the actual situation into the more desired one. The question of desirability – i.e. the normative one – may of course be set aside for later consideration or for consideration by others, or it may simply be discarded as unworthy of science. But when this is done, one is *not* left simply with a description, as often seems to be presumed. At least two elements are still left over from the idea of human action. First, there is a description, i.e. a diagnosis of the actual situation as well as whatever it is that leads one to expect to be able to transform that situation. Secondly, there is an imagined situation or guiding conception which, with normative considerations set aside, becomes simply a conception. We may call it an ideal conception. The word *ideal* has several meanings so that in this case it may take the meaning *confined to thought* and revert to the normative meaning *worthy of actualization* according to context.

There is then a first sense in which we may speak of ambiguity arising out of the mixed character of our legacy. Some economists treat equilibrium theory as an ideal conception with the normative meaning and others treat it as a description in some attenuated sense and yet others distinguish very poorly between the two. Some see it as an ideal system worth examining because it is taken – or should we say perhaps it is mistaken – to be the system economic liberalism advocates; others see it as one element in a projected though as yet unexplained series of successive approximations to the working of actual economies. Some treat equilibrium theory as a study of the conditions for one or other kind of economic efficiency, such as the optimum allocation of resources or simply market clearing; others treat it as a handy framework for explanations and predictions of what actually goes on, perhaps on the grounds that people never fail to meet the efficiency conditions, or fail in a predetermined way. Hahn, for instance, often treats general equilibrium theory as an ideal conception of economic efficiency. Textbook writers, he says, would be less inclined to declare free-trade equilibrium to be Pareto-efficient or -optimal if they spelt out the required assumptions, such as the absence of increasing returns and a complete set of futures and contingent-claims markets. General equilibrium theory, as Hahn sees it, deals with the question whether a decentralized economy relying only on price signals may be orderly. Its answer, he says, is that an economy with such properties may be described. 'But this of course does not mean that any actual economy has been described.'[175] On the other hand, Lucas could hardly expect the computer program he mentions in the passage already quoted (page 82 above) to accomplish what he has in mind for it unless it were a hypothesis which somehow captures certain constant features of actual economic affairs.

This kind of ambiguity is not new in economics nor did it start with Pareto. The change of character that general equilibrium theory underwent in passing from Walras to Pareto is noteworthy mainly because it highlights the contrast. But Walras himself, as we shall see, was not free of the ambiguity and it was certainly to be found in economics before his day, also in the *Wealth of Nations*. One may speculate that the ambiguity was due to the influence of dogmatic attitudes to the market economy, even on those who did not really hold dogmatic views. The dogmatist's prescription of economic liberalism takes the form of a simple anti-government stance according to which only the meddling of governments prevents the realization of the natural and desirable economic order. The description of the wished-for state of affairs, but for the intervention of governments, is the same as the description of the actual state of affairs. The natural economic order does not quite manage to become the actual state of affairs but it is always there, just below the surface.

That this is not so, that the market economy is an artifice which has to be promoted deliberately, is the pragmatic standpoint supported throughout this study. If it is correct, it is also quite evident that a conception of market order devised originally to guide policy is not at all the same thing as a description of the actual state of economic affairs; that an ideal conception of natural liberty and free competition is not at all the same thing as an abstract of the principles by which the quantitative configurations of actual economies are determined. A person who no longer distinguishes clearly between the situation in which he would like to find himself and the situation in which he actually does find himself would certainly be called confused. In equilibrium theory, however, there are so many complicating factors that it is proper to speak rather of ambiguity.

8.2. Three methods

Even quite casual observation shows that equilibrium theory is simply a bad description of actual economic affairs. It may, for instance, exclude predatory activity altogether and may include perfect foresight or surrogates for it such as a complete set of contingent-claims markets. That this does not describe the world we read about in newspapers is obvious. It is safe to say that all economists look upon equilibrium theory as something confined to thought, i.e. as an ideal conception. The ambiguity of equilibrium theory is due to the rather different ways in which the intellectual function of an ideal conception is perceived. At least three methods are applied in equilibrium theory and ideal conceptions have a different intellectual function in each of them.

The method used when theory is meant to guide action or policy we may call *pragmatic inference*. It may be explained as follows. An ideal conception is an inference that certain conclusions follow logically from certain premises. For instance, the ideal conception of a liberal economic order set out earlier (Section 6.2) is the inference that the successful efforts of each individual to procure for himself or herself the means to a good life add to the total that is available of such means if individuals are prevented from taking the means from each other. There is no assertion that people actually are prevented from taking from each other, nor that people actually do make productive efforts, successful or unsuccessful. In pragmatic inference, the ideal conception has no descriptive function. However, to be of practical significance as a guiding conception, it must be used together with some assertions of fact. For this purpose, the premises of the inference are to be understood as prevailing conditions and the conclusions as situations of a certain kind, i.e. situations to which some common feature may be ascribed, however different they may be otherwise. Pragmatic inference then shows that a certain kind of situation prevails if certain conditions prevail or *that it would prevail if certain conditions were to be made to prevail*. On the understanding that the same conclusions cannot also follow from other premises, pragmatic inference may also be used negatively to show that a certain kind of situation does not or cannot prevail if certain conditions do not, or cannot be made to, prevail.

Pragmatic inference may therefore be used either positively or negatively; either actively as a guiding conception, to show what the means for achieving some end would have to be, or passively as a heuristic device. For example, Smith's analysis of natural prices involves the inference that every good is 'sold precisely for what it is worth' unless factor mobility is impeded (pages 72–3 above). The inference is really a definition of value (as distinct from price). If it now appears that in many cases factor mobility is in fact impeded, the conclusion is that in many cases the prices and values of goods are not equal, i.e. goods are not sold for what they are worth. The analysis raises the issue of factor mobility, it draws attention and gives significance to institutions and other conditions which impede factor mobility. Used negatively and passively, the pragmatic inference is a heuristic device (see Sections 7.2 and 4.3.3). However, the inference may take another form, viz, if impediments to factor mobility were removed as far as is possible, the price and value of every good would be as nearly equal as is possible. Used positively and actively, the pragmatic inference is a guiding conception. Smith used pragmatic inference more or less intuitively and Walras used it rather more consciously, though both also resorted to the method which will be explained next. We have seen that Hahn has made use of negative and active pragmatic inference (page 86). In fact he has done so frequently.

The ideal conception in the case of pragmatic inference is not a description of any aspect of the world, i.e. it is not a model. Its relation to description is that it raises questions the answers to which are descriptions. More usually, however, the inference, of which the ideal conception consists, is taken to represent something in the world at large, something like the operation of a law or a cause intertwined in actual cases with the operation of other laws or causes. Walras, for example, apart from using his system for pragmatic inference (see Section 7.3), believed that the solution of his equations represented or corresponded to the outcome of a *tâtonnement* process in actual markets, at least in principle.

The method based on this notion of representation is sometimes referred to as that of *successive approximation*. This is the familiar method according to which a theory deals with one aspect of reality only. By dropping simplifying assumptions, combining theories and so on, one may bring other aspects into account and so approximate the 'real world' ever more closely. Since successive approximation may be regarded as the inverse of abstraction, ideal conceptions are often thought of as empirical generalizations or abstractions – so, for instance, Walras's recommendation that economics abstract by definition its *types idéaux* from *types réels* (page 78 above). It is well known that no strictly logical account of induction or empirical generalization has yet been, or perhaps can be, given and likewise the exact procedure of abstraction and successive approximation remains unclarified. However, analogies suggest themselves easily; for example, one may imagine how an ever fuller picture emerges as light is projected through an increasing number of superimposed transparencies. With such an analogy in mind and with a liberal use of the *ceteris paribus* proviso to separate the aspect under consideration from other aspects, one may develop theories on the vague understanding that one is dealing with one element of a description of reality.

Both methods discussed so far presuppose the 'realist' position that conceptual analysis by itself may be significant (page 79 above). The dominant method in economics at present, at least as set out in the early chapters of textbooks though probably not in practice, is the nominalist method of *testing positivist hypotheses*. We have already considered at some length an early exposition of this method by Pareto (pages 79–81 above). A valid positivist hypothesis is also part of a description, but the meaning of description differs in this case from that presupposed for abstraction and successive approximation. Description in the strictly nominalist sense is merely a mental expedient for relating facts by inference, and facts are to be related so that they may be predicted. The words or concepts used in a correct prediction are really immaterial. As Pareto put it: 'What alone matters is the objective relationship, whilst the means of expressing it is of secondary importance.' Thus if a model including perfect competition and perfect foresight yields correct predictions, one cannot for this reason conclude that there is anything in the world to which the words *perfect competition* and *perfect foresight* may be attached, only that events occur as *if* this were the case. This is what the debate on the realism of assumptions was about following the publication of Friedman's essay on the methodology of positive economics.

If a model including perfect competition and perfect foresight does indeed yield correct predictions, it is a matter of good luck that a successful formula has been hit upon. Any number of hypotheses might have been candidates for the job and there is little to go on in deciding which set of words and symbols is likely to be a successful formula. The impression that positivism is down to earth and matter of fact – which Pareto seemed to glory in when writing to Croce – is rather misleading. The search for a valid positivist hypothesis is in many ways like the search for a magic formula. What is wanted is a kind of *Open Sesame* for getting from one fact to another.

8.3. The ambiguity

We are now in a position to see that equilibrium theory is ambiguous in so far as it is treated variously as a heuristic and guiding conception in pragmatic inference, as an abstraction or empirical generalization in a projected series of successive approximations, as a positivist as–if hypothesis or as some combination of these.

When the distorting effects of tariffs are under consideration, equilibrium theory is used as a heuristic device. When the removal of tariffs is recommended for reasons of allocative efficiency, equilibrium theory is used as a guiding conception. When theories of imperfect competition are explained or developed, theory is likely to be regarded as an empirical generalization or abstract description. But as–if hypothesizing (e.g. entrepreneurs behave as if they equate marginal cost with marginal revenue) and pragmatic inference (e.g. advertising serves to differentiate products) may also be invoked. When attempts are made to predict the quantitative effects of policy measures, theory is likely to be treated as an as-if hypothesis. But the hypotheses may at the same time be presumed to be empirical generalizations as well; or tentatively possible ones, since there would be no need for testing them if they were known for certain to be abstractions or empirical generalizations.

The ambiguity is compounded by the apparently widespread conviction that the intellectual function of every theory is to be a simplified abstract picture, a model of the actual state of affairs. Thus theories which serve heuristic and guiding functions are thought to fail as theories unless they also serve a portraying or representing function. A guiding conception of free competition may therefore be squeezed into the role also of an abstraction to be used in successive approximation, as was Walras's system by Walras himself; or a conception of free competition which came to prominence through its guiding function may later be reinterpreted by others as an abstract picture. But heuristic fictions and guiding conceptions make rather poor pictures. The reinterpretation of guiding conceptions as descriptions has therefore led to some of the most intractable and bewildering problems of economic theory, such as the complex of knowledge problems which has received much attention in recent years. There has also been a temptation to adopt a different idea of description and to take to the as-if way of thinking.

The reinterpretation of guiding conceptions as descriptions has led to another development. As long as the market economy is a guiding conception, it is possible to have many variants of the market economy, differing by the institutional details that are imagined. Intent on making theory a description, however, one arrives at the notion of *the* one unique market mechanism, a kind of abstraction of what is common to all actual economies with markets. The notion is similar to the dogmatist's natural order, except that it is *the* market order for better or for worse, what may be called a denormatized dogmatism. As long as there are many imagined variants of the market economy, policy may be directed at achieving one particular variant. But this is not possible when there is only one market system. Denormatized dogmatism therefore has a problem with policy. The anti-government stance of dogmatism proper is not an option for denormatized dogmatism. Attention has therefore been turned, it seems, to a manipulation of economic aggregates within the one market system, to alternative quantitative configurations of actual economies with markets. In this way economists have ended up with the unenviable task of making quantitative predictions on the basis of Pareto's analogue of celestial mechanics.

8.4. Equilibrium theory and free-market pragmatism

At the beginning of Chapter 6, the question was posed whether equilibrium theory has developed and refined Adam Smith's idea of market order into something that may serve as a guiding conception for a programme of free-market pragmatism. In the last paragraph of that chapter, the question was answered by a qualified No. We are now in a position to give a fuller account of that qualified answer. Since equilibrium theory is understood in so many ways, it is not clear to which version the negative assessment applies. One may well interpret equilibrium theory in a way in which it could, one may imagine, guide free-market policy. What was meant by the negative answer is that such an interpretation, notwithstanding the ambiguity, would be far removed from anything that may be described as mainstream economic theory. It would be an interpretation rather of what might have become of the idea of market order than of what by and large has become of it.

It would be incorrect to say that equilibrium theory was entirely inspired by the idea of market order. The name itself in fact points to mechanics as the inspiration. But there have been theorists, Walras for example, and Smith in so far as he used an equilibrium concept, whose intention to articulate the idea of market order in equilibrium theory is quite plain. Let us consider some areas where the idea of market order and equilibrium theory are associated in this way and contrast what by and large has become of the idea of market order with how it might have been developed to be of use to those who want to promote free markets. We shall not concern ourselves with a chronological account but rather with a drift of ideas that may occur at one time or another.

An initial overview may help us. In many cases theories embody implicit definitions, for example of what constitutes production and exchange or the optimum state of allocative efficiency. These definitions implicit in theories (or ideal conceptions) may be and are used in pragmatic inference for heuristic and guiding purposes. But there also comes into play the ever-present presumption that every theory describes or represents some aspect of the world around us, or ought to do so. It may then be hard to tell whether the role of a theory in a particular context is that of some kind of description or of a definition used in pragmatic inference. There can be little doubt, however, that the tendency, especially in this century, has been to look upon all theories as descriptions, whatever their actual roles may be. This has created problems of an exegetical kind and also for policy. A description of what already exists cannot by itself guide policy because the execution of policy, like any human action, needs also some (guiding) conception of the end sought. It stands to reason that theory may guide free-market policy only if it is used as a guide.

8.4.1. Production and exchange

The liberal order of the invisible hand, it was argued earlier (Section 6.2), is one in which individuals do not dissipate their energy in taking from each other and so have no other option than to produce and exchange. Those who make such an order their ideal come up against the problem of identifying production and exchange. One has to be able to tell producers from predators and that is not easy (Section 7.1). The distinction is fundamental for individualism. Purposeful acquisition by individuals (as opposed to passive receiving of gifts and inheritances) may take many forms. Some of these may be deemed to be production and exchange while others may be deemed to be successful moves in zero-sum games. To identify the one kind of acquisition is also to identify the other kind, i.e. they are mutually exclusive and exhaustive in sum.

This idea played a role in Smith's analysis of natural prices and in the earlier groping attempts to formulate an equilibrium concept to articulate the notion of a fair price (Section 7.2). Such versions of equilibrium may be said to have embodied an implicit definition of production and exchange. The equilibrium of natural prices which Smith put forward in Book I Chapter VII of the *Wealth of Nations* applied to an imaginary state of perfect liberty from which all predatory activity was precluded by design because it was meant to articulate an intuitive notion of production and exchange. Smith used this equilibrium construct as a heuristic device, for example to identify the multifarious forms of monopoly, though his mode of expression (e.g. the natural price is the average price) sometimes exhibited the ambiguity which is still with us today. Later in the book, the equilibrium of natural prices in a state of perfect liberty served as a guide for liberal policies in opposition to the idea of accumulating bullion, which, according to Smith, was put forward by not disinterested parties to guide mercantilist policies.

If Jaffé's view of Walras is correct – and Jaffé was surely the foremost authority in this field – Walras's system of general equilibrium was built upon a concept of what constitutes production and exchange, as opposed to predatory taking, which is very similar to that which underlay Smith's equilibrium of natural prices. According to Jaffé the *Eléments* was designed 'not as a "study of men as they live and move and think in the ordinary business of life" … but as a theoretical representation of a just economy from the standpoint of "commutative justice"', i.e. the ancient notion of justice in exchange, which, Jaffé explained, 'in the traditional Aristotelian-Thomistic sense relates to acts of voluntary exchange in which the market value received is equal to the market value given up'.[176] Such justice in exchange was also the basis of the ancient distinction between fair and extortionate prices.[177] Incorporated into general equilibrium theory, it quite obviously would make no sense at all unless equilibrium price was a 'market value' distinct from market price. As we have seen (Section 7.1), equilibrium price then also implies a certain concept of productive contribution.

A preoccupation with defining production and exchange may seem quite unnecessary. The definition is not a problem in modern equilibrium theory. Within the framework of equilibrium theory this is no doubt so, but only because that theory was largely derived from a construction designed to articulate an intuitive notion of production. It may be otherwise when one looks at the world the theory is supposed to describe, if it is supposed to describe it. Clearly, shoplifting, car theft and housebreaking are not productive activities because, one may presume, there is no demand for them, at least not from the side of the victims of such activities. But is there a derived demand, for instance, for advertising, for 'aggressive' selling techniques, for massive sponsorship of sport or for 'image-building', 'social-responsibility' company sponsorship of artistic, educational and research projects? Is all the human effort associated with this kind of thing to count as productive effort? It would be difficult to find an answer to this question in either Smith's or Walras's scheme. In any case, their concept of production and exchange was derived ultimately from an ideal of the good society, which to many may not seem such a desirable state of affairs at all. But it is at least conceivable that the idea of market order might have been developed into an economics which analyses various criteria (i.e. premises in pragmatic inference) for production and exchange and so have given us greater clarity on the issue and a choice of answers.

8.4.2. Prices and allocation

Mainstream economic theory of course did not take this direction. Nor was it ever likely to because the prevailing perception of how science is conducted was pointing in another direction. The perception of science and of intellectual work in general is important. One has to see how different it may be to appreciate how a theory, in being passed on to other thinkers, may undergo a complete change of character even though there may have been little change in outward form.

Jaffé has translated an undated manuscript in which an apparently very youthful Walras expresses his philosophical convictions in the resounding tones of youth.[178] It reads in part:

> I am an idealist. I believe that ideas reshape the world after
> their own image and that the ideal a man conceives for his
> century commands the attention of all humanity. I believe that
> the world has striven without success for eighteen centuries
> to realize the ideal of Jesus and the first of the Apostles. I
> believe that the world will take another eighteen, or perhaps
> twenty, centuries, in trying, without better success, to realize
> the ideals of 1789, which we now perceive more clearly and
> which our successors will illuminate. How happy would I be
> if I could imagine that I had shed one ray of light, however
> small, on this vision. In this respect, I am swimming against
> the current of my century. Facts are now in fashion: the
> observation of facts, the investigation of facts, the acceptance
> of facts as laws. In stormy times, political power falls into the
> hands of the ignorant masses. Art, science, philosophy are
> swept away. Facts become masters; empiricism triumphant
> reigns supreme. Analytical minds closely study the explosion
> and wait for chaos gradually to take over as an object of fond
> description and serene glorification. As for me, I will have
> no part in this.

If Walras was not a man of his century, Pareto certainly was. As Jaffé remarked in another place, Pareto saw perfectly clearly what Walras was driving at and did not like it. Pareto apparently wrote to Pantaleoni, apropos Walras's theoretical aims, that he found it inadmissible to study what ought to be rather than what is.[179] This outlook is probably even more common and entrenched today than it was in Pareto's day. A recent critic of Jaffé's view of Walras, while arguing convincingly for what in our context would be one side of the ambiguity in Walras's thought, wrote the following:

> There is a major difference in character between the work
> of a scientist who strives as best as he can to achieve what he
> believes is objective truth – an accurate description of facts
> or a theoretical explanation of their behavior – and the work
> of someone who develops a system as a means of showing
> how his ideas about social justice can be distilled into rules of
> proper conduct, and as a way of demonstrating the desirable

consequences those rules would have if they were adopted. In arguing that Walras's work was of the latter character, Jaffé made a very serious allegation about Walras as a scientist, about his theory of general equilibrium, and about the critical work of many theorists.[180]

There is in this passage a tone of indignation, as though it has been alleged that a revered saint practised witchcraft. The tone conveys very well the current rather stilted perception of science.

This ideal of science, if the former perception may be applied to the latter, reshaped the idea of market order after its own image. What amounted in a certain context to a definition of an ideal was seen as 'an accurate description of facts or a theoretical explanation of their behavior'. The kind of theory inspired by Smith's equilibrium of natural prices and Walras's system of general equilibrium underwent a change of character without undergoing any substantial change of form. In the conversion it acquired its peculiar quality as well as many of its peculiar difficulties.

A feature of equilibrium theory is that it excludes predatory activity from consideration (with some possible exceptions being made in the case of monopoly theory). But, as Bastiat observed (page 60 above), predatory activity is practised on too vast a scale for economics, least of all, to be able to ignore it. Considered as a definition, the theory excludes but does not ignore predatory activity. The point of the construction is to exclude it so that production and exchange may be distinguished from it. Considered as a description, however, the same theory both excludes and ignores predatory activity. It is simply relegated to the welter of sociological factors one abstracts from in arriving at the economic aspect of social life. Sometime in the future perhaps, with interdisciplinary cooperation, the simplifying assumption may be dropped and a fuller picture built up by successive approximation. In the meantime economists concentrate on the economic aspect.

What is the economic aspect of social life described by Smith's equilibrium of natural prices and by Walras's system of general equilibrium? When the question is posed like that, i.e. when it is already presumed that the theories were meant to be accurate descriptions or theoretical explanations of the behaviour of facts of a certain kind, the answer seems fairly obvious. The theories try to describe how prices established in markets bring about an allocation of known resources such that their product is fitted to the demand, i.e. to individuals' existing preferences actuated by incomes which the pricing and allocation process itself distributes among individuals. (Smith, though, failed to mention the closing of the circular flow – see page 72 above.) That this is the kind of thing the theories are about is plain enough. But as descriptions, as abstract moving pictures as it were, the theories raise many problems and puzzles, as is well known.

Walras already had difficulties in this regard, a kind of foretaste of what was to come. He embraced as methods both pragmatic inference and successive approximation. (Jaffé called the *Eléments* a 'realistic utopia'.[181]) Walras stated his faith in successive approximation at the end of paragraph 164 of the *Eléments* (4th edition); and paragraph 322, for instance, begins with successive approximation and ends with pragmatic inference. Early in the book he said that from the competitive standpoint markets are *best* organized as auctions where prices are cried out and information is centralized.[182] His conception of free competition and ultimately his ideas on the *idéal social* presumably guided him in deciding what was best. But he also thought his theory described actual markets and not only stock exchanges and certain commodity markets, but all markets. To this end he introduced his well-known *tâtonnement* or trial-and-error groping towards equilibrium in markets, apparently unaware initially of the difficulties created for his theory by transactions concluded at non-equilibrium prices.[183] When a few years later he brought production into his model, he had to overcome the difficulty that non-equilibrium quantities of products could not be unmanufactured. As far as production was concerned, Walras noted in the preface to the fourth edition, he supposed the *tâtonnements* to be made by means of tickets and no longer as they were actually effected ('faits non plus effectivement, mais *sur bons*').[184] The tickets were something like contracts, which became effective only if market-clearing equilibrium was reached. Walras could no longer pretend that he was describing actual markets.

However, the fact that one or other equilibrium theory is not accurate as a description, not true to life as a picture, need not deter anyone from trying to improve the equilibrium picture. After all, there are good and bad descriptions, good and bad pictures, and the road to excellence is always a long one. It happens easily along that road that one comes to think of what one is trying to describe as the basic economic aspect of social life. Price determination and the allocation of resources tend to be established as the core of economics, as the proper domain of economic interest. Economists of course may concern themselves with all sorts of other issues, but it becomes accepted that a proper economic analysis of such issues must place them into the context of prices and allocation, i.e. into the basic framework of equilibrium.

Moreover, the tendency to ambiguity is such that the equilibrium framework is not always regarded as a description but is also used as a definition in pragmatic inference. Once it is accepted that economics is basically about prices and allocation, the old definition of production and exchange becomes a definition of allocative efficiency. This may be seen in the way the question of monopoly is handled. In Smith's analysis (page 73 above), a monopolist impedes the mobility of factors of production (or the flow of goods to the same effect) for the purpose of making gains he would not make otherwise. Something of this still remains in the analysis of monopoly profits along Marshallian lines in elementary textbooks. But in more specific studies the tendency is to identify monopolies by market shares or concentration ratios and to see the significance of monopoly purely in terms of its effects on the allocation of resources. When a theory of perfectly competitive equilibrium guides antimonopoly policy, it is not a description but a criterion for allocative efficiency or a definition of the optimum allocation of resources. However, since the equi-marginal conditions set out in the theory seem to be well-nigh unattainable in practice and yet leave out of account other important considerations, such as questions of innovation, analyses of specific cases of monopoly are often inconclusive, more so at least than when the analysis was based on predatory activity.

8.4.3. Allocative efficiency

Optimal allocation clearly played a leading role in Walras's 'ideal fiction of "commutative justice" subject to economic efficiency', as Jaffé called it.[185] When Walras argued that factors which interfere with freedom of production are obstacles to the attainment of individual utility maxima, he was using the theory as an ideal or definition of allocative efficiency (page 75 above). When he regarded the same ideal as a description, as we have just seen, he got into difficulties. Smith's equilibrium of natural prices, in which the quantity of labour, capital and land 'suits itself … to the effectual demand', also implies optimal allocation (page 72 above). Smith likewise used it as an ideal or definition of allocative efficiency when he spoke of the allocative effects of monopoly (page 61 above). He also used it in descriptions. For instance, he said that in the process of economic growth, with a rising demand for beef and an increasing shortage of 'wild pasture', the price of beef rises in relation to the price of wheat until a time is reached when it is as profitable to cultivate fodder as it is to cultivate wheat. He then related this analysis to the development of Scotland and England.[186]

In a few places Smith also spoke of a natural division and distribution of labour and a natural balance of employments or industry.[187] This sounds like an optimum allocation of resources actually achieved. However, he used these expressions in the context of 'that general objection which may be made to all the different expedients of the mercantile system; the objection of forcing some part of the industry of the country into a channel less advantageous than that in which it would run of its own accord'.[188] The channels into which industry runs of its own accord (Smith used this expression frequently) are not necessarily the most advantageous that are conceivable in terms of a particular definition of allocative efficiency. Nor did Smith have to claim this since he merely wanted to compare his idea of market order to the mercantile system and for this it was sufficient to claim merely a *greater* allocative efficiency for the former.

The claims made in the *Wealth of Nations* for the allocative efficiency of a market order are really quite modest. Moreover, they are overshadowed in emphasis by an argument repeated several times about the incentives created by government and laws which afford to everyone the confidence that one may enjoy the fruits of one's own labour and industry (i.e. incentives due to the absence of predatory activity in a liberal order).[189] Every individual is continually exerting himself and endeavours as much as he can to find the best uses for whatever capital he may have. But to try is not necessarily to succeed. On this score, Smith merely maintained that every individual in his local situation is able to judge *much better* where his capital is *likely* to be most productively employed than a distant mercantilist administrator could judge for him (page 62 above). No doubt, one could think of cases where this would not necessarily be so. Still, it was a reasonable comparison that could reasonably be made without any far-fetched assumptions about foresight and faultless coordination.

One may at least imagine that from such beginnings an economics might have been developed whereby alternative forms of economic organization might have been compared on the basis of features of market order that have been considered important and perhaps on the basis of some new ones. It has often been said rather vaguely that a system of free enterprise in free markets creates strong incentives for everyone to produce what is wanted, to use resources effectively and to innovate. Hayek has said that markets disseminate information efficiently and that competition is a discovery procedure (page 56 above). Such features presuppose various ideals against which we assess the effectiveness of institutions. Loose assessments of this sort are in fact very common. Stock exchanges rate highly in making current tendencies in valuations widely known; certain commodity markets in making the current balance between the availability and use (or expected use) of commodities widely known. Patent laws promote innovation but not competition. Progressive income taxes rate fairly well on the score of promoting egalitarian ideals but very poorly on those of promoting the ideals of enterprise and honesty. The principle of making such assessments might have been analysed and rigorously articulated to yield various efficiency criteria and efficiency definitions, i.e. premises and conclusions in pragmatic inference. These might have been applied in a comparative institutional analysis, i.e. in studies of how various rules of conduct and ways of doing things compare in meeting certain widely held ideals. Alternative proposals for institutional modifications might have been compared one with another, while they were still figments of the imagination, or these might have been compared with the existing institutions which a heuristic use of the criteria might well have laid bare. An economics which makes such comparisons possible would be very useful to those who want to promote free markets.

This of course is not at all the direction economic theory has taken. It so happens that comparisons of allocative efficiency may be taken to a logical conclusion, that they lend themselves to an inquiry into the ultimate state of efficient allocation or the optimum allocation of resources. Not all comparisons lend themselves to such treatment. One may say that one person is taller than another, but it does not make sense to inquire into the ultimate state of tallness. Likewise, it does not make sense to inquire into the ultimate economic incentive or the ultimate state of innovativeness. The questions of incentives and of innovation have therefore more or less fallen by the wayside in the development of equilibrium theory. They play a supporting role, but the leading role is played by allocative efficiency. Of all the features of market order that have been considered important, it is this one feature which from quite modest beginnings has come to dominate theory. Perhaps because the optimum allocation of resources could be investigated comparatively easily with mathematical techniques developed for other purposes in other fields of study, virtually every nook and cranny of the idea of allocative efficiency has been explored and consequently this aspect of market order has become almost synonymous with economics.

One should understand what is set out by the definition of allocative efficiency implicit in equilibrium theory. Given certain property rights, a certain distribution of resources, certain preferences and certain input–output relations, the theory states, in terms of variables and parameters of varying specificity, the interrelation of economic magnitudes which constitutes the corresponding optimum allocation of resources. The ultimate state of allocative efficiency is implicitly defined by being exemplified in a quantitative configuration. There are certain dynamic theories in which the time path of one or other variable is postulated and in such theories temporal magnitudes and a temporal ordering may have a role in the quantitative configuration. But equilibrium theories are not usually of this form. The definition of allocative efficiency implicit in the usual form of equilibrium theory has no place whatever for the passage of time and the here and now; and therefore by implication it has no place for much else.

As a rule, the optimum interrelationship of magnitudes is looked upon as a point of convergence, as the limit of a process. However, the time-taking equilibrating process is a vision which accompanies equilibrium theory but is not an integral part of it. In the vision, markets are being cleared while people are bargaining and competing, buying and selling, seeking and finding the most remunerative employments and industries and so on. If the equations of the usual form of equilibrium theory capture any part of this vision, they depict not the supposed journey to equilibrium but the destination. Walras's system of equations, for instance, makes no allowance for entrepreneurial and arbitrage profits[190] – Walras in fact said that entrepreneurs, like money too, may be left out of the equilibrium picture.[191] Whatever function entrepreneurs and arbitrage may have in the vision of the *tâtonnement*, the job is done and finished when equilibrium is reached. Walras's equilibrium prices, like Smith's natural prices, are equal to the sum of the (equilibrium or natural) costs of the services employed in providing goods – this is the condition for justice in exchange – and since the visualized service of entrepreneurs and arbitrageurs is to bring the system *to* equilibrium, it is no longer needed *in* equilibrium and therefore entrepreneurial and arbitrage profits are not part of the equilibrium solution, nor of the formal theory as opposed to the vision that accompanies it.

The link between a formal theory and an accompanying vision arises only when equilibrium theory is presumed to be some kind of representation of what actually exists. As the definition of an ideal of allocative efficiency, the theory merely sets out an interconnection of magnitudes. Time, the moment of decision, expectations et al have nothing whatsoever to do with it. Of course, when we aspire to the ideal, we discover our uncertainty, the limitations of our knowledge and all kinds of other things – this is the heuristic part of pragmatic inference. Ideals do not have to be entirely attainable. They may guide us, they may be aimed at, as long as they may be approached, i.e., in colloquial terms, as long as it is not a case of a miss being as good as a mile. Thus, the introduction of any scheme that facilitates the dissemination of information through markets, such as standardization of commodities and centralization of transactions in one place as on stock exchanges, would seem to be a step towards the ideal of efficient allocation, provided that the necessary incentives are there and competition is free. Of course, it may be a good idea always to define ideals, if at all possible, in such a way that they are attainable. For instance, the portmanteau ideal of allocative efficiency might be broken down into separate ideals concerned with incentives, freedom of trade, and information dissemination. It may be easier so to define these separate ideals, or so to imply them in theoretical constructs, that they may be attainable, especially if one can resist the temptation of positing an ultimate state of information dissemination, i.e. a state in which everybody knows everything, and instead can frame the definition in a way that incorporates the sequence in which decisions are made and thus could be known to others.

The omission of time from the definition of allocative efficiency has the effect of making the ideal of efficient allocation very difficult if not impossible to reach, though it does not deprive it entirely of significance. The effect is somewhat different when this apparently unattainable ideal is regarded as a representation of what actually prevails. Since economic activity necessarily takes time and since decisions necessarily are made in a present moment that divides the future from the past, the omission of time from the formal theory as a description must entail the omission of much that is familiar. In practice the descriptive deficiency of the formal theory is offset by an informal vision accompanying the theory. It is of course not only entrepreneurs and arbitrageurs who cannot be accommodated in the interpretation of Walrasian equations and must be content with a place in the informal vision. There is also no formal role for capital when it is not simply a piece of equipment but a fund for financing enterprise and time-taking production processes. Without any moments of decision on the brink of an uncertain future, the desire for financial liquidity is unintelligible and hence money, when it is more than simply a numeraire, has no formal role in the theory either.

What is perhaps realized less often is that all the bargaining and competing in markets, in fact most of the activity usually associated with a market order, also has no place in the interpretation of the formal equations of equilibrium theory, though conventional market activity often plays a lively role in the informal vision. Specialization, private property or some similar arrangement and some way of transferring ownership seem to be the only institutions which are an integral part of the definition of allocative efficiency or of the formal interpretation of the equations of equilibrium theory. The optimum state is defined as one in which individuals optimize their objective functions separately and for this the means for doing so (the constraints) must also be separate and therefore some arrangement whereby means are separated is presupposed. Prices are then implicit in the interconnection of individual preferences, technology and the availability and ownership of resources. Their function, rather than that of signalling, is a legacy of justice in exchange, i.e. the value (price times quantity) of the assortment of goods accruing to each individual must be equal to the value of the product of the resources owned by the individual while a similar equality must hold in any transfer of ownership in resources.

The informal vision is the repository for everything else, conventional market activity, money and capital in fuller senses and other institutions. Since the purpose of formal theory is rigorous analysis, all that is accommodated in the informal vision escapes the rigour and is merely a picturesque appendage to the analysis. One really has much leeway in deciding how colourful the informal vision should be. One may suppose, for instance, that allocative efficiency is enforced by a dictator and his bayonet-wielding retainers. Perhaps it is not easy to imagine how an optimum allocation of resources may be brought about with bayonets, but then it is not clear either how it is supposed to come about by so-called market forces.

8.4.4. Optimization and the market mechanism

The analysis of resource allocation is necessarily about a configuration of quantities (or at least of cardinal and ordinal magnitudes). A preoccupation with allocation problems therefore easily diverts the attention of theorists from the institutional character of market order and free-market policy to a quite different perception of market order and the conduct of economic policy. Market order comes to be seen as a quantitative configuration of a specific kind and policy as an attempt to change one configuration into another, i.e. as a manipulation of quantities, usually in the form of economic aggregates. Let us also look into this particular drift of ideas.

Comparative statics involves the comparison of equilibria corresponding to different values of the exogenous variables or parameters. Strictly interpreted, the same implicit definition of allocative efficiency is being exemplified in different sets of interrelated magnitudes. However, since equilibrium models are usually formulated in terms of differentiable functions – without such functions it would of course be difficult to define optima – the method lends itself to the idea of tracing the effect on quantitative interrelations of some 'exogenous shock', i.e. of an unexplained change or a change made deliberately in pursuance of policy. In practice, comparative statics usually takes the form of deducing the algebraic signs of partial derivatives from the assumptions made for and the restrictions imposed on models, thus showing the direction of change in an endogenous variable consequent on a (small) change in an exogenous variable. While differentiable functions therefore make the connection between equilibria mathematically intelligible, they do not, as is generally recognized, represent or describe the equilibrating adaptation process to which the conventional market activities in the informal vision refer, postulated stability conditions and Samuelson's correspondence principle notwithstanding. Comparative statics at most may compare the quantitative configurations that *would* prevail *if* the equilibria *were* reached.

Nevertheless, comparative statics is used very commonly, in elementary demand and supply as in more sophisticated analysis, to show the effects of some change as if there were no problem about the transition from one equilibrium to another. In this regard there has arisen a certain terminology, namely that the analysis shows how and by what this, that and the other, everything in fact apart from an exogenous shock, *is determined*. The terminology easily translates itself into something which is part formal interpretation and part informal vision. To have a picture of the *determination* in question, one has to imagine some peculiar things. To depict smooth functions one has to imagine that a utility function, i.e. a set of consistent and comprehensive preferences with certain mathematical properties, is programmed into each human head and that technical input–output relations also take the form of mathematical functions with certain properties. In itself that does not take one very far. Finding the equilibrium solutions corresponding to different sets of exogenous variables and parameters is a mathematical technique in which the question of the timetaking transition from one set of solution values to another does not normally arise. To depict that technique, one has to imagine a state in which (a) everybody adheres strictly to certain rules of conduct and (b) everybody knows everything, including his own utility function and those of others, and nobody can do anything really novel because everyone already knows all the possibilities. When an exogenous shock hits such a state of things, each individual *could* straight away optimize again within the limits set by commutative justice. The limitation is due to the way in which, owing to its forebears, equilibrium theory has been formulated. If individuals did not adhere to conduct which ensured justice in exchange as implicitly defined, then, in the modern denormatized terminology, there would be income effects from false trading and these would themselves constitute exogenous shocks which shift the equilibrium solutions in a way that the mathematical technique for finding them does not.

If one can imagine all that, one can imagine what has been criticized by Shackle under the name *rational determinacy*[192] and by Simon under the name *substantive rationality*.[193] Under the imaginary conditions described in the previous paragraph, human choice or, rather, decision in general, no longer has the meaning it has in ordinary discourse. Every decision is a mere calculation that may be done by anyone, the person whose decision it is, the observing economic scientist or anyone else. With such rational determinacy, it is possible in principle to calculate the effects of any change from outside an economy on the quantitative interrelations within an economy. (Whether policy decisions would be exogenous or endogenous is a moot point.) Unfortunately, this vision of an economy is not easy to live with.

The most obvious question is how do people manage to optimize when to do so seems to require knowledge which they cannot reasonably be expected to have. Preoccupation with this question has shown that the description of market processes is far more complex than Walras ever supposed when he talked of *tâtonnement*. The link between an individual's preferences and his actual decisions appears to be a complicated mental process which involves (a) his particular interpretation of events and the world around him and (b) the expectations he forms on this basis. Even if preferences really were fixed and comprehensive, it would not be enough to know them. One would have to know also the mechanics of the mind (or of each mind separately). In this way a complex of problems about knowledge and uncertainty has come under close scrutiny. How far, for instance, do people take the search for information? How do they form their expectations? How do they make decisions when as always they are uncertain about what the future holds?

The motive for investigating these mental processes may be simply to show that the neoclassical picture is not a true picture – this was the context in which attention was first drawn to knowledge and uncertainty. There may be various other motives. But the mainstream motive appears to be to preserve that determinacy of human action which came in when the ideal of allocative efficiency was turned into a description. Optimization, in a loose analogy with gravitational forces, is to remain the explanatory principle of that determinacy. But optimization within the limitations of human mental capacity, which research into the characteristics of mental processes may reveal, would not necessarily lead to an efficient allocation. That would hardly matter if disequilibrium economics allowed predictions of what from many points of view are the disorderly quantitative configurations of actual economies. Development in this direction leads to a vision of a kind of social mechanics, to the fulfilment of Pareto's ideal for positive economics as an analogue of celestial mechanics (page 80 above). The economic scientist would be able to predict the quantitative consequences – 'the operating characteristics of time series we care about' as Lucas put it (page 82 above) – of policy measures and of any other exogenous changes. If the populace at large should learn to do the same trick, then they too might form their expectations rationally and one would be back more or less in a state where potentially and eventually everybody would know everything that is relevant.

The vision of an ambitious social mechanics adds to the ambiguity of equilibrium theory. Is the theory still in any way about market order or is it purely about determination by optimization? Or is it perhaps that these two amount to the same thing? We shall see that the two are in fact not the same but that equilibrium theory is about both. However, we shall also see that equilibrium theorists, by concentrating entirely on optimizing behaviour and related questions, have committed themselves, perhaps unwittingly, to what amounts in certain respects to a dogmatic belief in the existence of a natural market order or a unique market mechanism. Finally we shall see that the effect of this is that the policy options which may be inferred from equilibrium theory are based on the principle of determination by optimization and that such policy is of little or no use to those who want to promote free markets.

Even if the epistemological mechanics of the mind could be modelled perfectly on a computer, or if there were fully rational expectations or the mind-boggling state of perfect knowledge, the question of the institutional character of economic order would still remain a separate issue. That issue turns on the *manner* in which the separately conducted optimizing actions of individuals impinge on each other. In a shared physical environment, the optimizing of one person almost certainly impinges on the optimizing of all the others and for any one person the optimizing of all the others constrains his own best course of action. This mutual impingement is central to the idea of equilibrium, though it is usually called mutual determination. The manner in which the mutual impingement takes place depends upon the institutions of a society and therefore no visualized equilibrium can be independent of institutional considerations. In the simplest case in which a number of individuals want a unique non-reproducible object, it is the rules of conduct and conventions of society which resolve the potential conflict. In the standard vision that accompanies equilibrium theory, mutual impingement is regulated by the price system and the rule that no one may take more in value terms out of the system than his resources, including his own ability, put into it. But whether the institutions we actually have really meet the ideal embodied in the vision is an open question and, moreover, one that is hardly ever considered by mainstream theorists.

Hayek, as we have seen (page 56 above), has pointed out that market order requires not only that individuals should be free to pursue their interests in their own way, but also certain moral rules and mores of honourable market conduct which restrain and temper that pursuit, i.e. regulate mutual impingement. Adam Smith's liberal order of the invisible hand, by trying to draw the thin line between economic freedom and economic power over others (page 64 above), sets out one possible manner of a mutually beneficial impingement. Market order is distinguished from other economic systems by the manner in which mutual impingement occurs and that depends on the nature of the rules of conduct and social conventions which prevail. Optimization and the associated questions of knowledge, uncertainty and expectations are not peculiar to market order. Individuals may be expected to optimize within the limitations of their mental capacity, i.e. to do the best they can, whatever the institutions, however they are constrained by the actions of others. A person born into a society with state socialism presumably does the best he can within the constraints of the bureaucratic and Party structures – for some individuals, of course, that may entail breaking out of the constraints altogether. In the limiting case where there are no institutions at all – no conventions, no mores of ethical conduct – the manner of mutual impingement would be set by the physical possibilities and the mental faculties and ingenuity of the contenders. An equilibrium may well be reached under such conditions, but it would be a deadlock in the war of all against all, which may not accord with anyone's idea of market order.

It does not seem that equilibrium theory considered as social mechanics is meant to describe this state of lawlessness. Preoccupation with the determination of quantities has diverted attention from institutions, but certain institutions nevertheless are taken for granted and with them a certain manner of mutual impingement. Whether by accident or design, the practice of taking institutions for granted makes equilibrium theory akin to free-market dogmatism. It is as though market relations are inherent in nature, as though natural law governs mutual impingement or as though spontaneous evolution, if allowed to run its course, may always be counted on to create those unique economic relations among individuals which constitute the natural market order.

Equilibrium theory differs from dogmatism in that it professes to make quantitative predictions and is infused with a spirit of scientific neutrality appropriate to a science which aspires to the idea most of us have of mechanics. Nature is not represented in the dogmatic manner as mankind's wise benefactor. In so far as social mechanics is associated at all with market order, equilibrium theory is often tied to that widely but loosely used expression *the market mechanism*. At some level of abstraction, there is something common to all economies with markets, namely, the unique market mechanism. As such it is simply there. Its desirability, or lack of it, is in the eyes of the beholder, as is the case with any other natural phenomenon. With changed sentiments about what constitutes a science, natural law (Section 4.1) has simply become a law of nature. Equilibrium theory in this sense may be described as a *denormatized dogmatism*.

In this sense also, equilibrium theory is of little or no use to those who want to promote market economies, to a pragmatic free-market policy. Social mechanics or denormatized dogmatism does have something to offer the policy maker (especially when its scope is extended to macro-economics), namely the hope of finding coefficients which are stable enough to make alternative configurations of economic aggregates into policy options. However sanguine one may be about that hope, and the work of Shackle, Lachmann and others has shown that there is a great deal that stands in the way of its realization,[194] it can lead only to a policy based on determination by optimization, with the market mechanism taken for granted as though it were a natural phenomenon. But a theory which takes the existence of the market mechanism for granted can hardly be a guide for promoting market order. In fact, determination by optimization does not in principle require market order. With the right coefficients, equilibrium theory could predict the reactions of people who live on collective farms in Russia, in the forests of New Guinea or the Amazon basin or anywhere else. Optimization and the whole issue of expectations does not relate specifically to market order.

To guide policy, a theory must be a guiding conception and to guide the promotion of market economies, a theory must be a guiding conception of market order, an ideal we may analyse and strive towards, and not a theory which takes the existence of markets for granted. Theory as guiding conception unfortunately runs against the current perception and ideal of science, which is to describe and not to dabble in ideals. But if one is inclined to go along with D.H. Robertson's opinion that 'as an intellectual pastime economics is rather a drab and second-rate affair' and that 'it is mainly worth pursuing not for its own sake, but with a practical object',[195] then ideals or at least the ends sought certainly cannot be ignored (though there may be other good reasons for not ignoring them). It is not very useful, for instance, to have a theory which is taken to show what is common to all market economies because, in a world of great diversity, it is not at all clear which actual economies are to count as market economies. It would be more useful, it would better serve a 'practical object', to have criteria for telling *where* there are the kind of institutions which, on the basis of certain ideals, are necessary for market order, and some guides for possibly promoting them where they are not or exist in a very imperfect form. There is in fact not much difference between setting out the conditions common to all market economies and setting out the conditions that have to be met for an economy to qualify as a market economy, but it is the difference between description and pragmatic inference. We have seen that pragmatic inference shows that certain conclusions follow from certain premises (page 88 above). Where the conclusion sets out an ideal, say one that is part of the composite ideal of market order, the premises in the inference are both criteria and guides. When we want to promote markets where there are none or where they are imperfect, it is sufficient, as Walras said, that we should be able to form a conception of them.

There is in fact a criterion that may be derived from equilibrium theory. The theory presupposes private property or at least some arrangement whereby certain goods accrue to certain people irrespective of opinions on what the distribution of income should be, since otherwise the optimum allocation of resources remains undefined (page 102 above). The theory therefore does not apply, as is generally agreed, to the economy of the Soviet Union nor probably, though this is more problematical, to the experimental versions of market socialism in Yugoslavia and Hungary, because property rights are not of the required kind. In a strict sense, it also does not apply to western economies with substantial political programmes of income redistribution, which is to say that it applies strictly to virtually none of them. But since there is nothing in formal equilibrium theory about how equilibrium is reached, so that not even central planning is logically precluded, one cannot derive rigorous criteria for the market institutions associated with equilibrating processes, i.e. with market processes which are presumed to make individual activities impinge on each other in such a manner that economic activity becomes coordinated in the equilibrium sense. Such institutions do of course appear in the informal vision that goes with the theory, but they are not captured in the mathematics or in the essential logic of the equilibrium construct and thus escape the rigorous analysis.

From a dogmatic standpoint, this gap in the formal theory is not very serious. If government were kept out of economic affairs, the part missing from the theory, according to the dogmatic view, would be the part played by nature or by a benevolent spontaneous evolution and thus need not really concern us. But for those who find this hard to believe, to whom it seems that virtually anything may happen in the spontaneous course of history, an ideal or guiding conception of market processes with its attendant criteria must be an indispensable precondition of free-market policy. From a pragmatic standpoint, it is highly significant that institutions are never quite the same in any two countries or even in different industries or different regions of the same country. In highly industrialized countries the differing technical economies of scale in different industries make markets deviate to a greater or lesser extent from the informal vision of the market process accompanying equilibrium theory, while in so-called developing and less developed countries there usually are also unmistakable regional variations in institutions. In such circumstances it is surely more useful to have criteria and guides based on an ideal or on several ideals of market processes than to have a theory of optimization which takes the market mechanism for granted.

It is the latter kind of theory, however, that we do have. The theory of optimizing behaviour can in fact handle institutional oddities if these may be translated into restrictions on parameters. But when no oddities are specified, certain relations between economic magnitudes are presumed to arise quite naturally and spontaneously. Equilibrium theory becomes the analytics of exchange in the natural state, a denormatized dogmatism. The all-important question of institutions is relegated to a lower-grade economics as though it were unworthy of the attention of high-powered analytical theorists.

If market order were a guiding conception, a composite of ideals in competition with various socialist ideals, free-market policy would be seen as an attempt to make a rather amorphous reality more orderly. The approach to economic policy is quite different when the market mechanism is seen as something we all have anyway as long as we have private property, contract and not too much state control. Anything and everything that is considered undesirable about actual economic conditions may then be taken as evidence of 'market failure'. The market economy is not seen as an ideal on an equal footing with socialist and welfare-state ideals. It is seen instead as the often rather unfortunate reality we live in, whose 'unacceptable face' all well-meaning people deplore. But fortunately for everyone, there is economic theory which shows us how to counteract and make up for market failures by changing undesirable quantitative configurations into more desirable ones. In so far as those responsible for policy have accepted this scenario, the manipulation of economic aggregates is the kind of policy we have, though, given the limitations of theory, little more is expected of demand management policy than to inflate or deflate.

8.4.5. Positive economics and pragmatic inference

We set out to contrast what by and large has become of the idea of market order with how it might have been developed. For this purpose we contrasted its use in description and in pragmatic inference. In its association with equilibrium theory, the idea of market order has become embedded and more or less neglected in a theory of optimization which seeks, but in its formal part has not managed, to describe how economic magnitudes are determined in actual economies. Market order in pragmatic inference is a guiding conception, a composite of inferences the conclusions of which set out ideals and the premises of which are both heuristic criteria and policy guides. Our argument has been that a programme of free-market pragmatism would require the idea of market order to be used in pragmatic inference. Sometimes it is in fact so used by economists (page 90 above), but such cases are rare. The prevailing perception of science favours positive economics and its evolution into a kind of social mechanics. Some remarks on this will round off this part of our discussion.

> The idea that one thing depends on another is one of the basic notions behind all science ... Thus gravitational attraction is a function of the mass of the two bodies concerned and the distance between them; the incidence of murder is a function of the severity of the punishment for it; and the quantity of a product demanded is a function of the price of the product.

> Economic theory is based on relations among various magnitudes.

> The *magnitude* of the change that occurs in one variable in response to changes in another variable is extremely important in economics.[196]

These sentences, taken from Lipsey's *An Introduction to Positive Economics*, indicate the familiar character of economic models. If the business of determining economic magnitudes is to be taken seriously, there has to be more than a mere postulation that certain variables are functionally related in some way. As the last of the sentences indicates, the form of functions and the numerical values of parameters have to be found. Economists have of course taken the matter seriously and a great deal of their time and effort in recent years has been spent on econometric work.

This project has been made possible by the positivist idea of testing hypotheses and the rather different notion of description that it involves (see page 90 above). If the responses of economic agents had to be described by tracing lines of causation through the mental processes of millions, through a maze of individual preferences, expectations and institutional rules of conduct, positive economics would be a quite fantastic undertaking, even if we were all far less fickle and capricious than we seem to be. But to postulate functions as hypotheses and to fit them to statistical data is quite feasible. If a reasonable fit is found, the whole mass of detail that otherwise would have to be considered is reflected in the numerical values of a few parameters. It may then be maintained that the parameter values have no other significance than that the parameters worked out at such values with the data used. If a more lasting significance is disclaimed altogether, however, positive economics is not a science but just a game of fitting curves. There must be something to discover. There must be stable response patterns, hidden coefficients on which the economy turns. The economist's job is to find them, to make scientific discoveries, to reveal nature's secrets, just as the scientists in the white laboratory coats do.

To someone who sees scientific respectability in such terms, pragmatic inference must seem extremely odious. The context in which pragmatic inference was introduced in the preceding pages seemed to be all about value judgements, ideals and visions of the good society. Perhaps, contrary to his image among economists, that kind of context did excite an idealistic young Walras, but it is not about observable facts, neither an accurate description of them nor a theoretical explanation of their behaviour (see page 95 above), and thus hardly a suitable preoccupation for economic scientists. However, the context need be no other than that of plain prosaic everyday living. Pragmatic inference is simply a name we have given to the way that reason *may* guide action. It is the way we may articulate ends and the means for achieving them and therefore necessarily does involve purely imaginary situations. In the context of economic order, the imaginary situations *are* ideal situations. But, as the Hayek of some years ago said (page 55 above), a guiding conception of the overall order is 'not only the indispensable precondition of any rational policy, but also the chief contribution that science can make to the solution of the problems of practical policy' – though Hayek may now be convinced that it is better not to let reason loose on the overall economic order.

We have considered pragmatic inference only in the context of economic order. But it applies also in other contexts. Computers, jumbo jets and nuclear power stations, for instance, all had their beginnings in the imagination, in ideas that reshaped the world to some extent after their own images. However, that raises another question. In a sense, technology is based on ideals or at least on what is desirable. But it can serve desirable ends only once science has accomplished its task. Inference in technology as elsewhere must be based on established *regularities* and it is the prior task of pure science to discover them. Positive economics similarly has the task of preparing the ground for economic policy by finding stable coefficients. The scientific search for regularities cannot be avoided.

This is no doubt a complicated question. But at least in the area of the organization of human affairs, which from a pragmatic standpoint includes market order, the requisite regularities may be deliberate, consciously sought and sometimes deliberately imposed; and when this is not so, the possibility of a deliberate regularity is still significant. Let us consider the following inference: if drivers travelling in one direction keep to one side of the road and drivers travelling in the opposite direction keep to the other side of the road, then (if the road is wide enough) there will be no head-on collisions. In so far as the traffic rule derived from this inference is followed deliberately, is enforced or becomes an ingrained rule of conduct, i.e. in so far as the regularity is observed, there are no head-on collisions. But even if many people refuse to follow the rule, say because they regard it as impudent government interference with their personal freedom or because they do not agree that head-on collisions are undesirable or simply because there is some gain to be had, the inference still leads to a rule of practical significance, which is what Walras (page 74 above) also said of free competition.

The road-rule example is of course not an isolated case. Enforced regularity is the basis of legislation. But deliberate and voluntary regularity is more far-reaching. A positivist researcher who shuts out of his mind all he knows about the way human beings organize their affairs might discover, with the help of questionnaires and data kindly supplied by airlines and after testing many hypotheses, that of all the people in the world those booked on airline flights appear at the relevant airports at times which are a function of the times of departure of their flights, that there is a fairly stable lag and that there is some correlation between anomalous lags and persistent indistinct noises coming over loudspeakers; furthermore that there is an unbelievable correlation between the wished-for destinations stated by the passengers on any particular aircraft and the places at which the aircraft actually lands. It is easier of course to bear in mind how human beings in some cases organize their affairs by applying reason to their circumstances. Walras, it may be remembered, criticized Say for treating production, distribution and consumption as though they occurred in a manner independent of the will of man (page 76 above). It may perhaps be argued that positive economics does not deal with anything as trivial as traffic rules and timetables. However that may be, deliberate regularity of the familiar sort based on pragmatic inference would be quite sufficient for market order.

Hayek is of course correct when he says that not everything people do, not even a great deal of what they do, is reasoned out (Section 5.4.1). One would have to be more than blind not to be aware of the role played in everyday life by conventions and myriad rules of conduct. Furthermore, one may agree with Hayek that very many of these institutions arose spontaneously, i.e. that they were not at any stage reasoned out, thought through and adopted deliberately. From a pragmatic point of view, one would balk only at Hayek's further and latest contention (Section 5.4.4) that the rules which have never been reasoned out are always to be preferred to those which have been reasoned out and are followed deliberately.

The prevalence of institutions clearly has a bearing on the question of regularity. Here it seems possible to draw an analogy with the regularity of the so-called natural kinds in the natural sciences. Physical science describes a substance by the conjunction of various properties, e.g. a certain density, specific heat, coefficient of friction and so on. What is regular is that pieces of substance answering to this description are found in various places. Medical science describes human anatomy and physiology and it so happens that the surface of the earth is teeming with creatures answering more or less to such descriptions. If this is what at least one kind of regularity in the natural sciences consists in, then we have it also. Unless we are quite mistaken about institutions, it must be possible to investigate and describe a rule of conduct and then find a variety of individuals following it on a variety of occasions. When we speak of institutions, we surely imply just that kind of regularity.

In so far as it is the ideal of economists to emulate the natural sciences, one may commend institutions as a more promising field for empirical investigation than the possibly quite fortuitous events recorded in statistical time series. A knowledge of institutions may at least enable us to gain a reasonable understanding of whatever economic order there may be in various parts of the world. But it would not, just as the idea of market order does not and market order actually achieved would not, enable us to predict the quantitative effects of our reactions to exogenous shocks, let alone to make plain forecasts of what will happen. It would not give us positive economics as social mechanics or macro-economic hydraulics. It would give us only the grammar, the rules of economic activity (Section 5.3). It would tell us *how* things are done and not *what* is done. To know the rules of chess is not to know the sequence of moves and the outcome of every chess game that is ever played.[197]

Individualism and Public Spirit

9.1. The public interest

Individualism is the basis both of pragmatic and of dogmatic views on free markets. However much they may differ otherwise, they have this in common or else, on the stand taken here, they would not be about free markets at all. Individualism may be both a norm or ideal (page 64 above) and a methodological conviction or view of society. The latter is the conviction that only individual human beings and not organic social wholes or collectivities, such as socio-economic classes, the community, the State or 'the people', may be said to have preferences, values and interests, to make decisions and to take action.[198] Individualism does not of course preclude the possibility that a number of individuals may have common interests and may share certain values, such as individualist, collectivist or nationalistic values. Nor does it preclude the possibility that there may be an overall order in the relations among individuals, i.e. regularities in the manner in which the separate actions of individuals impinge on each other in a shared physical environment. It is not on the question of individualism but on the question of how economic order may come into existence in an individualist setting that pragmatic and dogmatic views on free markets are divided.

The issue of individualism and economic order raises a further question. The proponents of natural, libertarian and spontaneous order argue that market order should be allowed to come about of its own accord while the pragmatic argument is that it should be brought about by deliberate policy measures. In either case the prescription implies that there is something beneficial and desirable about market order. Methodological individualism requires that one should be able to say who benefits from market order and who finds it desirable. But, contrary to what their critics sometimes suspect, free-market supporters in general do not think that free markets benefit certain individuals only but, in a sense at least, everyone, though they would have to admit that not everyone regards market order as desirable. However, they are unlikely to feel that their arguments stand or fall by whether the idea of market order titillates everyone's fancies nor even by whether each and every individual would gain from free markets. Adam Smith, as we have seen (page 26 above), thought that the private interests of many individuals irresistibly oppose free markets and yet he evinced not a hint of misgiving about invoking the public interest in support of free markets (see e.g. Section 6.3). It is as though *the public interest* is an objective criterion quite distinct from the partial interests of, say, a monopolist who runs a successful predatory scheme. But this notion does not seem to be compatible with individualism. The public is not an individual and therefore, on the individualist thesis, it cannot have an interest.

Rothbard says quite simply in a footnote that '"public interest" is a meaningless term … and is therefore discarded by libertarians'.[199] In one way he is of course quite right. The notion of the public as a social entity with an interest of its own distinct from the interests of the individuals who compose the public is nonsense, at least from the individualist standpoint, while the 'general will' in the sense of unanimity of interest is possible but, on the evidence of history, exceedingly unlikely. But while the notion of the public interest cannot satisfy the quest for objectivity, it is not for that reason necessarily quite meaningless. If no meaning whatever may be attached to the term, one is left wondering why, for instance, Rothbard bothered to publish his views at all and to whom he is recommending libertarian order and on what grounds. One could give an interpretation purely in terms of personal gain. But would one have got it right?

Let us look at this more closely. Rothbard more than most economists is quite aware of the part played by predatory activity in economic life. He presumes, though, that government is the only avenue through which it may be practised (or perhaps that governing and predatory activity are synonymous) and hence he calls it hegemony. He concludes two of his books by listing the consequences, in terms echoing Quesnay (page 32 above), of the market and hegemonic principles respectively: 'The former breeds harmony, freedom, prosperity, and order; the latter produces conflict, coercion, poverty, and chaos.' Having exposed the hell of hegemony and the heaven of market order, he says with impeccable scientific decorum that analysis can go no further, 'the citizen – the ethicist – must now choose according to the set of values or ethical principles he holds dear'.[200]

Let us imagine, for the sake of argument, a libertarian who is addressing a gathering of individuals whose financial health depends in a large measure on licences, permits, subsidies, control boards and so on, as also on the support of unofficial governments such as trade unions. As the speaker senses that he is losing his audience, he appeals to them not to consider the libertarian order in any narrow perspective but according to the values they hold dear as citizens, as ethicists. Would it have made much difference if he and Rothbard had referred to the public interest? In this sense obviously it is an individually conceived public interest. As such there may be many versions of the public interest and they are unlikely all to favour the same economic system. To avoid confusion with the public interest as an objective criterion, one may perhaps speak of a *public-spirited interest*.

Our libertarian may object that he was merely appealing to enlightened self-interest. But, given the preconception of a social contract, such interest amounts to public-spirited interest. The idea that others are much like oneself is a necessary part of public spirit. It may be thought of as the basis of compassion for the suffering of others and so on but also of the social-contract idea. If I rob my neighbour, I may expect him also to rob me. When I think of how much an exclusive licence would let me extract from others, I must think also of how much the same strategy would let them extract from me. If we agree not to do such things to each other, we may all benefit. The social contract would be motivated by enlightened self-interest.[201] The social-contract idea may of course be quite misleading. But if one cannot conceive any but private interests, one may speak of enlightened self-interest. Clever self-interest is to prey upon others and to pre-empt their predilection for the same.

Disputes about economic order always revolve on appeals to the public interest rather than the interests of particular individuals. Unless the sincerity of the disputants is in question, such disputes may be said to be conducted in a public spirit. This terminology merely recognizes that people do have opinions, moreover a diversity of opinions, on what is in the public interest. Adam Smith, as also Hayek, Rothbard and all economists who appear to have recommended some version of economic order, wrote, one may presume, in a public spirit. Smith considered increases in the means to material prosperity to be in the public interest. This opinion would seem to have very wide support, but even it does not receive universal assent. The ancient Spartans are said to have considered virtually the opposite to be in the public interest, while many throughout history have thought it in the public interest to give priority to the spiritual side of life. One may accept diversity of opinion without prejudice to the question whether there are any absolute ethical standards. One may analyse opinions on what constitutes a good economic order without deciding the question whether values go any further than the individuals who hold them.

9.2. The social condition

Frank Knight devoted an entire paper to arguing that there are no definable objectives, no distinctly economic wants, which serve to separate any of our activities from the body of conduct as a whole; that man is an aspiring rather than a desiring being, or, as Buchanan interpreted Knight, that man wants to want better things.[202] When speaking of public spirit, one has to bear in mind the open-ended nature of human aspirations. Moreover, public-spirited interests are, so to say, second-order interests, being themselves derived from the moral precepts and the rules which modify our conduct as a whole. All the same, a public-spirited interest, such as an interest in a particular form of economic order, is often pursued with greater fervour and vehemence than when narrow pleasure seeking is the predominant interest. When various parties pursue diverse and especially dogmatic public-spirited interests, they can hardly avoid prescribing to each other how they are to conduct themselves and, as Adam Ferguson remarked (page 26 above), 'he who would scheme and project for others, will find an opponent in every person who is disposed to scheme for himself'. Public-spirited interests and therefore also ideals of economic order are major contributors to the perennial bickering and fighting that seems to be the social condition. We shall make this context the setting for our final assessment of free-market dogmatism and pragmatism.

9.2.1. Tacit and articulated moral precepts

Rules of conduct and more generally our moral precepts modify, temper and restrict our interests − 'in their very nature morals are traditional restraints placed on the pursuit of human pleasures', as Hayek put it.[203] Without such restraints, our interests, intentions and plans would be different from what they are. This may be seen in the ordinary organization of production. The available resources include not only raw materials, machines and equipment, but also human beings. The ideal of efficiency demands that all the resources be put to effective use and yet the inert and the human resources are treated rather differently, though in some cases the difference may be no more than a pretence. As long as only inert resources are involved, any technique whatever that makes difficult material yield a product is laudable. If this were also the case with the human resources, then, for instance, lies, deception, subterfuge, intimidation, blackmail and flattery would not have the connotations they do have but might have the status of a sophisticated know-how acquired through long experience, an enviable expertise in getting the most out of available resources.

We have throughout included such moral restraints among rules of conduct or the institutions of society. Following Hayek, we have used the term *rule*, as he put it, 'irrespective of whether such a rule is "known" to the individuals in any other sense than that they normally act in accordance with it'.[204] It is of course Hayek's point (see Section 5.4.1) that in the most usual cases rules of conduct are quite tacit, i.e. unarticulated, a knowing-how as grammatical rules are a knowing-how. In general, people are not aware of following rules nor conscious therefore of what may be the consequences of not following them. (For this reason, it may be observed, rules of conduct are very unlikely to have arisen in social contracts in any literal sense.)

It was Polanyi who drew attention to the overriding importance of the tacit dimension of knowledge, but it was also his contention that the capacity to articulate some possibly small fragments of tacit knowledge sets human beings apart from animals.[205] Tacitly known rules of efficient and honourable conduct, it seems, are no exception to this. There may be occasions, for example, on which one has to choose between two courses of action of which one seems financially more rewarding while the other seems more correct, decent and honourable. One may then become conscious of a rule of conduct and try to put it into words, just as grammatical rules also have been articulated. Whatever the occasions, rules of conduct and especially moral rules have of course often been articulated, perhaps seldom to the extent that they may be written down succinctly as in the decalogue, but at least to the extent that they may be thought and talked about.

The articulated moral precepts of one person need not disturb the affairs of others. Like Albert Schweitzer, one may withdraw to a remote place and observe the precept of reverence for life without pressing one's convictions on others. However, articulation and especially a very fragmentary articulation of moral rules, easily leads to that sometimes vicious sort of morality which is not about how one should conduct oneself but about how others should conduct themselves. Once a rule of conduct has been articulated, it is not uncommon for the thus enlightened to be gripped by a missionary zeal for moving heaven and earth to see others observe the rule. When economists and others are moved by a public-spirited interest to recommend one or other form of economic order, they would seem to be recommending what appear to them sound rules of conduct to the population at large because economic order is a matter of sound economic relations among people. For this they must not only have articulated certain rules to some extent but must also be prepared to tell others how they are to conduct themselves.

Knight's argument that it is not possible to categorize human aims and ambitions becomes very apposite in the context of a meddling crusading morality. All kinds of things may be done in pursuit of public-spirited interests, but individuals seldom have only one interest at heart. The distinction between self-centred private and public-spirited aims and ambitions (as opposed to interests) is extremely fuzzy and even the notion of sincerity may become irrelevant because individuals may be hard put to apply the distinction even to their own motivations.

One may, for instance, have to make many sacrifices to conduct oneself with integrity and even more to seek fair treatment for others, but it is also a pleasure to feel virtuous, and rules of just conduct are never so unbending as when insisted on by those who are far removed from the consequences. One has to uphold moral values if for no other reason than that without them social life would indeed be a war of all against all. But to play on the moral feelings of others has always been the most effective strategy for making others yield what one wants, even if it is not very clear what that is. It is also the main gateway to power, that ultimate form of freedom for one or a few individuals. And how could one do good if one is not free to do so? People so much yearn to live in peace and harmony with each other that everywhere they bicker with each other over the issue. Emotive words like 'outrage', 'abhorrence', 'affront to humanity', 'shocked and saddened' become holier-than-thou weapons wielded with bitterness in the perennial battle in which faction fights faction for peace and harmony on its own terms.

9.2.2. The regress of conflict

It was necessary to attempt this characterization of what we may call the social condition. Economics is not only concerned with scarcity, with human beings in relation to a niggardly nature, but also with human beings in relation to each other. Many of the questions which have fallen within the purview of economics may be said to be about resolving conflicts, about rules for reconciling interests – economic questions are to a large extent questions of civilized conduct. Perhaps this was more apparent when the subject was still known as political economy than it is now when economics has become so largely an arithmetic of economic aggregates and a mathematical analysis of the idea of optimal allocation turned into a description. Even 50 years ago when Knight and Ayres debated their differences, as Buchanan has observed, they had the common ground that 'the function of economics is to offer a theory of social order, of social interaction'.[206] Social order and interaction are of course favourite subjects for the perennial bickering we have called the social condition.

Here it is necessary to distinguish between differences among people which may be resolved into an order by certain rules, and differences among people about what these rules should be. The distinction follows on from one made previously (Section 5.3) between an order in economic activities and the rules of conduct or institutions which make the activities orderly. An economic system may of course accommodate a wide variety of tastes and inclinations. It may accommodate those who like to relax in the solitude of a mountain hideaway as well as those who like to relax amid much laughter, shouting and noise, just as it may accommodate the wishes of those who like apples and of those who like bananas. But in a shared physical environment, potential conflicts must eventually arise both among those with different and among those with similar inclinations (as among all the many who long for the solitude of a limited number of mountains). Such conflicts, however, may be settled in an orderly and civilized way by a host of rules of conduct which in effect lay down a sanctioned manner of mutual impingement. In the case of an ideal market order, the potential conflicts are resolved by the rules which create the impersonal constraint of market prices (see page 106 above). The price system, as elementary textbooks sometimes state, is a rationing device.

But what of the people who do not like the institutions of their society, who do not like the sanctioned manner in which conflicts are resolved, who, for instance, believe that differences of opinion are best settled by making only one opinion prevail, albeit that they call that one opinion the collective will? Or what of the people who, though they agree on the rule of law as an ideal, disagree among themselves about which laws should rule? Such conflicts are not normally considered in economics. Micro-economics presumes a world in which a coherent set of tacit rules is uniformly observed by everyone. Under such conditions, nothing that would be recognized as conflict would arise in the normal course of events. In culturally very diverse societies, on the other hand, where a large number of ill-matched rules are observed tacitly, conflicts are likely to arise in many specific cases of mutually incompatible demands on resources. Neither of these extremes seems to be the most normal situation, such as that of a society which is by and large based on ideals of free enterprise in free markets. Most normally, the set of rules is only tolerably coherent and only moderately well established or enforced by an authority. The rules are articulated to some extent and held up by some as the guardians of sound economic order but merely acquiesced in with varying degrees of reluctance by others.

Under such conditions, the resolution of potential conflicts by rules is not a final resolution. Conflicts are shifted on to the rules. Attention focusses on rules and they become the objects of disagreement. If there is a further set of rules for dealing also with these disagreements, such as rules of political process, the focus of disagreement and conflict is likely to centre on these rules and so on. Potentially there is an infinite regress. It is a type of problem that may arise in many contexts. Who guards the guards, who oversees the overseers, whose hand is behind the invisible hand?

9.3. The dogmatic tradition

What we have called dogmatic views on free markets must be seen against this background. There appears always to have been a body of dogmatic opinion which has sought to end the potential regress of conflict by an appeal to objective criteria, to absolute rules which are not a matter of opinion and stand whether mankind sanctions them or not. (The term *dogmatic* should not be understood in a derogatory sense.) In antiquity the Stoics enjoined men to live in accord with nature and to recognize providence and right reason. Their intense study of physics had the ultimate objective of demonstrating how men and mankind's affairs may partake in the order and harmony of the cosmos.[207] Stoic ideas in their great diversity passed on into the Christian era and, in the Middle Ages, aspects of Stoicism were merged in the natural law tradition of the Scholastics (Section 4.1). Schumpeter maintained that 'social science discovered itself in the concept of natural law' and that the Scholastics passed with ease from normative doctrine to analytic theorem, just as we nowadays may pass with ease 'from their just price to the price of (short- or long-run) competitive equilibrium'.[208] (See page 73 above.) Natural law doctrines flourished in the 17th and 18th centuries, the era in which the roots of economics as a distinct discipline are embedded. John Locke's enunciation of the 'law of reason' or 'original law of Nature for the beginning of property' was and still is influential.[209] So was the natural order discovered by Quesnay and the Physiocrats, and the Providence detected by Adam Smith in his younger days (page 33 above).

Modern conventions make it very difficult for any ordinary academic to claim that he has gained an insight into absolute moral rules or natural laws, but the point may be made in other ways. We have considered three very different cases in which the principles of market order are treated as objective and independent of shifting conflicting opinions. They are cases of dogmatism in the sense that market order is presented as something that either is or would be, if properly recognized, outside the regress of conflict. Two of the cases were meant to show what appear to be the main variants of freemarket dogmatism from which other dogmatic views on free markets borrow in different combinations. They are the libertarian order as rendered by Rothbard (Section 5.2) and the spontaneous order based on tradition, as reinforced by the 'ethics of success' of the Hayek of recent years (Section 5.4.4). The third case is the denormatized dogmatism of equilibrium theory. It will be held over to the final section.

Rothbard's rendition of libertarian order is in line with a long tradition of dogmatic views, particularly with Locke's appeal to a law of reason. Libertarians must appeal to reason rather than simply adopt existing legal custom (page 44 above). Reason, it seems, is not the slave of the passions, as Hume put it, but reveals rules of correct conduct, i.e. obligations with corresponding rights. This outlook on reason probably accounts for the paucity of institutional considerations in the libertarian order and contrasts sharply with Hayek's views, but not with the denormatized dogmatism of equilibrium theory, for Rothbard maintains that the 'laws of economics apply whatever the particular level (of development) of the economy'.[210] The libertarian order, however, is not denormatized. Reason apparently reveals that 'in the profoundest sense there *are* no rights but property rights. The *only* human rights, in short, are property rights.'[211] These rights follow closely Locke's natural law for the acquisition and transfer of property, namely 'every man has the absolute right of property in his own self and in the previously unowned natural resources which he finds, transforms by his own labor, and then gives to or exchanges with others'.[212] (The same absolute ownership applies to what is received in exchange or as a gift or inheritance.) The whole libertarian order is then deduced with remarkable consistency from this sole human right.

The principle of voluntarism (page 45 above), for instance, is subservient to property rights. The scope of anyone's voluntary action is established by his property rights and limited only by the property rights of others. But respect for absolute and all-embracing property rights is definitely not voluntary. The choice of economic system falls outside the scope of voluntarism. The attitude to voluntary associations and therefore to monopolistic practices not enforced by government has a similar base. It distinguishes libertarians from classical liberals, particularly those we have called pragmatists. Adam Smith, for instance, seemed to take it for granted that a voluntary association in the economic sphere usually has the purpose and certainly the effect of restricting the scope of the voluntary actions of non-members (see Chapter 3 and Sections 6.2 and 6.3). Classical liberalism had the problem of defining freedom in a way that distinguishes between freedom and power, and hence also between economic freedom and economic power (page 64 above). Rothbard states: 'The libertarian doctrine … advocates the maximization of man's *power over nature* and the eradication of the *power of man over man*.'[213] But he considers the concept of economic power and concludes that it has an 'inherent contradiction' and 'makes no sense at all'. He offers a long argument, the gist of which is, quite correctly, that to concede that anyone has the right not to be restricted by the economic power of another would be to concede that the right to do with one's property as one pleases is not absolute and unconditional.[214] There is a natural law of property and everything else follows from it; in particular a 'society built on libertarian foundations – a society marked by peace, harmony, liberty, maximum utility for all, and progressive improvement in living standards'.[215]

Libertarians find themselves in the same dogmatic tradition as modern liberals or welfare-state humanists, who also rest their case on various human rights. In the general strife over the form of economic order, libertarians and modern liberals are of course implacable opponents. But the tradition is the same; the absolute human rights revealed by reason are different.

In Hayek's argument from cultural evolution, private property, the family and other institutions associated with market order are not justified by human rights revealed by reason, but, quite the contrary, by their being independent of rational inquiry. Their justification rests on the fact that they are spontaneously evolved, traditional, tried and tested or, as he has put it recently, shown scientifically to be superior by (as he sees it) the proliferation of people who have these institutions (Section 5.4.4).

It is not clear whether this is also a natural-law argument, but it is definitely different from that which lies behind the libertarian order and welfare-state humanism. Hayek himself considers the question in several places. He presumes that the opponents of his views (the constructivists) would represent his position as a natural-law theory. He would apparently have no objection to this if natural-law theory were understood as an articulation of traditional rules and values; nor if it were understood in the sense in which at times in the Middle Ages natural law was given an evolutionist interpretation, especially by the late Spanish Scholastics, principally Luis Molina, who, for instance, interpreted natural prices as cases of what amounts almost to Hayek's middle category, i.e. the unintended consequences of the purposeful actions of many people (see page 50 above). However, these beginnings of an evolutionary approach,

Hayek observes, were overshadowed by laws of reason in the age of reason.[216] Hayek then explains his position:

> Though there can be no justification for representing the rules of just conduct as natural in the sense that they are part of an external and eternal order of things, or permanently implanted in an unalterable nature of man, or even in the sense that man's mind is so fashioned once and for all that he must adopt those particular rules of conduct, it does not follow from this that the rules of conduct which in fact guide him must be the product of a deliberate choice on his part; or that he is capable of forming a society by adopting any rules he decides upon; or that these rules may not be given to him independent of any particular person's will and in this sense exist 'objectively'.[217]

Buchanan puts Hayek's 'ideology' into a category he calls *Panglossian*, as opposed to his own, which falls into the *meliorist* or *constitutionalist-contractarian* category. Panglossian, as Voltaire cognoscenti might guess, implies 'that there is really nothing that can be done to improve matters; hence we live in the best of possible worlds'.[218] This is the kind of natural law view expressed by the invisible hand in Smith's *Moral Sentiments* (page 33 above). It has already been observed that the ethics of success in all consistency should also lead to this conclusion (page 57 above), but that it does not seem to be Hayek's conclusion at all, or else it would not be necessary to rail against constructivism (Section 5.4.2).

On occasion Hayek does in fact express the opinion that some spontaneously evolved institution is regrettable. One such occasion arose when he was dealing with a matter some way into the regress of conflict, namely the 'unlimited democracy' of our time in which legislative powers and executive powers to direct government are vested in the same assembly, so that members of such assemblies do whatever they 'find expedient to do in order to retain majority support' and decisions 'rest on a sanctioned process of blackmail and corruption' (e.g. economic policies intended to buy certain votes).[219] In this connection Hayek says:

> The great tragedy of the historical development is that these two distinct powers were placed in the hands of one and the same assembly, and that government consequently ceased to be subject to law. The triumphant claim of the British Parliament to have become sovereign, and so able to govern subject to no

law, may prove to have been the death-knell of both individual freedom and democracy.[220]

There could hardly be a more spontaneously evolved institution than the British constitution. Hayek surely would not have such an opinion of it if he really believed that we live in the best of all possible worlds and spontaneous evolution always has a favourable outcome. He does not appear to hold this Panglossian view. It is rather that he believes that deliberate attempts to devise social and economic institutions almost *never* have a favourable outcome. Hayek's respect for tradition seems to be based on a great distrust of the intellect and reasoning of his fellow men, especially when they think that reason may reveal moral rules of conduct. This is surely what he means to say in the following passage:

> It is the humble recognition of the limitations of human reason which forces us to concede superiority to a moral order to which we owe our existence and which has its source *neither* in our innate instincts, which are still those of the savage, nor in our intelligence, which is not great enough to build what is better than it knows, but to a tradition which we must revere and care for even if we continuously experiment with improving its parts – not designing but humbly tinkering on a system which we must accept as given. Human reason's greatest achievement is to recognize not only its own insurmountable limitations, but also the existence of a gradually evolved set of abstract rules of which it can avail itself to build better than it knows.[221]

In so far as Hayek holds a dogmatic view, it is that we may escape the perennial conflict over the form of social and economic order because traditional institutions are a far surer foundation for sound order than the various opinions which are party to the conflict. Traditional rules of conduct exist 'objectively' and we may and should take them as given. This kind of dogmatic standpoint no doubt does frequently enter the defence of free markets. But the dogmatic mantle fits Hayek rather awkwardly. One may venture the opinion that it is more a matter of expedience than of principle, or if not of expedience then at least of practical wisdom for a world inhabited mainly by fools. It would be understandable if, in a long life in which he has been much exposed to what people in public life and in certain academic circles present as the fruits of their reflection, he has come to think that man would be far better off with the intellectual elegance of a dog or a horse and that it is better to sit on Pandora's box as tightly as one can rather than to encourage mankind to play havoc with itself.

As practical wisdom there may be much to be said for Hayek's anti-rationalism. But as a principle on which to defend market order – and there can be no doubt that this is the use Hayek puts it to – it raises some difficulties. Given the vague perception many people have that western societies have emerged from a laissez-faire era and are moving towards some form of socialism,[222] it is easy to present market institutions as traditional institutions and socialist and other new ideas as rationalist constructions. But there was a time not so long ago when the ideal of market order as the principle of the overall economic order of society must have seemed very new-fangled indeed. Dogmatic antirationalism would have had to dismiss the *Wealth of Nations* as constructivist folly, as the product of the fatal conceit of a cloistered academic who could not appreciate the inherent wisdom of feudal institutions or of whatever was considered traditional. If the advent of the ideal of market order was sound cultural evolution, then why does not the same apply, for instance, to the strides made by social-democratic ideals in this century? The problem is how one should distinguish between spontaneous evolution and rationalist constructivism. Is spontaneous evolution not at least to some extent the common outcome of the bickering that takes place between various people who come up with constructivist schemes in a public spirit? Does it help to speak of 'unintended consequences', as Hayek does? If constructivist schemes usually end in disaster, then surely these are unintended consequences.

It may be helpful to consider a parallel lower down the regress of conflict. Newcomers to economics may often be puzzled by the idea of a price established under conditions of perfect competition. Such a price may change continually and yet no one may be singled out (leaving the Walrasian auctioneer aside) as the person who changes it because everyone takes it as given, while furthermore a price is hardly the sort of entity that moves by its own volition. It may then be instructive to enlarge upon the elucidation of market price that the theoretical construction is meant to provide. Individuals may well be involved in setting prices, such as when they engage in bargaining, but no one has the power to force his will on others either by raising or lowering a price. The spontaneity of a market price implies that not only one person's will was involved in setting the price.

Hayek's idea of the spontaneous evolution of institutions may be looked upon as the analysis of market price moved to the second stage of the regress of conflict – a kind of perfectly competitive market in opinions on rules of conduct, in which no one has the power to force his opinions on others and whatever rules emerge are the product of many minds. Individuals may well proffer all kinds of constructivist schemes but none is powerful enough to make his particular scheme prevail. Hayek himself has not been averse to trying his hand at constructivist schemes, such as his suggestions for the denationalization of money and his proffered model constitution.[223] But he does not have the power to make his schemes obligatory and perhaps would not even want to have that power. His objection to the socialist schemes of this century, it seems, is that certain groups of people have appropriated the power to make their schemes prevail. The market in opinions has been characterized by monopolistic practices. The game has not been played according to the ground rules of spontaneous cultural evolution.

These ground rules are of special interest to us. For them, we must look to the third stage of the regress of conflict since they are the rules which govern spontaneous evolution at the second stage. Hayek speaks of the principles of a liberal social order.[224] We may call them the principles of a free society for short and interpret Hayek's elaborate analysis as follows: the principles of a free society should govern a process of cultural evolution which produces the rules (or economic systems) which in turn govern the mutual impingement of ordinary everyday economic activities. It is not clear whether the principles of a free society, if applied, would always lead to a free-market system. Hayek seems to think so. Perhaps he would argue that any system arrived at without coercion is by definition a market system. The point is debatable.

It is quite clear, however, that for Hayek the rules at the third stage of the regress of conflict, i.e. the principles of a free society, are not negotiable. They are permanent and of timeless significance. They are no more subject to further spontaneous evolution than respect for property rights is voluntary in the libertarian order. They are the basis from which he argues. If Hayek invoked natural law, human rights or some other outside authority to support the principles of a free society and thus end the regress at that stage, he would be a dogmatist by our criterion. As far as one can tell, he has never done so. The principles of a free society are also rules of conduct and, as we have just seen (page 124 above), he does not think that such rules may be represented as 'part of an external and eternal order of things'. Twenty-five years ago, when Hayek explained why he did not regard himself as a conservative, he described himself as 'an unrepentant Old Whig' and spoke of the tenets which go under that name simply as his conviction or a creed of which he approved.[225] If that is still so, then by our criterion Hayek is really a free-market pragmatist.

Furthermore, if Hayek is prepared to stand up for his convictions – and he obviously is prepared to do that – he is very much embroiled in the conflict over economic order. A mild way of conducting that fight is to denigrate one's opponents. Surely Hayek is doing just that when he speaks of 'those secondhand dealers in ideas who regard themselves as intellectuals' and who may almost be defined as 'those who are not intelligent enough to recognize the limits of reason'; or when he says: 'I sometimes have the impression that in a world that depends on traditions which the individual cannot rationally justify, some of the most intelligent men can become the most dangerous fools, aliens to and disturbers of the civilization in which they live'.[226] Hayek has not escaped the social condition.

9.4. Pragmatism in the realm of principles

There is no corresponding tradition into which free-market pragmatism falls, unless it is classical liberalism. We have attributed pragmatic views on free markets to certain writers – Smith in his mature years, Walras in the way he saw the significance of his theory, Hayek in some of his moods, Simons and his positive programme for laissez-faire, Eucken and *die Soziale Marktwirtschaft*, Buchanan and Tullock and public-choice theory. But their respective work is too different and the pragmatic element in it too implicit for one to be able to speak of a common tradition. In the discussion which follows an attempt will be made to bring out the characteristics which make a pragmatic position on free markets distinct from other positions. However, these characteristics may not be found in their entirety in the works of all the writers mentioned above.

Free-market pragmatism must seem like a contradiction in terms. The first part indicates an ideal and the second may be understood as the eschewal of all ideals and principles. Nevertheless, free-market pragmatism may be described as a pragmatism in the realm of ideals and principles. It is pragmatism at the second stage of the regress of conflict. The explanation of this rather curious concept will unfortunately be rather complicated. Three aspects have to be explained: that free-market pragmatism is not pragmatism in admittedly the most usual sense, which we may call ad hoc pragmatism; that in its opposition to ad hoc pragmatism it sometimes takes on the guise of a pseudo dogmatism; and the sense in which it is a pragmatism. A further part will be added to illustrate the rather difficult material.

9.4.1. Ad hoc pragmatism

There is an ad hoc pragmatism observed by people who pride themselves in taking problems as they come, making day-to-day accommodations, moving from one stopgap to the next and generally muddling through without any principles or guiding conception at all. Free-market pragmatism is not this kind of pragmatism. The matter is, however, not as simple as that. There are many cases in which principles and guiding conceptions do come into play and some form of order arises as a result, but which nevertheless fall into the category of ad hoc pragmatism. Such cases are difficult to deal with. The general idea is that they are cases in which a specific person or group of persons, guided by certain principles or by certain ideals, wishes to achieve specific objectives which, however, can be achieved only if other people are not free to use their knowledge for their own purposes, as Hayek often puts it.[227] This is to be contrasted with cases of order in which everyone does have the freedom to use his knowledge for his purposes, though only in the sense that he is subject to *impersonal constraints*. Freedom subject to impersonal constraints is the economic equivalent of freedom under the law.

One area in which this distinction finds application is that of organizational structures and command hierarchies, such as in military establishments and business corporations. Hayek has long been preoccupied with trying to distinguish the rules on which organizations are based from those on which market order is based. The latter, he says, are universal, general and abstract and are not the conduit for specific commands. General rules tell us only the abstract character of an order while organizational rules aim at deliberate detailed arrangements. He also borrows some terminology from Oakeshott, who called organizational order purpose-governed or telocratic and market order and the like law-governed or nomocratic.[228] On this basis a law laying down that verbal contracts are binding would be general while legislation providing for agricultural marketing boards which set prices would probably be analogous to the administrative rules within a company. But what about banking legislation? No doubt there are many doubtful cases. The distinction between the general and the particular, which is what all this is about, is an important question of logic. It has been a major preoccupation of western philosophy since antiquity. Yet there do not seem to be any rigorous criteria which may be applied in economics, not even, as far as one can tell, a useful working rule. Eucken, like Hayek, regarded the distinction as vital (see page 54 above). Both seemed to assume that their readers would more or less understand it.

If the same assumption may be made here, we may see that the scope of ad hoc pragmatism extends very far – in fact to all cases in which some authority is trying to control the economy to achieve a specific result. Central planning therefore falls into the category of ad hoc pragmatism. So does planning in various other forms of socialist organization. While there are of course many forms of socialism, it is surely quite evident that in many of them the political or revolutionary leaders and their planners are trying to put into effect some notion they have of a good society by doing whatever seems to come closest to using their hands to push people and mould society into the desired order. That such manipulation sometimes leads to totalitarian oppression is not necessarily part of the plan. The vision of a good society may not include anyone lingering in prison. Things simply work out that way when some people fail to see the good intentions of the planners and insist, like the political or revolutionary leaders themselves, on using their knowledge for their own purposes.

More interesting is the question whether full-employment or demand management policies also fall into the category of ad hoc pragmatism. Clearly, an authority is trying to manipulate the economy to achieve an objective, but whether that objective is to be regarded as 'specific' is hard to say because there is no rigorous criterion for deciding the question. Furthermore, the fiscal and monetary policy measures used for the manipulation do not prevent anyone from using his knowledge for his purposes, but they do seem to be based on the assumption that people use this freedom in a predictable way. If knowledge, perhaps newly acquired knowledge, is used for purposes rather different from the predicted ones, demand management could hardly be effective. Some explanations for the rather mediocre success of such policies have in effect taken this line of argument.

Both Eucken and Simons were more than a little unsympathetic towards full-employment policies and for more or less the same reasons, namely that reform of the monetary system and policies to discourage monopolistic practices would remove the need for such policies.[229] Eucken, while conceding that crisis situations call for immediate ad hoc measures, did not take the view Keynes took, namely that 'apart from the necessity of central controls to bring about an adjustment between the propensity to consume and the inducement to invest, there is no more reason to socialise economic life than there was before'.[230] Eucken did not think that one could by such means simply add the unemployed on to the active part of the economy while the latter ran on undisturbed. Basing himself on German experience, he thought full-employment policies threw so many other aspects of the economy out of line that there was an increasing tendency to centralized state control of the economic process.[231]

This question brings out an important feature of free-market pragmatism. Demand-management policies are based on an implicit denormatized dogmatism. The market mechanism and certain economic laws are just there and beyond our control, like the law of gravity. From a normative point of view, the market mechanism fails in certain respects and the economic laws may be harnessed for counteracting market failures with ad hoc measures. In contrast, the freemarket pragmatist does not regard the so-called market mechanism and economic laws as immutable. In his view, policy should undertake the difficult task of modifying institutions, i.e. the rules of economic conduct (e.g. reforming the monetary system, discouraging monopolistic practices). If one looks to the rules of the economic game, all the rest looks after itself. As Eucken put it, there should be state planning of the economic system (forms) but not of the economic process (page 54 above). The essential thing is to be able to tell the difference.

9.4.2. Pseudo dogmatism

This difference in approach to economic policy warrants closer examination because policy directed at changing the economic rules is sometimes confusingly represented as a do-nothing policy of inaction. A leading principle of market order is that constraints on what people may do should be impersonal, i.e. not directed by anyone in particular against anyone in particular. A market price is an impersonal constraint because it prevents sellers from setting prices more favourable to themselves though no person or persons may be pointed out who are deliberately preventing them from doing so. Some, though not all, forms of what we have called ad hoc pragmatism violate the principle of control by impersonal constraint. Someone is deliberately restraining others in order to achieve an objective of his own. For free-market supporters such conduct is objectionable since it may be defined simply as conduct incompatible with market order. When they urge people to desist from conduct incompatible with market order, they are of course urging them to confine themselves to conduct compatible with market order. That these are merely two ways of saying the same thing is taken for granted as obvious by, for instance, Simons and Eucken. However, sometimes essentially the same arguments as theirs are presented in a different guise, namely that the institutions of market order establish themselves of their own accord *under certain circumstances*. On closer examination, it may turn out that these circumstances are nothing other than the absence of conduct incompatible with market order.

We first characterized a dogmatic view on free markets (Chapter 2) as one according to which the hand behind the invisible hand is invisible too. We also indicated that apparently the most common dogmatic assertion is that the institutions of market order establish themselves of their own accord in *the absence of government interference*. We are now in a better position to see what is dogmatic about that assertion. It is dogmatic because it singles out government as the only agency capable of conduct incompatible with market order.

This attitude to government may stem in part from the conviction of the libertarian property-rights anarchist that government is incompatible with absolute property rights (see pages 44–5 above). Respect for property rights, as he sees it, is the fundamental and the only moral obligation. The institution of government is therefore immoral and should be done away with, its law-enforcing (i.e. property-rights-protecting) and judicial functions being taken over by private enterprise. Whatever social and economic conditions would emerge, then, would constitute, by definition, a wholesome order. It is, however, misleading to say that such order comes about by itself since it would require the active efforts of certain individuals to abolish government in all its forms.

This position may influence many free-market dogmatists who do not fully comprehend what it entails. It is seldom spelt out as clearly as Rothbard expounds it. It would seem, however, that not many free-market supporters who berate government for its burgeoning role in the economy adopt this extreme position. Milton and Rose Friedman, for instance, say: 'To some extent government is a form of voluntary cooperation ...' and 'There is nothing "natural" about where my property rights end and yours begin.'[232] With a more flexible and tolerant approach to government and property rights, what could still be dogmatic about the assertion that the institutions of market order establish themselves of their own accord in the absence of government interference? It could be dogmatic in the sense that it is inspired either by the nature-loving, hands-off, man's-touch-sullies attitude (pages 31–2 above) or by a Panglossian reverence for tradition. Government would then simply be the most prominent agency capable of interfering in the natural course of things. But, whatever else may be said of such attitudes, they do not lend themselves very well to support of free markets. An unbiased interpretation of the natural course of things may recognize that spontaneous evolution does not necessarily create free-market institutions. Such interpretations of history were prominent in Germany at one time.

Menger contrasted social phenomena of *pragmatic* origin with those of *organic* origin. After some discussion, he concluded that the latter are best analysed as the unintended consequences of purposeful action ('das unreflectirte Ergebniss gesellschaftlicher Entwickelung'), i.e. in terms of the old idea which Hayek now expresses as the outcome of spontaneous evolution.[233] But when Menger said this, Hayek had not yet been born and the proponents of the organic view whom Menger had in mind were his chosen opponents, namely the members of the historical school of German economists. The gentlemen of this school were by no means free-market dogmatists. In fact, people of such persuasion sometimes called them *Kathedersozialisten* – socialists of the academic rostrum or chair. The historical school took the view that social institutions evolved in their own national idiom as an organic whole and this was often taken to mean that their changing character as time passed was a matter of inevitable historical evolution. On the organic wholeness of institutions and the inevitability of their evolution historical economists had something in common with Marxists. Under the influence of this way of thinking, as Eucken remarked, the formation of cartels was accepted as the outcome of a necessary process of historical evolution and therefore as progress. The German courts took a similar view of cartels and other monopolistic practices.[234] When later the economic oligarchy thus formed fell under the hegemony of the National Socialist German Workers' (Nazi) Party, a similar view might again have been taken. It would have been a consistent application of a theoretical standpoint.

But it is very hard to imagine, for instance, the author of *The Road to Serfdom* having contentedly regarded that development as yet another example of spontaneous evolution to be revered and cared for. Freemarket supporters who invoke traditions and spontaneity, who generally appeal to the sentiment that man's touch sullies, are doing something very different. They are advocating the principle of control by impersonal constraint, i.e. the principle of the invisible hand, and they are doing it by putting a Panglossian gloss upon the rather curious position they are in, namely of trying to restrain people from deliberately restraining each other.

People are told that market institutions establish themselves of their own accord in the absence of conduct incompatible with market order. At most this may be construed as the dogmatic assertion that people left to themselves never fail to develop market institutions such as exchange and production for a market, and never fail to respond to incentives to be enterprising for the sake of material benefits. On the evidence of subsistence economies, such an assertion would seem to be mistaken. But this is not the usual context in which free-market arguments are put forward. The usual context is that of a situation where market institutions already exist side by side with conduct incompatible with market order. It is in this context that everyone is urged to cut out the latter so that only the former remain. To say, therefore, that a situation *brought about* deliberately also and at the same time *comes about* by itself is just a bit of dogmatic-sounding mysticism about a natural or spontaneous order. It is a pseudo dogmatism that distracts attention from the fact that people are being told how they should conduct themselves. The conflict over economic order sometimes becomes rather devious.

Statements to the effect that something should be done to *make* (and subsequently *let*) things happen of their own accord may be characterized as pseudo dogmatic. Their intent may be characterized as pragmatic. Hayek's position amounts to pseudo dogmatism, as the discussion in the latter half of Section 9.3 was meant to show. His arguments about cultural evolution and tradition rather obscure the fact that he is urging everyone to observe the principles of a free society and to appreciate the free-market institutions which he thinks would then prevail. Such institutions do not come about by themselves. Hayek is doing whatever he can to bring them about.

The same may be said of Smith's famous statement (quoted on page 33 above) that the 'system of natural liberty establishes itself of its own accord' in the absence of preference and restraint, so that everyone may be left alone 'as long as he does not violate the laws of justice'. It may be, as Hayek has said, that Smith made explicit the principles of an order that had already come into existence in an imperfect form, so that he could demonstrate the desirability of their general application.[235] But Smith's arguments against the mercantile system and the 'wretched spirit of monopoly' show that he thought there was much room for improvement (see pages 61 and 66 above.) Smith also did what he could to bring about what in his famous statement he said came about by itself. Moreover, he had a large measure of success, albeit posthumously and against his expectations.

9.4.3. Intimations of a well-ordered society

A libertarian may also agree that one has to do what one can to bring about free-market institutions. We have not yet shown in what sense freemarket pragmatism is distinctly pragmatic. This will be rather difficult. It will be convenient first to distinguish between dogmatism and pragmatism in the realm of principles and only then to add the qualification that the latter takes the form of free-market pragmatism. The contrast we want to show is with dogmatism in the sense that some principle is considered fundamental and all other considerations are subservient to it. Such is the case when an appeal is made to natural law or, more likely nowadays, to a fundamental human right.

A dogmatic attitude becomes apparent only in some contexts. All freemarket supporters may agree, for instance, that private property is the best safeguard for individual freedom and that some inequality in property holdings is a strong incentive to effort and efficiency. But libertarian attitudes will manifest themselves when it is said that extreme inequalities in property holdings passed on from generation to generation leave some with rather less freedom than others, with colossal incentives and minimal freedom to be enterprising. The libertarian is likely to say that this involves a jaundiced idea of freedom. If respect for property rights is the fundamental principle from which all else follows, if it is the only moral obligation, he could come to no other conclusion than that the idea of freedom being mooted is immoral. However, a dogmatist of a different hue may see this kind of freedom as the fundamental principle, the fundamental human right, i.e. a freedom which implies some access to physical things with which a person may be enterprising. The same argument would then run the other way and arrive at the conclusion that absolute property rights are immoral. Most dogfights we see are between dogmatists of different breeds. The subject of their disputes is which principles are fundamental and which principles are subservient to the fundamental ones. This is where the pragmatist in the realm of principles differs from them because he, in a very peculiar sense, seems to regard all principles as subservient. But subservient to what?

We may find a clue in the following statements by Henry Simons (referred to already on page 37 above):

> The representation of laissez-faire as a merely do-nothing policy is unfortunate and misleading. It is an obvious responsibility of the state under this policy to maintain the kind of legal and institutional framework within which competition can function effectively as an agency of control. The policy, therefore, should be defined positively, as one under which the state seeks to establish and maintain such conditions that it may avoid the necessity of regulating 'the heart of the contract'– that is to say, the necessity of regulating relative prices.[236]

Simons went on to propose some extremely drastic measures, which included the abolition of private fractional-reserve banking and the dismantling of large corporations. These measures were to be taken to make competition an effective agency of control, which in turn was meant to obviate the necessity of an alternative kind of control, namely the direct regulation of relative prices. A free-market dogmatist might well wonder why it should ever be *necessary* to control relative prices. If freedom of contract is a fundamental human right, it is an end in itself and may surely be maintained in relation to prices without curtailing it in relation to banking and large corporations. But Simons seems to regard freedom to contract at any prices merely as a preferable means of control. What end is supposed to be served by such means of control?

Simons, if he had been asked this question, might have found it embarrassing. He might have managed no more than to make some vague remarks about the public interest and the general well-being. It is a problem for anyone who has not latched on to a single idea which then looms large in the mind to the exclusion of all else. Public-spirited standpoints are easily formulated when one is guided by a single idea, whether it is the freedom of contract that comes with property rights or whether it is the exploitation of workers by capitalists. It is not so easy in other cases where there is only a vague and ill-articulated notion of a well-ordered society to which all principles are subservient.

Simons did in fact attempt an articulation of his notion of a well-ordered society but, by his own admission, he managed only 'fragmentary ideas and opinions' and even with these he did not do very well. His notion of a well-ordered society was that which he thought had inspired the tradition of classical liberalism:

> The distinctive feature of this tradition is emphasis upon liberty as both a requisite and a measure of progress. Its liberty or freedom, of course, comprises or implies justice, equality, and other aspectual qualities of the 'good society' … its good society is no static conception but is essentially social process whose goodness is progress – and progress not only in terms of prevailing criteria but also in the criteria themselves. Liberalism is thus largely pragmatic as regards the articulation or particularization of its values; but its ethics, if largely pragmatic, also gives special place to liberty (and nearly co-ordinate place to equality) as a 'relatively absolute'.

Furthermore: 'Economics properly stresses competition among organizations as a means to proper resource allocation and combination and to commutative justice. But effective competition is also requisite to real freedom of association – and to real power dispersion.' But he is undogmatic even about these rather equivocal tenets. He makes a point which has grown in significance since his day: 'How unfree societies may start toward freedom, … how economic progress may be made to prevail against inordinate birth rates – these are social problems for which Western liberalism offers no clear or simple answers, only dubious conjectures and earnest hopes.'[237]

But it is on the institution of property (which he calls an institutional device) that he is most equivocal. Security of property is essential and has many economic advantages. But the good society would have 'the maximum dispersion of property compatible with effective production', the liberal ideal of equality of opportunity requires 'substantial restriction on family accumulation of wealth' and he speaks of a liberal process of 'continuous, experimental development in the institution of property'. Liberal policy contemplates a property law with the curious feature of being 'both stable and flexible'.[238] But as Simons said, if we can 'apprehend fragments or aspects' of the well-ordered society 'we apprehend something of how the firm substance may gradually be realized'.[239]

Simons's attempt to articulate the notion of a well-ordered society was hardly a model of clarity. But this should not be held against him; perhaps it should be regarded as a sign of intellectual honesty. Over the centuries many have made similar attempts and the study of economics in particular has in many cases had its origin in such attempts. Yet notions of a well-ordered society are still so little articulated and articulated in so fragmentary a way that certain ideas loom large in some minds and none of us may be sure to what extent the public-spirited interests of different people are simply incompatible. Clearly, there must be many public-spirited aspirations which, unlike the separate wishes of apple and banana lovers, could not all find accommodation within the same political boundaries. But it is not clear whether the incompatibilities extend as far as it often seems they do. The issue is beset with much logical obfuscation and with antipathies trumped up in the heat of conflict, such as when the principles of a free society are represented in certain quarters as the chains of bondage.

However, the problem is mitigated by the fact that institutional compromises are possible in the sense that a set of institutions may serve a number of ideals. One does not always have to make up one's mind nor argue with others about which principles take priority. A wide variety of public-spirited points of view held by a wide variety of people may find accommodation in an institutional compromise. Such an accommodation may be looked upon as a compromise at the second stage of the regress of conflict analogous to the way the composition of the output of ordinary economic goods and services is a compromise at the first stage.

Market order itself is a composite of ideals, serving, for instance, (as a guiding conception) the ideals both of individual freedom and of material prosperity, the links being provided by the information and incentive aspects of market order. An institutional compromise depends on the detailed characteristics of the rules of conduct that make up a set of institutions. We may consider just one example. Among businessmen it is quite laudable to vie openly to take away another man's customers but plain criminal to take away his stock and equipment, even though the loss suffered may often be greater in the former case than in the latter. The fact that these particular rules of conduct are not normally found among professional people shows that there is nothing natural about them. Individual freedom, stability, incentives and so on are served by respect for the ownership of stock and equipment; efficient allocation and hence material prosperity by competition for customers.

One way of investigating the potential for institutional compromise is to carry out *Gedankenexperimente*. A thought experiment of this kind amounts to an attempted articulation of the notion of a well-ordered society and is often called by the name Sir Thomas More gave to his own endeavours in this regard, though *guiding conception* may be a term with less troublesome associations. After discussing 'the required courage to consider utopia', Hayek summed up his idea of the function of a utopia in the following words, however consistent they may be with others of his statements: 'Yet it is only by constantly holding up the guiding conception of an *internally consistent* model which could be realized by the consistent application of the same principles, that anything like an effective framework for a functioning spontaneous order will be achieved' (italics added).[240] Immediately after this passage, Hayek alluded to Smith's work as an example of such a guiding conception and to the influence it had on the course of events. Jaffé, we may recall (page 97 above), also said that Walras looked upon his theory of general equilibrium as a realistic utopia.

Our discussion therefore suggests that the distinction between dogmatism and pragmatism in the realm of principles amounts to the following: dogmatism is based on one or a few principles, regarded as fundamental, from which are deduced the properties of social and economic order as it should be or, in a denormatized version, as it is. Pragmatism in the realm of principles is based on ill-articulated notions of a well-ordered society from which are educed or extracted various principles in a process of articulation which progressively formulates these notions into ideal institutional compromises (guiding conceptions, utopias), i.e. into sets of envisaged rules of conduct which combine a number of principles and serve a number of ideals.

What makes a pragmatist in the realm of principles into a free-market pragmatist is the insistence that the ideal institutional compromise should include the principle of control by impersonal constraint, the principle of the invisible hand, as the agency of control by which social and economic order is maintained.

There is, however, a problem with this. It may be said that our distinction amounts to no more than that a different dogmatic fundamental principle looms large in the mind of a so-called free-market pragmatist, namely, the leading principle of classical liberalism. One may say in response that the desirability of control by impersonal constraint is simply a conclusion reached when well-ordered societies are contemplated. The response to this may be that the contemplation of a well-ordered society is just the process, if pursued with great intelligence and much effort, by which reason arrives at the only true and fundamental moral principles. There is of course no way in which one can say that this cannot be so. One can only say that, with the intelligence and effort that has been applied, people have reached very different conclusions. Compromises, where they are logically possible, therefore seem to be the best expedient we have – though this is of course also the expression of a value.

The pragmatic attitude does, however, make a considerable difference in the ongoing conflict over social and economic order that seems to be the social condition. Socialist thinkers also come in dogmatic and pragmatic varieties. Schumpeter, in commenting on the influence of early utopian writers and the contempt in which they are held by scientific (and we would say dogmatic) socialists, said that nevertheless 'much of the propelling force of socialism' comes from the 'longings of the hungry *soul* – not belly'.[241] Socialist principles incorporated in guiding conceptions may of course emerge from attempted articulations of what hungry souls long for. Free-market dogmatists are likely to spurn such guiding conceptions either because they are founded on false principles, disregard immutable economic laws or are unnatural and therefore bad since man's touch always sullies. The free-market pragmatist, by contrast, may in many cases consider them provided that they may be incorporated into internally consistent compromise-guiding conceptions which also make allowance for control by impersonal constraint. It is in this sense that free-market pragmatists are pragmatic.

9.4.4. Walter Eucken as a free-market pragmatist

Let us present a very short profile of Walter Eucken as a free-market pragmatist to illustrate what has been said so far.[242] It is also of interest because of the influence Eucken and his followers are said to have had on the economic policies of West Germany more or less from the time of its inception as a state.

Eucken addressed himself to the question 'How can modern industrialized economy and society be organized in a humane and efficient way?' and said: 'That is the problem with which every nation is confronted.'[243] It is the question of a well-ordered society. Eucken's particular vision of it presumably gave meaning to *humane* and *efficient* and to how possible conflicts between these criteria were best resolved.

He does not appear ever to have spelt out such a vision but fragments of it show in his attitude to various problems.

Before we may have a look at Eucken's attitude, however, we have to say something about his analytical scheme. Eucken was preoccupied with what he called the Great Antinomy, the apparent schism between theoretical and historical (or 'descriptive') approaches to economic problems, or simply between theoretical analysis and the 'real world'. The issue was very much on the minds of German economists because of the legacy of Schmoller and the earlier historical schools and the *Methodenstreit* which had carried on for many years. Eucken had the idea that any actual economy may be seen as 'a fusion of a limited number of pure economic forms'. The underlying idea is that all economic action proceeds from planning and that the circumstances under which planning is carried out may be analysed as a configuration of a number of pure forms. Theory would investigate pure forms while a 'morphological analysis' would show the particular configurations of forms found in actual historical situations. All forms fall into either one of two primary classes, namely the centrally administered economy (including that of e.g. a firm) and a free economy. The distinction between these is similar to that, referred to above (page 130), made by Oakeshott between telocratic and nomocratic order, or that between ad hoc controls and control by impersonal constraint.[244]

In one place Eucken referred to the scheme just outlined and said: 'Just as innumerable tunes can be constructed from a few notes, so innumerable economic systems are formed by the fusion of a limited number of pure forms.'[245] The ambiguity in this analogy was perhaps intentional. It may be seen from the point of view of a person analysing a tune (its primary meaning) and from that of a composer of a tune. Eucken was far from underestimating the difficulties of constructing or even modifying institutions, but his attitude to the conduct of economic policy was analogous to that of a composer to his art. Just as a composer assembles notes in the quest for aesthetic ideals so the policy maker tries to assemble pure economic forms in the quest for an ideal of a well-ordered society. Just as the composer may make his task easier by analysing the music of the past so the policy maker may make his task easier by analysing history. Eucken always referred to 'German experience', by which he meant events prior to 1945. 'Roughly speaking, we can distinguish three methods of control applicable to the industrialized economic process: control by central state authorities, by groups, and by competition. Analysis of German experience strongly suggests that, given an adequate monetary system, control by competition is far superior to both the other methods.'[246] Clearly, competition was a means to an end, as it was with

Simons. Moreover, it was not a natural competition he was thinking of. The setting for it had to be carefully prepared.

> Thorough investigation of the forms of system realized in the *laissez-faire* period reveals varying degrees of efficiency. Certain market forms – for example, bilateral monopolies, oligopolies, etc. – or certain monetary systems, such as the linking up of money and credit, do lack equilibrium; but other market forms and monetary systems are far more efficient. The fact that the price system in the *laissez-faire* period was not in perfect running order does not mean that the price system is quite incapable of governing the economic process. What experience of *laissez-faire* goes to prove is that the economic *system* cannot be left to organize itself. So there is no question of any return to *laissez-faire*.[247]

By *laissez-faire* Eucken meant what we have described as the dogmatic view that the hand behind the invisible hand is invisible too. In the early years of the 20th century, he said, there was of course a comprehensive legal system and much legislation that affected economic relations. 'But the economic system and the shaping of it were not regarded as a special responsibility of the state.' 'The conviction prevailing in Germany and elsewhere at that time was that, within the limits of the law, social forces would spontaneously generate a good economic system. Such was the economic policy of *laissez-faire*.'[248]

But why did laissez-faire policy disappoint expectations? Here Eucken dwelt incessantly on a concept which the libertarian considers meaningless. 'First and foremost there is the problem of *economic power*.'[249] With the combination of a laissez-faire policy and the organic view already mentioned cartels were not only accepted but also given legal sanction.

> This attitude to the cartel problem was of fundamental importance, for it meant that the right of freedom of contract could also be used to eliminate competition and to restrict the freedom of others by means of sanctions, boycotts etc. The principle of freedom of contract thus came into open conflict with the competitive principle.[250]

But how should the problem of economic power be dealt with?

> German experience therefore enables us to state precisely on what lines a solution of the problem of economic power

should *not* be attempted. The solution is not a policy of *laissez-faire* which permits misuses of freedom of contract to destroy freedom; nor is it a system of monopoly control which permits the formation of monopolies while merely seeking to check abuses. Over and above … the problem of economic power cannot be solved by further concentrations of power, whether in the form of a corporative system – as in German coal mining – or of centralized economic control, or of nationalization. Power remains power whoever may exercise it, and it is in public rather than private hands that power reaches its zenith.[251]

What then is the answer? Should the state do more or less? 'Friends of compromise solutions seek a middle way. They would like the state to plan and, at the same time, to give scope for private planning and initiative.' But it is not a compromise between more or less but rather a division of functions. 'The answer is that the state should influence the *forms* of economy. but not itself direct the economic process.'[252]

It has already been mentioned how this conclusion coloured Eucken's attitude to full-employment policies. 'Social conscience forbids us to tolerate mass unemployment, and so does reason of state.' Full-employment policies did, at least in his day, achieve their immediate objectives. But there were drawbacks. 'Economic policy is faced with a dilemma: on the one hand, mass unemployment necessitates a full employment policy; on the other, the policy of full employment makes for an instability on other markets …'

So it was with fiscal measures. 'The dependence of income levels on market conditions can … lead to grave injustice and certainly poses a considerable problem; but no less dangerous is dependence on state officials who are called upon to carry out large scale investment programmes …'

Monetary measures were used in an attempt to make up for neglect of policy in other spheres.

In general, it is very typical of the age of experimental monetary policy that disproportion should first of all have been caused in the price system by the formation of pressure groups in industry, agriculture and labour, and by the introduction of a very unstable monetary system, and so on. Then, after the event, monetary policy was given the task of clearing up the damage done.

His own recommendations were those of a free-market pragmatist.

> The time has now come to dig deeper, as it were, and attend generally to the development of systems which will prevent disturbances of equilibrium. The policy of full employment will then no longer be necessary …

> It is not enough merely to restore equilibrium to the labour market … the achievement of general equilibrium requires the establishment of certain market forms and monetary systems; and this is the primary task of economic policy.[253]

To accomplish this task is of course no easy matter. Eucken did not shirk the issue. But he saw it as an art and this is not easily summarized. Let us consider one example. Eucken disagreed with the widely held view that technological development militates against competition because it makes concentration inevitable. The tendency to larger plant sizes, he felt, was more than offset by a widening of both product and factor markets, a greater availability of substitutes and greater flexibility in varying production programmes. This made for more rather than less competition and in fact called forth even more vehement efforts to stifle competition. 'The true characteristic of concentration is rather *the bringing of many works under unified control*.'[254] This then was one area where competition policy could operate by changing economic rules. Simons had a similar idea. He wanted the right to hold shares in companies to be restricted to natural persons and genuinely inactive investment trusts.[255]

There is, however, one overall prerequisite for the conduct of economic policy, whatever its detailed aims may be. In the terminology we have used, it is that policy must be based on internally consistent guiding conceptions.

> Speaking more generally, any single measure of economic policy should, if it is to be successful, be regarded as part of a policy designed to establish and maintain *economic order as a whole* … No measures … can have any real meaning, unless they are conceived within the framework of a comprehensive policy designed to establish and maintain some general system. The general line of economic policy should be considered *before* any individual measure. That is the conclusion I wish to emphasize as an important matter of principle.[256]

> Modern economy is a vast system of interrelationships. All acts of economic policy therefore affect the economic process as a whole and should be attuned to one another. General

principles of economic order need to be developed and acted on, in order to assure the unity of economic policy.[257]

However, the question still remains who is to decide what goes into the guiding conceptions that formulate institutional compromises. Eucken did not have an answer. Without authority and positions of power, he said, there can be no social life. But power provokes arbitrary action and destroys mature and good institutions. He conceded that it is a dilemma.[258] Simons seemed to evince the American faith in democracy – somehow, sometime better people would reach the highest elected offices. Hayek of course has no such illusions. The institutional compromise in his scheme, as we have argued, would emerge from a kind of perfectly competitive market in ideas. But this would require observance of the principles of a free society. The problem has simply been shifted one stage further in the regress of conflict. For this reason, it seems, Hayek has taken an interest in the reform of the 'unlimited democracy' of our time (see page 125 above.) In his scheme, the executive function would be more effectively separated from the legislative (in the sense of general-rules-making) function. The members of assemblies entrusted with the latter function would enjoy some independence and some protection from the temptation to respond to the extortion and rapacity of voters. But whether such people would then see things Hayek's way appears not to be beyond doubt.

There is here a connection with public-choice theory. This theory has taken the current methods of economic analysis into the realm of governmental processes. As such it is a positive analysis of how such processes work. But it may also be seen as a study of how governmental processes are related to economic analysis; a study of how governmental processes bring about, or fail to bring about, the institutional compromises which in turn govern the ordinary operations of the economy. At least one of its leading exponents has seen it that way. Buchanan has said: 'Public choice is a theory of "governmental failure" … in the precisely analogous sense that theoretical welfare economics has been a theory of "market failure".'[259] The value-laden term *failure* establishes a connection with notions of well-ordered societies – and this Buchanan fully realizes. He disagrees with the view he attributes to Friedman that positive analysis is enough; 'that a demonstration of the "is" must necessarily lead to some consensus on the "ought"'.[260] Public-choice theory, Buchanan suggests, should become more normative, not in the sense that it discusses ad hoc measures ('end states') but that it expresses opinions on 'process' or 'procedure', i.e. on the rules of conduct in public administration. He does not share Simons's faith. 'It is folly to think that "better men" elected to office will help us much, that "better policy" will turn things around here.'[261]

Buchanan continued immediately: 'We need, and must have, basic constitutional reform, which must of course be preceded by basic constitutional discourse and discussion.' Only a frightening fanatic would not value highly and therefore welcome wide discussion of his ideas. But there is here one last point to make in the characterization of free-market pragmatism. It is not equivalent to the contractarian position though it has something in common with it. In which respects is it different and in which the same?

In the following passage Buchanan expresses the pragmatic free-market position in what appears to be a contractarian way, i.e. as though the rules of market order were established in a social contract of some kind.

> If man can envisage himself as a product of his own making, as embodying prospects for changing himself into one of the imagined possibilities that he might be, it becomes relatively easy for him to envisage changing the basic rules of social order in the direction of imagined good societies … Individually man invests in becoming that which he is not. Collectively, men agree to modify the artifactual rules within which they interact one with another so as to allow individualized pursuit of whatever men may choose.[262]

It should no longer be necessary to show that the part before the last sentence expresses a pragmatic outlook very well. It may also find approval among contractarians. But the last sentence is rather odd. It says that men make social contracts and that their contracts always make allowance for the principle of control by impersonal constraint, i.e. for the principle of the invisible hand. But surely not all contractarians have assumed this nor even thought it desirable. Did Hobbes make this assumption? On the other hand, could freemarket pragmatists assume that social contracts, however conceived, would always be of a kind that they would favour? They would be foolish if they did. Free-market pragmatism is of course a normative position. However much discussion there may be on constitutional reform, there is no guarantee that a majority would favour a constitution that incorporates the principle of the invisible hand. It is an essentially dogmatic idea that all of us would agree about everything if we thought long and hard enough. Perhaps this is in fact so. But it seems to be a very precarious assumption on which to base public-spirited aspirations.

Adam Smith did not presume that the economic system he was advocating would necessarily have the weight of popular support behind it. He did not always express the ideas he presented in the *Wealth of Nations* in the form we have called pseudo dogmatism. Often he distinguished between economic process and economic system as clearly as Eucken was to do. He advocated that the economic process should be entrusted to individual choices constrained by an appropriate economic system. The choice of an appropriate economic system, however, was an altogether different matter. When Smith wrote the following passage, his tongue was no doubt in his cheek. But it does reveal his attitude to public choice.

> The laws concerning corn may every where be compared to the laws concerning religion. The people feel themselves so much interested in what relates either to their subsistence in this life, or to their happiness in a life to come, that government must yield to their prejudices, and, in order to preserve the public tranquillity, establish that system which they approve of. It is upon this account, perhaps, that we so seldom find a reasonable system established with regard to either of those two capital objects.[263]

.

10.

Economics and Ideals

The idea of market order clearly falls within the intellectual domain which economists have always regarded as their own. Yet economists seem always to have been in two or several minds about what to make of the idea. The reader of the *Wealth of Nations*, for instance, is left with the impression that Smith described the economic system of his time and place as market order but that his overall purpose nevertheless was to recommend the adoption of just such a system. Many passages may leave the reader in some doubt whether they were meant to analyse certain features of the economies of the 18th century or to illustrate economic relations which perforce must always prevail or to show what would be the case if certain conditions were met. Where Smith's intention was the last of these, the pragmatic inference, as we have called it, was a guide to action, a policy recommendation, but the line of reasoning has also been interpreted as a description of what is natural. It is in this area especially that perplexity arises. Walras faced up to the question squarely in the opening chapters of the *Eléments* but in the event his work was equivocal enough for Jaffé and Morishima a century later to disagree completely about what he was trying to do.[264] Pareto also sought clarity on the issue and wanted Walras's analysis of interrelated markets to be an analogue of celestial mechanics by means of which the course of economic events may be predicted. But, as we have argued, this approach has led to a theory nowadays which is ambiguous on the question whether it deals with actual or ideal situations. Hayek, on the other hand, is quite clearly urging an ideal, but he also appears to be making positive assertions about a connection between market order and spontaneous evolution. Ideal and actuality are firmly interwoven in most economic discussions.

It is perhaps unlikely that such eminent economists were simply unable to distinguish clearly between ideals and actuality or that they failed to see the need for doing so. The problem is of a different kind: how to make economics *wertfrei*, how to maintain a spirit of scientific disinterestedness when dealing with a subject matter that bristles with issues in which all manner of people may have passionate and factional interests. The rule is: science deals with what is the case and not with what ought to be the case. A fair inference from this rule is that scientists should observe, describe and explain but not urge, prescribe or direct. It is apparently in deference to this rule and to the way it has been applied in the natural sciences that market order has been represented in many cases, though rather ambiguously, as an actually existing economic order, perhaps immutably inherent in nature like gravitation, or as a hypothesis for explaining and predicting the actual course of economic events. Represented in these ways, market order appears to be either a suitable object or a suitable tool for scientific observation, description and explanation.

However, what if other considerations lead one to believe, as we have argued, that market order is not an order inherent in the nature of things nor a hypothesis that may be expected to yield the kind of explanations and predictions positivist economists look for; that it is an ideal or a complex of ill-articulated ideals which have been realized only to some extent in some places at some times? The reader may have gained the impression that the present writer believes that market order cannot be treated in accordance with accepted scientific procedure and that he is out of sympathy with the rule that science ought to confine itself to observation, description and explanation. Such an impression would be incorrect. The present writer fully shares the view that it would be a pity for economists to become embroiled in the general conflict over economic order and to forsake the role of disinterested analysts. Moreover, he believes – and some might be inclined to argue the point – that there is no way of discovering or proving what ought to be in some objective impersonal sense and that an inference can lead to a conclusion that is an 'ought' statement only if at least one of the premises from which it starts is also an 'ought' statement. But one may hold this view and yet have misgivings about a certain perception of science which currently seems to predominate among economists and about the way the idea of market order has often been treated apparently in accordance with that perception. These misgivings and a proposal for bringing ideals into economic analysis will be the subject of this concluding chapter.

10.1. Scientific disinterestedness

The rule that scientists should not indulge in 'oughts' is itself of course an ideal of what 'good' science ought to be. There is no paradox in this. But it does show that the term *wertfrei* – literally *value free* – is rather misleading. It conjures up a vision of science completely cut off from human values and human concerns – a disembodied eye that simply reflects reality like a mirror. In so far as it is a vision of the natural sciences, it may often have seemed quite apposite since the natural sciences, unlike economics, deal with topics that for the most part are far removed from the issues that excite the passions of mankind. Nevertheless, it is not really tenable. Science is very much a human endeavour. It is the hallmark of a human being to be striving after something and one surely misunderstands science if one does not recognize a human striving to attain the ideal of 'good' science. The modern growth-of-knowledge literature has drawn attention to what with a little reflection might have been obvious all along, namely that there is a community of scientists distinguishable by its allegiance to a complex of little-articulated ideals of what makes 'good' science – standards of what constitutes, for instance, correct reasoning, sufficient evidence, accuracy and rigour as well as coherence, consistency, simplicity and even intellectual elegance.[265] Above all there is the ideal which is perhaps better characterized as scientific disinterestedness than as *Wertfreiheit*.[266]

Thus while science does not discover or prove what is right and what is wrong, it nevertheless is not independent of values. Nor are the ideals of scientific excellence the only values on which it depends. It has often been pointed out that values do enter science in so far as the scientist has to select his subject matter or have it selected for him. This selection is not made on the basis of the criteria of excellence in science – though we shall argue that this is rather a moot point in the case of mainstream economics – because normally such criteria come into play only when the selection has already been made. The ideals of 'good' science do not lay down that it is, for instance, continental drift, butterflies, inflation or unemployment that should be studied, only that a scientific investigation should proceed in a certain way once the subject has been chosen on other grounds, i.e. for reasons involving other values. In recent decades it has also begun to appear that the influence of such other values may be far more pervasive than was once suspected. There is the question of the conceptual framework, the *Betrachtungsweise* or the paradigm that is chosen. It is as yet little understood how choices in this regard are related to the values of the chooser or even whether *choice* is quite the right word in this context. Nevertheless, anyone who, for instance, has pondered the contrasts between the Walrasian analysis of market order and the Marxian analysis of capitalism, i.e. the differences between analyses of what in some sense is supposed to be more or less the same thing, could hardly escape the notion that the values of the analysts are somehow involved. But while, for instance, the Walrasian analysis is individualist and the

Marxian is not, they are both public spirited. When the purpose behind economic analysis is not a public-spirited one, when, for instance, it is motivated by the wish of some party in business to gain a competitive advantage, or even to wheedle money out of other people's pockets through asset-market speculation, the factual position may be grasped in terms of yet a different kind again. When the world is viewed through theoretical spectacles which differ in such ways, each paradigm-bound field of study may come with its own set of theory-laden facts. Adherents of different paradigms, such as members of rival schools of economic thought, are quite likely to grasp the factual situation quite differently, even incommensurably, in Kuhn's terminology – as is evident in the case of mainstream and Marxian economics. What then becomes of the idea that economics is *wertfrei* as long as it is confined to statements of what is the case? What-is-the-case may not be independent of values after all.

Thus while science does not discover or prove what is right and what is wrong, it seems that the pursuit of science is guided as much by a whole array of values as any other human activity. Let us now try to interpret the ideal of scientific disinterestedness with this consideration in mind. We want the word *scientific* to refer to the human endeavour to attain 'good' science, to observe the rules that have gradually evolved in efforts to gain understanding. Such an interpretation would therefore be rather different from the idea of science as a disembodied eye. The ideal of scientific disinterestedness would be analogous to the ideal of impartial justice. One takes it for granted that a judge has values, interests and opinions like any ordinary person and that the administration of justice has a place in some ideal vision of a well-ordered society. But when he is hearing and deciding a case, one would expect a judge (or that at least is the ideal) to strive to follow correct judicial procedure, to follow the rules that have gradually evolved in this regard, and not to have some other motive or cause uppermost in his mind. One may similarly expect a scientist to have values, interests and opinions, and scientific activity to fit into a scheme of things into which various values enter. But when he is doing science one may expect him to strive to follow correct scientific procedure, to try to observe the norms of excellence in science, and not to have motives and causes other than understanding uppermost in his mind. If, for instance, academic promotion or victory in a dispute is all that matters, even though, to achieve it, one has to deceive and dissemble; if certain conclusions are sacrosanct and finding arguments for them is one's only task; if the tone of scientific disinterestedness is used to deliver a telling blow for one's cause – then presumably the spirit of scientific disinterestedness is not being honoured. Something other than understanding is being given priority. Conversely, the spirit of scientific disinterestedness *is* honoured when the cause of understanding is put above (but not necessarily to the exclusion of) all other causes, at least in so far as this is compatible with normal moral obligations. In this interpretation, scientific disinterestedness amounts to intellectual honesty, but this is perhaps the most reasonable way of looking at it.

The pursuit of 'pure' science is often said to be motivated by curiosity. Perhaps the ideal of scientific disinterestedness evolved in this context. When one is motivated by the plain wish to find out, anything other than complete intellectual honesty does not make sense. But while curiosity may often be the sole stimulus to inquiry, it would surely be going too far to say that this is always so. It seems to be, one might almost say, an affectation among some scientists to claim to be moved by nothing more worldly than curiosity. It may well be a sincere attempt to establish for themselves the credentials of disinterested scientists. An innocuous childlike curiosity seems to distance one from the hurly-burly of social conflict. But there is a drawback. A subject then has to be divided into several compartments – both Menger and Walras went in for this wholeheartedly[267] – e.g. a pure economics as the product of curiosity and applied, practical and social compartments of economics with more utilitarian ends in view. Once one has divided a subject in this way, one is committed to believing what sometimes in fact may be the case, namely that it is quite fortuitous, a happy coincidence, when a finding of pure science proves to be relevant to some contentious issue. Walras, for instance, despite many remarks that indicated his ideological interest in the questions he investigated, assumed the air of one moved only by curiosity and was then forced to suggest a happy coincidence:

> Do these pure truths find frequent application? To be sure, the scholar has a right to pursue science for its own sake, just as the geometer has the right … to study the most singular properties of geometric figures, however fantastic, if he finds that they excite his curiosity. We shall see, however, that the truths of pure economics yield solutions of very important problems of applied economics and social economics, which are highly controversial and very little understood.[268]

When one considers all the avenues that Walras's curiosity might have led him into, it seems to have been good fortune indeed that his pure theory yielded useful solutions in matters pertaining to an *idéal social* which is known to have been close to his heart. It is not this, of course, but rather that a particular interpretation of disinterestedness may force one to adopt attitudes which one may otherwise not have been inclined to adopt at all.

We have looked into the question of *Wertfreiheit* and interpreted it as scientific disinterestedness to see what it may reasonably be said to force on us and therefore also what it does not force on us. We have done so because it is on this score that one may have misgivings about the way the idea of market order has been treated apparently in accordance with a perception of science currently dominant among economists. In view of what is to follow, it may be useful to set out the main conclusion, even though it may seem quite obvious once stated.

The ideal of *Wertfreiheit* forces on us no other obligation than to observe the norms of 'good' science and to be honest in interpreting such norms so that the intention really is to find out, analyse and understand. It does not force us, for instance, to pretend that understanding is always an end in itself and never a means to another end, i.e. it does not require us to become disembodied eyes cut off from the concerns and values that motivate us in other spheres of life. Scientific activity, like all human activity, must have a motive. To pretend otherwise would hardly be honest. The concerns and values which guide the choice of subject matter and probably the choice of paradigm or conceptual framework are distinct from the ideal of *Wertfreiheit* in science. The latter comes into play only once such choices have been made and then distinguishes scientific activity from other activity.

A corollary of the above is that *Wertfreiheit* in science is a property of the scientist's approach to his subject matter and *not* a property of the subject matter itself. Whether or not science is *wertfrei* depends on the intentions of the scientist, on whether he really intends to find out and understand, and not on whether the subject matter he treats is devoid of any suggestion that there are values and ideals. For this reason the term 'scientific disinterestedness' may be preferable. Only a person may or may not be disinterested whereas there may be doubt about what it is that should be 'free of value'. The ideal surely is that investigation and analysis should be conducted in a disinterested way and not that only 'value-free' subject matter should be investigated and analysed. In itself *Wertfreiheit* or scientific disinterestedness places no restrictions on the choice of subject matter.

This conclusion, namely that the ideal of scientific disinterestedness does not in itself restrict the choice of subject matter, has an obvious bearing on the issue we raised at the outset. That issue concerned the ambiguous treatment of market order in economics and the question whether market order recognized as a complex of ideals is amenable to scientific treatment. If the mark of the scientific is a certain disinterested way of conducting investigation and analysis, whatever the subject matter, there would seem to be no reason why ideals such as the ideals of market order should not also be investigated and analysed scientifically.

Clearly, ideals are now entering our consideration in two quite distinct ways. There is an obvious difference between looking upon ideals as objects of inquiry and being guided by ideals, such as we may be both when selecting subject matter for inquiry and when deciding on how to conduct the inquiry. Ideals which guide us and which we believe in may be, and perhaps in the majority of cases are, only tacitly known, like the rules of conduct we considered earlier (see pages 49–50 and 118–19 above). Such ideals are not necessarily articulated in thought, not necessarily known, as Hayek put it, in any other sense than that individuals normally act in accordance with them. The believer in them is not necessarily conscious of them. In the ordinary welter of life we may become aware of ideals only because it is on their account that certain individuals and groups and certain social institutions are approved of or criticized, venerated or denigrated, worshipped or reviled. Ideals as objects of inquiry, on the other hand, must be articulated because that is the purpose of analysis. Furthermore, it is a matter of indifference whether or not the person conducting the inquiry also believes in the ideals he investigates. But detachment from ideals is perhaps not the right expression in this context. An ideal may become an object of inquiry when the person conducting the inquiry acts in accordance with the ideals of 'good' science and understanding takes precedence over other ideals; when, in other words, it is scientific inquiry that is venerated. To a person who puts the cause of understanding above all other causes, and perhaps only to such a person, an ideal may be as much an object of dispassionate scientific contemplation as interstellar dust.

10.2. The influence of physical science

All this may be so well known as to be uninteresting. But then it is all the more puzzling why market order should have been treated so ambiguously in economic theory. After all, it is not difficult to distinguish between ideal and actuality. Who would deny that it is quite possible to discuss various criteria of efficiency without being thrown into a state of perplexity over whether the questions under discussion concern what ideally should be done or what actually is done? Yet uncertainty of precisely that kind often arises when it comes to an efficiency criterion such as the equi-marginal conditions in equilibrium theory, let alone when it comes to the broader questions of market order. It was suggested earlier (pages 149–50 above) that attempts to make economics *wertfrei* have had something to do with this state of affairs. That is why we have taken the trouble to look into *Wertfreiheit*. Before we go into the question again, however, let us briefly go over some ground we have covered already.

10.2.1. Successive approximation again

The ideals of market order find expression in arguments that have the form of pragmatic inference. For example: if individuals could not procure what they want by taking it from each other, then they could procure it only by production, i.e. by augmenting the wealth of nations. If competition were perfectly free, then equal values would pass hands in every transaction, i.e. all prices would be fair and commutative justice would prevail. If all equi-marginal conditions were met, then resources would be allocated optimally for some distribution of endowments. These particular 'if … then' statements amount to definitions (of production, value and efficiency respectively). They also articulate ideals or values, fragments of a vision of a well-ordered society. Some of the premises for the inferences, if they were set out formally, might be assertions of fact. But in each case the part between the 'if' and the 'then' is a supposition which does not imply an assertion of fact. The suppositions in the above inferences do not imply that competition always is perfectly free nor that the equi-marginal conditions are always met. With some suppositions the contrary is the case. 'If wishes were horses, beggars might ride' prompts a denial of the premise to make a statement about wishful thinking and the limitations of supply. In pragmatic inferences where the conclusions formulate desired states, or in the special cases where the inferences define ideals, the premises are usually contrary to fact though not obviously beyond the realm of possibilities. In human action, as von Mises said, individuals conceive conditions which they prefer to the actual ones. There could be no striving after goals (except in those cases when the status quo is to be preserved) unless the conditions aimed at were as yet contrary to fact.

However, these logical constructions have also come to be regarded as descriptions and explanations of the conditions that actually prevail. It was suggested earlier (Section 8.2) that the notion of successive approximation makes this possible in so far as the logical and mathematical constructions may be regarded as first approximations to reality, i.e. as greatly simplified descriptions or models. Moreover, not too fine a distinction is often made in economics between this descriptive function of models and the function of positivist hypotheses as instruments for prediction which have no significance until they have been successfully tested. One may therefore become engrossed in the logical and mathematical structure of models and, when the occasion appears to demand it, also proceed on the presumption that economic models do in some, though dimly perceived, way explain actual conditions that have already been identified in everyday terms.

Seen from this standpoint there is much that theories based on the idea of market order may describe and explain. In everyday discourse, after all, we are forever speaking of the market for this, that and the other. The everyday terms contain no hint that we mean anything else than that there are markets in the world, that they are very much part of the actuality we live in. The term *market*, however, has become a very broad one. In its narrower sense it referred to a congregation of a large number of independent individuals for the purpose of buying and selling wares which were on open display. In such markets some of the ideals of market order, such as the ones mentioned above, may have been realized to a considerable extent. It may well be, as Hayek has suggested, that the ideals of an overall market order were derived from contemplations of spontaneously evolved though somewhat isolated markets. But one seldom speaks of markets in this sense anymore. The term *market* used in the plural has been broadened, especially in economics, to refer to an economy-wide communications network for individuals who specialize, including all those who specialize in selling their labour services. Whether the ideals of market order are also realized to any great degree in such markets is often recognized as being questionable. But a theory based on the idea of market order may be regarded as a first approximation. Further approximations have to account for deviations from the ideals of market order.

There is a further stage of this development. The first approximation mentioned above has lost its status as an approximation, or at least it has receded into the background. In what we have called denormatized dogmatism, the pragmatic inferences defining the ideals of market order have been interpreted as statements of what is natural, what is inherent in the nature of things (see pages 91, 107–8 and 109 above). The institutions of market order are taken for granted. The first problem of theory then would seem to be to analyse the interrelations that would prevail if all individuals managed to optimize their objective functions, whatever they may include. It is a reasonable observation that all individuals do want something, do have objectives, and, since the theory is formulated in non-specific terms, it seems possible at least in principle to insert those objectives into the theory. Once more, therefore, equilibrium theory appears to be a reasonable first approximation to actuality, though not a very close one. Further approximations will have to show how difficulties about knowledge and uncertainty affect the situation. Such further approximations appear to occupy the minds of many economic theorists at present. The origins of equilibrium theory in the ideals of market order, derived possibly from isolated actual markets, have been in some circles almost completely forgotten.

10.2.2. Scientism and the physicalist schema

There can be no certainty in interpreting the thought processes of others. From what one knows has been said and done in economics, one has to surmise apparent presuppositions and intentions to arrive at an intelligible account of what economists are trying to do, what they are 'getting at', always on the assumption that they are striving to achieve coherence in such matters. Our interpretation of how theories derived from the idea of market order are meant to describe and explain had to be done on that basis. On that basis also it seems that something more deep rooted is at work, namely the influence of what may be described as scientism. The *Oxford English Dictionary* defines scientism as the 'habit and mode of expression of a man of science' and in the Supplement published in 1982 adds the meaning:

> A term applied (freq. in a derogatory manner) to a belief in the omnipotence of scientific knowledge and techniques: also to the view that the methods of study appropriate to physical science can replace those used in other fields such as philosophy and, esp., human behaviour and the social sciences.

We have seen already how Pareto evinced this kind of faith in physical science when he expounded to Croce a parallel between general equilibrium and celestial mechanics (pages 79–80 above). Prior to that, J.S. Mill also had maintained that 'the backward state' of the social sciences could 'only be remedied by applying to them the methods of Physical Science, duly extended and generalized'.[269] More recently, for example, Samuelson wrote that economic theory should aspire to a form of theory borrowed from physical science, or be regarded with suspicion.[270] There is of course nothing wrong with trying to emulate and learn from an immensely successful intellectual enterprise. If successful innovations were never copied, they would be of little benefit to mankind. But the question of just what it is that is copied is important, since, after all, the copy is not complete. It is a case of doing economics *like* physical science and only some aspects are copied.

We would be emulating an aspect of physical science if we adopted only the rules or norms of 'good' science and the spirit of disinterested inquiry. In itself this would not restrict our choice of subject matter. Our interest might have been aroused by the observation that certain possibly contradictory ideals were so widely held and acted upon that they affected economic affairs to a considerable extent, even though none were actually realized to any great degree. We might therefore study such ideals, including the ideals of market order, in a spirit of scientific disinterestedness. We might do so both to gain a better understanding of economic affairs and to investigate the possibility of a greater realization of the ideals. It would not be unscientific to do that.

Evidently this is not the way the physical sciences have been emulated by mainstream economic theorists. Though the case necessarily must rest on surmises, it appears that mainstream economic theory has taken over not only the spirit of disinterested inquiry, but also something like the techniques and language (the habits and mode of expression) of the physical scientist. We have already seen the influence of such emulation in the drift of ideas sketched out in Section 8.4. The leading idea is that the function of an economic theory is to find determinants, that almost everything of interest in economics is functionally related to other things and either is a determinant, has determinants or both determines and is determined. The work of the economic theorist is therefore done once he has shown, even if only in principle, how the values of certain variables are implied by the values of other variables or by the mutual interrelationship of all the variables. The demands of this paradigm are such that quite familiar things of economic life have to be recast in a mould in which they assume the character of the entities of physics. Human action within familiar economic constraints takes on the character of a pre-programmed reaction, choice becomes something like a readjustment resulting from the activation of a propensity by an external shock while almost everything partakes in the continuity characteristic of time and space. Lachmann has referred to this paradigm as *late classical formalism* and the present writer has dealt with the issue elsewhere under the heading of *mechanomorphism*.[271]

The techniques and terminology of a science may seem to be mere instruments for dealing with a subject matter which may well be borrowed by others for approaching their own subject matter. But techniques and terminology are very much part of a conceptual framework or paradigm and, as noted earlier, a paradigm appears to come with its own set of theory-laden facts (or perhaps in this case 'facts'). The entities entering formal economic theory differ so much from the familiar ones of everyday discourse that they constitute what amounts to a different subject matter. In other words, the injunction only to describe, analyse and explain, the injunction to be scientific, has come to govern not only the way inquiry is conducted, but also the choice of subject matter. In choosing a subject matter which has a distinct affinity with that of the physical sciences, economic theorists have in effect chosen a 'value-free' subject matter.

The physical sciences simply do not have the distinction between ideal and actuality or between any kind of desired state and the actual state. The absence of this distinction may even serve as a criterion of what the physical or, more generally, the natural sciences study. Value, purpose, a striving to attain what is merely conceived have been deliberately excluded from consideration. The period during which the physical sciences began to impress mankind by their great achievements was also the period during which teleological and anthropomorphic elements were systematically taken out of these sciences. This refining of their subject matter, by making for greater clarity, may well have contributed to the success of the physical sciences. But for the economic theorist who sees in it the essence of science it creates a dilemma. Economics without human beings, like *Hamlet* without the Prince of Denmark, is hard to conceive. His perception of the essence of science pulls him in one direction. The common perception of the questions he is dealing with pulls him in the opposite direction. This, it is suggested, is the ultimate source of the ambiguous treatment of the idea of market order. Representing ideals as attenuated descriptions is one way of attempting to overcome the dilemma.

The theory of consumer behaviour and demand is perhaps a good example of how human beings have been represented in a schema resembling those of sciences which have deliberately excluded human characteristics from consideration. The merely conceived conditions individuals plan to attain in pursuance of their interlinked private and public-spirited interests, i.e. the ends of human action, are reduced to well-defined preference orderings of 'bundles' of consumer goods and services. The sort of mental life the theory ascribes to an individual – that he would rather have two apples and five bananas than three apples and two bananas, but that three apples and two bananas would give him as much satisfaction as one apple and six bananas – is really a disposition. The apples and bananas are of course mere blanks. But whatever is written in their places, the schema allows only for a disposition in the choices among 'bundles' of different quantities of the same things and only for purposes of appropriation or consumption. That is a far cry from the mental life of people who propose, contrive, anticipate, fear, prepare, forestall, prevent, avoid and perhaps want to be other than they are; from a mental life that involves ideals and personal ambitions and may lead to an earnest striving or a scheming and conniving. In this respect, the beings who inhabit economic models are distinctly sub-human, whereas in the comprehensiveness and consistency of their preferences, and in their ability as producers to foresee and calculate, they are quite super-human. The schema may be represented as an approximation, a simplification. But it is not convincing that economic theorists favour such an extremely distant approximation for reasons of verisimilitude. It is more convincing that they favour it as a compromise for the dilemma mentioned above. Conditions are postulated and determinants are found. All the while individuals are moving along indifference curves or are pushed on to higher or lower ones, i.e. ostensibly the analysis is still about human beings.

Another sign of the tension inherent in the economic theorist's dilemma may be found in economic jargon. Every discipline of course has its jargon and some jargons may well be a lot more peculiar than economic jargon. However, the most striking peculiarity of economic jargon is that certain familiar words from everyday discourse about economic affairs are combined either with mechanistic-sounding words or with words that accompany mathematical techniques developed not for dealing with economic questions but for other purposes in other fields of study. There are utility surfaces, commodity spaces, indifference maps and diminishing marginal rates of substitution as well as income elasticities of demand and linearly homogeneous production functions. Again, the volatility of money supply aggregates may be aggravated by destabilizing capital movements that filter through the transmission mechanism as stochastic shocks and may set off a wage–price spiral. Economic jargon creates the impression that rigour is to be simulated by a clinical tone and references to mental activities are to be eliminated as far as possible. Its effect is to restrict the vocabulary to such a narrow range of words that it becomes difficult to express the distinctively human though admittedly unrigorous things that mankind has learnt to say about itself over the millennia. It is a convention that has been avoided deliberately throughout this study. But that could be done only at the cost of foregoing the tone requisite for modern economics. The end result, as the reader will have noticed, does not sound like economics. Terms such as 'social conflict', 'moral restraint', 'rule of conduct', 'public spirit', 'guiding conception', 'ideal' and 'intimations of a well-ordered society', it must seem to many, are too contaminated by the smell of humanity to be admissible in the science of economics.

However, one should be careful not to overstate the case. If all economic theorists wholeheartedly embraced the physicalist schema we have been describing, there would be no question of an ambiguity nor of a dilemma. Moreover, it could be said that the difficulties of adequately treating distinctively human issues in terms of the physicalist schema are, so to say, a by-product of the emulation of the techniques and language of physical science. Economic theorists do not want to exclude human issues from consideration. Quite the contrary. They want to be able to deal with them rigorously or at least to have some analytical methods for coming to grips with them. It is in this context that the exemplar of physical science and its method of functional analysis presents itself.

The so-called New Welfare Economics is a case in point. The physicalist schema is here used to investigate what amounts to an ideal of efficiency, i.e. to construct a guiding conception, and that is intelligible only in human terms. It provides a relatively simple basis for the investigation. But even that rather barren representation of mental life and technology has led to conclusions about a multiple infinity of Pareto optima and the impossibility of pinpointing the most efficient position without a further preference ordering represented by the peculiar notion of a social welfare function. Criteria of efficiency could probably be based on other simple schemata. But could one make much headway if one started off with a highly complex idea of the mental life of a person? It is a valid question. Whether conclusions based on a barren representation of mental life have any significance for a world in which people appear to have much fuller mental lives is a question the answer to which is not immediately obvious. Welfare economists seem to think that they do.

10.2.3. Questions of language

There is a related issue. One may imagine it put as follows: granted that there is an ordinary way of talking about what people do and how they think about what they do, it still does not follow that ordinary language is sacrosanct. Scientific theory is meant to give new insights and improve on everyday understanding. It goes beyond ordinary language to do so. We still say the sun rises every morning but a strictly scientific account of the phenomenon would run quite differently. In developing its own idiom, economic theory borrowed words and mathematical techniques from the much older physical sciences because they were palpably successful at gaining new insights. The borrowed words and phrases obviously were used metaphorically. Early physical scientists presumably also improvised with metaphors. How else could anyone embark on a new intellectual venture if not by making do with the linguistic material available at the time? Ordinary language has a way of assimilating metaphors and specialist terms. It has been absorbing words from the physical sciences for a long time and from economics more recently. Ordinary language eventually changes to accommodate new conceptions and new beliefs about what things are really like. There is, therefore, nothing very significant about the state of ordinary language at any one time. In other words, it cannot be held against formal economic theory that its treatment of human beings does not accord with the way we ordinarily speak about people at present.[272]

Arguments of this kind challenge any attempt to judge an economic theory in the light of ordinary experience. They therefore call into question the misgivings about the physicalist schema set out above as also the arguments of those who have advocated a subjectivist approach to economics – notably Mises, Hayek, Lachmann and Shackle – and who in effect have also appealed to the common understanding of human beings as formulated in ordinary language. The present writer has tried to deal with the question elsewhere.[273] We may confine ourselves here to a few observations.

Hayek once remarked:

> That the objects of economic activity cannot be defined in objective terms but only with reference to a human purpose goes without saying. Neither a 'commodity' or an 'economic good', nor 'food' or 'money', can be defined in physical terms but only in terms of views people hold about things. Economic theory has nothing to say about the little round disks of metal as which an objective or materialist view might try to define money.[274]

Let us put this into a more purely linguistic form. Words such as 'commodity', 'money', 'food', 'tool' and even 'house' cannot be understood without reference to purposes; 'profit' and 'loss' or 'success' and 'failure' presuppose a notion of objective or aim and 'improvement' and 'deterioration' presuppose a notion of value or ideal. These and other common words would be meaningless in a domain of thought which does not recognize mental life, as we have called it. But it is just this which is missing, or rather has been deliberately excluded, from the domain of physical science. Hayek also remarked in another place that 'the progressive elimination of all "anthropomorphic" explanations from the physical sciences' has been 'the most marked tendency of the development of scientific thought in modern times'.[275] By developing and refining those parts of everyday discourse which do not presuppose mental life or other teleological elements, physical science arrived, it appears, at the concept of determination as this is understood in the context of a functional (relational) formulation.[276]

Though to argue the case would take us too far afield, it appears on further investigation and as far as one can tell that these subjective and physical domains of thought are simply quite separate in the sense that what is stated or even conceived in terms of the one cannot be rephrased in terms of the other without losing the connotations that were intended. Within each domain of thought there is a complex of cross-implications between words which does not extend to words in the other domain. So, for example, the statement that cold air in contact with one's exposed skin makes one shiver cannot be translated into terms of deciding to shiver or indulging in shivers without acquiring a completely different meaning. In ordinary discourse words from both domains are used together but the separate meaning complexes are always understood. So, for example, if it were said that someone planned or intended to shiver, one would understand that he wanted either to simulate shivering or to expose his skin to cold air in order to shiver (i.e. to take action with the object of letting his shivers be physically determined). For the same reasons, and this is the point we want to come to, a statement to the effect that a decision was made to purchase a certain article cannot be translated into terms of determination without losing the intended connotations, unless 'determination' is turned into a metaphor by being conjoined with other words in the subjective complex of cross-implications.

It does not appear that the use of 'determination' in economic theory (as in 'the determination of prices') is metaphorical in the above sense. It is rather that expressions such as 'consumer choice' have been conjoined with words in the physical meaning complex. Let us try to illustrate this. To make the illustration more graphic, we shall at first leave the utility function aside and substitute for it a shiver function. Later we shall reverse the substitution. We assume that a person's shivering is determined by, or is a function of, the temperature of the air around the person, the proportion of the total surface area of skin covered by material(s) and the total thickness of such material(s) multiplied by a factor determined by the heat conductivity of the material(s). That is the function – the lower the temperature the more intense the shivering and so *mutatis mutandis* for the other determinants. We may also postulate the signs of the partial derivatives. Otherwise, however, we assume that individuals differ in susceptibility, i.e. each has a certain unique propensity to shiver and therefore also e.g. measurable temperature elasticities of shivering.

Apart from the fact that a lot of guessing is involved, there can be no objection to this formulation. Shivers are not contemplated or decided upon; they are physically determined and that is that. Now we observe that people who shiver usually put on more or thicker clothes. This operation may well be contemplated and decided upon. A person may, for instance, decide to adjust the thermostat of the heating system instead or decide to refrain from doing anything because he may have reasons for wishing to evoke pity in another person, though he would find that pity is not physically determined. However, if we go in this direction we shall become bogged down in all sorts of considerations that do not combine nicely with our shiver function. We therefore assume, perhaps on the analogy of a conditioned reflex, that a shivering person naturally continues to put on clothes, which continues to reduce shivering until the equilibrium condition of zero shivers is reached. A little reflection shows that temperature has become (via the shiver function) a determinant of the demand for clothes. But there are other propensities and every person's budget to consider. We therefore introduce the utility function and budget constraint. Since we have taken so much trouble, we shall presume that we have not merely found the determinants of the demand for clothes, but the determinants of the consumer demand for x, where x is anything.

This is not of course an allegory of how demand theory was developed. It was meant to make the point that a functional formulation with its language of determination is quite appropriate in certain cases of involuntary reactions but that voluntary conduct may be treated in this way only if words like 'choice' and 'decision' are severed from their usual connotations and given those of a word like 'shivering' in the physical meaning complex. Choice has to be regarded as an automatic response to the environment like shivering. It may seem that it does not matter much whether one says that a purchase is determined or decided upon. However, the connotations (cross-implications) in the physical and subjective meaning complexes respectively are very different. The difference becomes more marked and begins to matter more as one moves, in the one domain of thought, from the determination of demand to the determination of prices and, in the other domain, from wants (which in any case are ambiguous between subjective wishes and physical needs) to values and ideals. It is then that the language of determination becomes incapable of expressing many issues of importance to economic affairs as ordinarily understood.

The attitude one often finds among economists towards the idea of a fair price may be regarded as an indication that the determination language of economic theory has this incapacity. We have on a number of occasions indicated that the question of what constitutes a fair price had something to do with the genesis of the idea of market order and of the concept of general equilibrium. The attitude of many modern economists steeped in the analysis of price determination, however, is that 'fair price' is an emotive but meaningless term, or at least a notion which economics cannot help to explicate. If their thinking is set within the physical meaning complex, their attitude is entirely consistent with their presuppositions. A price is determined and that is that. It makes no more sense to ask whether a price is fair or unfair than it does to ask whether the moon's orbit about the earth is fair or unfair. But it is unlikely (though not impossible) that the population at large will stop talking about unfair prices and unfair economic practices just because economic theorists have taken this view of the matter. It is even less likely that they will stop orienting their conduct to ideals of fairness either to conform to them or to appeal to them in order to prey upon others and get what they want. Revolutionary wars have been fought and established societies overturned on issues of perceived economic unfairness. At some remove from the narrow concerns of theory, few economists probably would deny that such issues have significance for what economics studies. We have already argued that such issues cannot be insufficiently *wertfrei* to be open to dispassionate analysis because that term should apply to the conduct of analysis and not to the issues analysed.

These observations do not refute the contention that economic theory cannot be judged by whether it treats human beings as they are treated in ordinary language at present. Nor do they refute the rationale of emulating physical science in economics. But they do offer an alternative interpretation of that rationale. One may explain the matter as follows:

A specialist terminology such as the language of determination evolves in the course of scientific investigation. The phenomena to be investigated may have been expressed in a prior specialist terminology but, since the same reasoning may be applied to this and any other prior terminologies, there must have been a time when the phenomena to be investigated were expressed in the ordinary language of that time. It is well known that the modes of expression of bygone eras were heavily influenced by what we now call mythical and animistic beliefs and that, for instance, the sun and moon and many natural phenomena were often personified as various deities and their doings. Even when the notion of natural phenomena had been established among sections of a people, such as the *physis* of the ancient Greeks, it did not necessarily correspond to the modern notion. According to Collingwood: 'Greek natural science was based on the principle that the world of nature is saturated or permeated by mind. Greek thinkers regarded the presence of mind in nature as the source of that regularity or orderliness in the natural world whose *presence* made a science of nature possible.'[277]

On the other hand, the ancient Greeks also had their atomic theory with the notion of matter in motion in empty space, and a Greek living in Alexandria in the Hellenistic period even found a method for measuring the circumference of the earth.[278] When more ordinary people, say metalworkers, set about their task they may have made incantations to their gods but when they spoke about the techniques they used they must have expressed concepts which presumably had at least something in common with what was said by metalworkers of more recent times. In other words, there is no reason to believe that ordinary language ever has reflected a single coherent conception. Though it has continually accommodated new conceptions and beliefs, it has not undergone comprehensive and uniform transformations. Wittgenstein likened ordinary language to a town that has been lived in for many centuries and has come to serve diverse interests. There are newer parts on the outskirts laid out in a regular and systematic fashion and older parts in the centre which, through adding or rebuilding and adaptations to new uses, have become heterogeneous, irregular, intricate, messy but versatile.

It is a reasonable interpretation that early physical scientists came, by much trial and error, to distil out of ordinary language a specialist terminology and way of seeing their subject matter. First they came to see that they were concerned with the composition, changes and motions of inert matter or substances. Much later they developed a relational or functional formulation as a prominent part of their disciplines and the search for determinants as understood in the context of this formulation became the regulative principle of their scientific inquiries.[279] In this way they achieved insights and explanations which by a wide consensus were better and more useful than earlier ones. One cannot prove or disprove that equal success is attainable by applying the same procedure to what are economic questions in the ordinary language of our time. But if 'same procedure' is taken to mean the adoption of a search for determinants as the regulative principle of inquiry, its application does entail shutting out a very dominant side of human experience as formulated in ordinary language thus far – a side in which in the ordinary understanding most economic questions are rooted.

There is an alternative interpretation of 'same procedure'. Economists would be following the example of physical scientists if they distilled out of our heterogeneous ordinary language the distinctively human, mental-life or subjective elements just as the distinctively physical elements were once distilled out of it; if they developed these by the 'same procedure' the physical sciences used, namely of specifying the usage and cross-implications of terms more explicitly.[280] (More will be said about such specification below.) Perhaps this rather than the more or less direct transfer of a specialist terminology is the lesson to be learnt from the physical sciences. Seen from this point of view, the position of present-day economists may be the inverse of that of the early physical scientists. The latter were hampered by the anthropomorphism in their language. Economists living in the shadow, or rather in the glare, of the accomplishments of physical science may be hampered by the 'mechanomorphism' in their terminology.

10.3. Economics as a social science

10.3.1. Intelligibility

The influence of physical science on economics is epitomized in the way the function of theory is most commonly perceived. The function of theory is not only to formulate coherent conceptual systems but to do so in order to represent the world as a determinate system. It is as though anything else is inconceivable. What other function could theory possibly serve if not to find determinants? What else could explanation possibly mean? How else could theory be of use to anyone? Determinate systems are not merely the subject matter of the physical sciences, the special preserve of these sciences, but the sum and substance of all science.

It is perhaps on account of this perception that the exponents of a subjectivist approach to economics have had a rather moderate influence on their colleagues. What they have had to say has no doubt been found interesting and relevant to economic questions understood in the everyday sense. But what can be done about their observations? They seem to defy almost all attempts at incorporation into determinate systems. They belong, as we have put it, to another domain of thought, to a different side of experience. The role of expectations in economic affairs is a good example of this. That decisions are based more on what is expected to happen than on what has already happened seems to be a reasonable proposition. Mainstream economic theorists have therefore bent over backwards to find some way of incorporating expectations into their representation of economies as determinate systems subject possibly to stochastic shocks. But did those who drew attention to the importance of expectations really regard this transfer from the subjective to the physical domain of thought as a prerequisite for the theoretical treatment of expectations? Writing on expectations in economics as a social science, Lachmann remarked in an early paper that 'it is *intelligibility* and not *determinateness* that social science should strive to achieve'.[281] In a later publication he said: 'In social theory our main task is to explain observable social phenomena by reducing them to the individual plans … that typically give rise to them. This is what Weber meant by the explanation of action "in terms of the meaning attached to it by the actor"' and

> Human action is not 'determinate' in any sense akin to the one in which natural science has to strive for the 'determinacy' of the events it studies. A mechanistic interpretation of action, couched, say, in terms of 'response to stimulus', would have to explain away such simple facts as that different men in identical situations may act differently because of their different expectations of the future.[282]

Our final task will be to suggest that the study of economic ideals, such as the ideals of market order, not only becomes feasible but gives us much scope for useful work when we try to achieve intelligibility rather than determinateness.

Inquiry in which intelligibility rather than finding determinants is the basic concern may take on a variety of forms. History is probably the best-known example of such inquiry (except of course when it is informed by theories of historical determination). Historical inquiry seeks intelligible accounts of how one thing led to another, and of the mental life that was involved, without implying that the course of events could not possibly have been otherwise, i.e. without implying that it was determined in the physical sense. Max Weber was a pioneer in the field of adapting this *method of interpretation* to the social sciences. Theory then has the role of providing conceptual schemes and conceptual clarification.[283] Menger also seems to have seen the role of his economic theory in this way.[284] Mises coined the term *praxeology* for the study of the implications of the concept of human action. Economic theory, according to Mises, is one form of praxeology.[285] Hayek speaks of a *compositive* (as opposed to an analytic) method. From simple features of mental life familiar to us all, compositive theory infers more complex social phenomena in very general terms, rather as a conjectured history of money has been constructed. He considers this to be the correct method for understanding the unintended consequences of human action (see page 50 above), i.e. for understanding spontaneous order, and it is, according to Hayek, the method of economic theory. He regards general equilibrium theory as a compositive theory explaining the general interrelations of prices as an unintended consequence of purposeful action.[286] The word 'consequence' has quite different connotations in the languages of physical science and of history respectively and it is not entirely clear which ones Hayek had in mind when he spoke of general equilibrium and the compositive method.

These forms of inquiry have in common a concern with the mental life of individuals in relation to their circumstances. The aspects of this relationship that usually come under consideration may be divided roughly into three kinds. First, there are the physical conditions that are obstacles to the attainment of human ends but which may also be exploited with the aid of technology to serve human ends. Secondly, there is the fact that individuals share a common environment and that their individual endeavours to achieve specific ends therefore impinge on each other. Thirdly, there are the ideals, values and moral precepts that are held. They create obligations which may modify the ends individuals seek but they also create opportunities for each individual to exploit the obligations of others to serve his own ends. Above all, they may be mutually contradictory and that creates problems in a one-world shared environment. Economic studies have usually emphasized only the first two aspects. It is, however, the third aspect which seems to have the potential for making economic studies empirically more specific, though considerable conceptual clarification would be needed. We shall argue this case first. Thereafter we shall try to give some indications of how such empirically more detailed analysis may enhance our understanding of issues of long-standing economic interest.

10.3.2. Identifiable ideals

Clearly, one may consider mental life in relation to circumstances in the case of each of billions of human beings and each case is likely to be in some respects unique. Historians may often have good reasons for taking an interest in one or a few individuals. It is quite feasible to interpret or draw up an intelligible account of the relations in the past between individuals' thoughts and circumstances if the number of individuals taken into the account is small. Economists, however, often take an interest in rather different questions. If one wants to understand economy-wide problems such as unemployment or inflation, and furthermore if one wants one's understanding also to suggest what could be done about the problems, interpretation of individual action is not really a feasible approach. It would be too unwieldy, it would simply not be feasible, to inquire into all the thoughts and circumstances of millions in order to build up a synoptic view of such problems. Usual practice therefore is to concentrate on what are considered or sometimes merely postulated to be typical conditions under which very many if not all individuals conduct their affairs. Conclusions are drawn from broadly stated premises such as that there is scarcity, specialization, uncertainty, a profit motive and that people act purposefully, make plans, have expectations and so on – just as in indifference analysis conclusions are not drawn from the detailed shapes of individual indifference maps (or dispositions to choose) but from assumptions made about all of them, such as those of transitivity and convexity. The empirical content of the premises from which conclusions are derived is therefore rather meagre or at least not very specific and one's ability to distinguish on such a basis between actual situations and to deal with one specific problem rather than another is rather limited. It would be helpful if something relevant could be found which may be stated more specifically and yet does not have the unmanageable diversity of the aims or specific ends pursued by a large number of individuals.

In this context there is something to be said for putting the focus of attention on ideals (values, moral precepts, rules of conduct, institutions). It appears from the loose way they enter everyday discourse that the ideals found in a particular society in a particular era are not infinite in their variety. Or at least it appears that certain ideals, including those of market order, acquire identities of their own, not in a sense incompatible with individualism, but in the sense that they are always held by a substantial number of people though one could not say of any one person that he would never change his mind or that he would always conduct himself in conformity with an ideal if once he did. If this is so (and one cannot at present be sure that it is), ideals may be regarded as economically relevant entities which are amenable to and, unlike the specific ends sought by each and every individual, manageable in empirical analysis. It may be feasible to specify and articulate at least some of the ideals current in a particular society and so get an empirically more detailed understanding of certain economic problems.

It has already been pointed out that a uniformly observed set of rules of conduct or tacitly held ideals is (or should be) implied when micro-economic theory is regarded as descriptive of an actually existing market mechanism (see pages 56, 106–7 and 121 above). A world is apparently described in which there are no incompatible ideals and social conflict does not arise because everyone abides by a set of rules which sets out the correct manner in which the optimizing activities of individuals should impinge on each other. If ordinary experience is anything to go by, that is not the actual state of the world. Our argument in this study has been that it is a picture informed by only one complex of interrelated ideals held by some people. Missing from the picture are the problems that arise (a) when different people, especially when associated in different organizations, are guided by mutually conflicting ideals, (b) when the self-same people are guided by a number of incompatible ideals and are undecided on priorities, i.e. when their guiding conceptions are logically incoherent, and (c) when the realization of ideals is impeded, restricted and even blocked by physical conditions. It is not suggested that this is all there ever is to economic problems. The role of ideals may well be minor when compared to that of personal ambitions of various kinds (though in general it is difficult to separate the two from each other – see Section 9.2, pages 118–22 above). Nevertheless, it does seem that the considerations listed above are features of many economic problems. It therefore seems that we could gain an empirically more detailed understanding of them if we not only recognized that ideals (values, moral precepts, rules of conduct) do play a role, but also tried to articulate at least some major ideals.

Such inquiries would rest on the supposition that it is in fact the case that ideals as identifiable entities are less varied and less subject to continual change (less protean, as Shackle might say) than the individual aims and expectations found among a large number of people. In the course of historical and other social and political studies, ideals or at least widely held standpoints and fashions in attitudes, are sometimes described, so these studies apparently rest on a similar supposition. Even so, the loose way such matters are dealt with in ordinary language makes it difficult to ascertain whether the supposition really is correct. This brings us back to the procedure apparently followed with great success in the physical sciences, namely that of specifying the usage and cross-implications of words more explicitly. Without the conceptual clarification and precision introduced in this way, investigations of factual questions are difficult simply because it is not clear what one is looking for.

We need not suppose that ordinary language is a hopelessly feeble means of expression. It is admirably suited to the task to which it is put. The variety of contexts in which it is used is completely open ended. We manage with a limited number of words and constructions in an open-ended variety of contexts because words assume ever-newer connotations (cross-implications between words) according to context, i.e. because, as one would ordinarily say, words take on different meanings in different contexts. This makes for the flexibility and versatility of ordinary language without which communication would be extremely limited. But it may also make the usage of words in any one context open to doubt and the connotations of words rather fuzzy. When the usage and cross-implications of words used in a particular context are deliberately specified, a specialist terminology is created. It is likely to be less flexible and less versatile than ordinary language, but in the appropriate context it is far more precise.

The usage and cross-implications of the word 'force' in classical mechanics, for example, were in effect specified distinctly in Newton's famous three laws of motion.[287] In comparison, the usage of the word 'force' in discussions of social issues is rather indistinct. It is not very clear, for instance, what is and what is not implied by the expression 'market forces', nor, as Nagel observed, by an expression such as that one of two influences has been the 'greater force' in the 'development of modern capitalistic society'.[288] Along what kind of dimension, for instance, is the comparison made? Our argument has been that this vagueness cannot be remedied by the wholesale importation of a more precise terminology from another field, such as by the transfer of the language of determination; at least not as long as the questions we want to deal with come to our attention in the terms of ordinary language, as is the case in economics. When such importations are made, words of ordinary language are very loosely understood to correspond to certain terms of the more exactly defined terminology (e.g. choice corresponds to a constrained maximum or minimum). With loosely used words loosely related to specialist terms, the vagueness is merely compounded. The lack of precision may be remedied, it seems, only by developing specialist terminologies appropriate to the context, i.e. by making more explicit the usage and connotations of the terms in which the questions we want to deal with come to our attention.

The want of precise terms is particularly acute in the context of ideals in relation to economic order, as the groping for words in the present writing may have shown. The expressions 'ideals', 'values', 'moral precepts', 'rules of conduct' and 'institutions' in general are not interchangeable. But in the context we have been concerned with, any two of them sometimes may be interchangeable and all of them share certain common connotations, though each of them may also have connotations which are not intended in the context. (Hence the expedient has been adopted in this study of using two or more expressions in conjunction in an attempt to narrow down the meaning.) It is difficult to conduct rigorous analysis when words may have different meanings every time they are used. Nor can one be sure that intended meanings are conveyed to others when the intricate interlinking of words is not made explicit and may be perceived differently by every user of the language. The term 'institution', for example, takes on a great variety of connotations, i.e. it means many things to many people according to the context they have in mind. We early on followed Hayek in adopting 'rule of conduct' instead because it has fewer connotations (Hayek has said he followed Hume in this). But a particular system of taxation, for example, is an institution which, though it consists of rules and regulations, does not consist of what is suggested by 'rule of conduct'. On the other hand, the specific form of a tax – say, a progressive income tax – is likely to be an expedient modified by the moral precepts or values which predominate in the society in question, and these are usually reflected in rules of conduct. For some the term 'rule of conduct' may connote that people are conditioned to react in a certain way to their environment, but this connotation is not intended in a non-determinist context. In the context we have been concerned with, 'rule of conduct' may often have a connotation of things being done rather unquestioningly and with a minimum of thought, but nevertheless of voluntary conduct tacitly adapted in certain ways to the circumstances at hand (see Sections 5.4.1 and 9.2.1). These certain ways are then spoken of in some cases as customs or conventions and in others as moral precepts or values and in yet others perhaps as reflecting a conflict between rule of conduct and personal interest, such as, in some circumstances, whether it should be integrity rather than more profits or vice versa.

Ordinary language therefore does not provide clear-cut words for dealing with ideals in relation to economic order, only intricately interlinked words whose meanings vary indistinctly with context. More precision is required if one is to know what to look for when investigating questions of fact, such as whether our supposition that ideals are manageably identifiable is correct. The first step towards such precision is to delineate the required context by analysing the usage and connotations of words, rather as economists have spelt out the implications of the word 'scarcity' (and often have maintained that they delineate the entire field of study of economics). Presumably it would be a good idea to articulate common usages as far as possible, but arbitrary stipulation may be necessary where usages vary or logical inconsistencies are found. In its most worked-out form, the delineation would consist of explicit statements showing the interrelations or cross-implications of a number of general terms.

It is not enough, however, to have a precise form of the general term 'ideal' (or some other word). There is also the question of what is to count as an ideal. We have suggested formulations of a few of the ideals of market order, such as the implicit definitions of production and of value or commutative justice (see, inter alia, pages 87–8, 93–4 and 156 above). Not everyone may agree to call them ideals. But what of the proposition that men and women should be remunerated equally for similar work? If that is an ideal, then what of the proposition that medical practitioners and farmers should earn more than they do, or more than café proprietors? There is here once more the problem of distinguishing between the general and the particular (see Sections 5.4.3 and 9.4.1). Somehow one would like to say that equal pay for men and women doing similar work is a particular application of some general ideal of fair play. But it does not seem to be as particular an application as the specific intention to raise the pay of Mrs Jones by 20 per cent from next month. It seems that whatever we actually do is specific by definition. But to what extent could we specify what we intend to do? Ordinary language does not require us to commit ourselves. Words such as 'intention', 'purpose', 'objective', 'aim' and 'end sought' are flexible and versatile and correspondingly imprecise. We need a criterion for what constitutes an aim, objective or specific end. In our context at least, an ideal or a value is not an aim, though it may enter the specification of an aim. It is not a target, but something that participates in placing targets in particular positions.

Let us suppose that we have achieved a measure of conceptual clarity and are able to use the word 'ideal' more rigorously in the context of economic order. An entirely different question now arises. How would we establish how widely an ideal is held? Conceptual clarity is a prerequisite for settling factual questions but does not in itself do the job. In this regard opinion polls are likely to come to mind. But a head-count would not provide the information we want. First, we would have to suppose that the opinions of any one person influence the course of events as much as the opinions of any other person. That supposition would surely be false. (The assertion of a democratic ideal that all should be equally influential is of course another matter altogether.) Secondly, if we knew that a certain number of people held an ideal when the poll was conducted, we would know very little unless we also knew the importance each of these people attached to it. Some may accord it a very low priority while others may be fanatical about it. The information would have to come in the form of an order of priority among all of a person's ideals, analogously to a preference ordering for consumer goods. But this introduces just the kind of unmanageable complexity we want to avoid. We would at least have to allow for the possibility that individuals differ as much with respect to the priorities accorded to values as they do with respect to their preferences for consumer goods. There may not even be anything analogous to the 'tastes' economics ascribes to individuals, i.e. people may not have fully worked-out opinions and comprehensive sets of values neatly arranged in individual orders of priority. The actual situation may be more fluid, with some people forever propagating values and enlisting new recruits and others who are forever in search of something to believe in and whose latest finds loom largest in the mind. It is in the more fluid situation that one would be more likely to find manageably identifiable ideals.

Historians cannot conduct opinion polls among the people of the past and yet they may on occasion account for a particular feature of an institution by the prevalence of, say, Calvinist or Catholic values or by the fact that the civil service conferred high status or successful entrepreneurial activity was held in high esteem, and so on. Such values are inferred from conditions of which the institution to be explained may have been a prominent part. This is normal procedure in inquiry in which intelligibility is the regulative principle. An intelligible historical account explains the social and economic issues of the past by the significance people apparently attached to their actions, even if only tacitly as in the illustrative cases above. The procedure is just as applicable to the economic issues of the present, i.e. it may yield information on ideals and values that may help to make current economic issues intelligible. Furthermore, the information would be in a form in which it is already weighted for the differences in the influence various individuals managed to exert and for the priorities accorded on balance to various values, so that one would not necessarily have to concern oneself with the shifting ground of individual idiosyncrasies (i.e. the two kinds of difficulties mentioned in the previous paragraph would be obviated). But in keeping with a more explicit and precise usage of the term 'ideal', one would need also a more explicit and precise term for the 'strength' or 'force' of the influence of current ideals and values. As already noted, this idea is often expressed rather vaguely in social studies. One may also have to develop new criteria for what constitutes sufficient evidence for the existence of values since these criteria presumably may be more stringent when the evidence is taken from a current rather than a historical setting.

However, for someone used to deterministic theory, and especially for someone used to thinking of determination as prediction, the procedure just mentioned must seem foolishly circular. If Y follows from X, can it then be said that X follows from Y? If an ideal or value is inferred partly from an economic issue, can it then be said that the ideal or value partly explains the economic issue? If 'explains' is taken to mean 'predicts', the procedure must indeed seem rather foolish. But, as noted, it is normal procedure when intelligibility is the regulative principle of inquiry. It is the procedure followed, for example, when an economist in an elementary way ascribes an increase in a market price to a change in tastes. An appeal to tastes hinges on intelligibility. That 'tastes' are a foreign body in the texture of deterministic theory was noticed by Stigler and Becker, who proposed to neutralize it by the rather surprising suggestion that tastes, like 'the Rocky Mountains ... are there, will be there next year, too, and are the same to all men'.[289] They were concerned to show that 'assumptions of differences in tastes' and of 'unstable tastes' 'have been a convenient crutch to lean on when the analysis has bogged down. They give the appearance of considered judgement, yet really have only been *ad hoc* arguments that disguise analytical failures.'[290] Analytical success apparently is to show how an independently ascertainable entity is determined by other independently ascertainable, rather than ad hoc or imputed, entities. Since economists are not qualified to say how tastes are determined and since tastes are suspect on the score of independent ascertainability, they should be replaced as determinants by incomes and prices, which Stigler and Becker appear to regard as independently ascertainable.

Even in the perspective of physical science, this is rather a narrow view of analytical success. Various sub-atomic particles in physics, for instance, are said to be merely imputed. Certainly in interpretations or intelligible accounts, there are imputed entities which make their appearance when coherence is sought, which appear, so to say, in the mind's eye when one reads between the lines. Intelligibility in this context implies something like coherence within the limits of one's knowledge. What is known about an issue is fitted together coherently and imputations are made to fill the gaps. Imputations may no doubt be made foolishly or sensibly. They are foolish when they are so construed as to be isolated from everything except what they are meant to explain, when each comes in a world of its own in which it cannot be corroborated by other evidence. A one-world-only assumption must underlie all sensible observation. One should not explain one policy measure taken by a government by the preponderance of ardent socialists among its supporters and another taken not long after by the preponderance of free-market dogmatists among its supporters. When something is imputed to exist in a particular setting, any other study dealing with what must count as the same setting must either accept its existence or challenge the previous finding.[291] In this way the ambit of intelligible accounts and their coherence may become ever wider and the criteria for accepting the existence, for instance, of ideals and values may be made ever more stringent. Interpretations of events and economic issues therefore become more definite as more factors are taken into (intelligible) account.

The terminology we have been using to characterize this method of gaining knowledge may be unfortunate in at least one respect. It may give the impression that knowledge so gained can have no other significance than to satisfy intellectual curiosity. It would then be of little interest to economists whose primary concern is to gather information which may also guide action and policy. Terms such as 'interpretation' and 'intelligible account' may have an outlandish sound about them in the economist's milieu, but the method described by these terms is by no means unfamiliar to economists. It is in fact the method used in elementary economic analysis where the language of determination of formal theory is not taken too seriously.

Let us say there is a sudden increase in the relative price of a commodity called X. It would be quite normal to inquire into the circumstances in which the increase took place and then to fit the various pieces of information together as best one can (i.e. into an intelligible account). It would make a considerable difference to the possible actions to be taken, depending of course on the capacity various parties have for taking action and on what they want to achieve, whether it appeared on the basis of intelligibility that the increase in price was due to a change in tastes, a new fashion perhaps, or to drought conditions or to collusion among the sellers. If it appeared that the price of X rose because of a new fashion, a manufacturer who uses X as an input may investigate the X industry and, if it appeared to be competitive and there appeared to be people able and willing to respond to incentives, he may expect the higher price of X to be temporary and therefore may decide not too look for a substitute for X. On the other hand, if it appeared that the price of X rose because of collusion among the sellers, the manufacturer may well look for a substitute, while a more powerful person in industry may find his thoughts turning to special deals or to retaliatory threats and a powerful person in government may contemplate yet other action, and so on. Intelligible accounts in these cases would not merely satisfy intellectual curiosity. Elementary economic analysis of this kind is probably a far better guide to action than is formal theory couched in the language of determination.

In these cases too, the intelligible accounts would be based on a knowledge of certain institutions and other conditions which are not once-off or very transient. They may include the number of sellers in the X industry, the technical limitations in the production of X, the kind of decisions that sellers gathered together are likely to consider in their interest and the way these are limited by legislation and by mistrust within the group, but also the rules of conduct observed in the X industry, among which are standards of honourable conduct with a minimum standard set by the state of financial exigency at the time. All in all, it would be a motley lot of considerations of varying degrees of haziness, but surely not atypical of the sort of analysis that precedes decisions. Such analysis could presumably benefit from a more formally organized and independently established knowledge of identifiable ideals and values.

However, intelligible accounts even of as simple an event as a rise in price may become immensely complex and may involve much guessing. When we try to deal with unemployment, inflation and other complex and necessarily economy-wide questions of economic order (i.e. in terms of intelligibility rather than of macro-economic aggregation), we simply do not have the capacity to keep track of the welter of considerations which would have to be taken into account, even if we called in a friendly computer with its greater capacity in this regard. It is with such questions that a knowledge of identifiable ideals and values may come into its own. We would be able to leave aside the intricate interrelations of individual activities and deal rather with questions of the compatibility and practicability of the various ideals and values which, so to say, form a framework within which the analytically unmanageable interlinking of the conduct of a multitude of individuals takes place.

10.3.3. The study of economic disorder

It was presumed throughout this study that the ideals of market order would qualify as manageably identifiable ideals. In the kind of research just suggested, a closer and scientifically disinterested study of the *ideals* of market order would be part of a wider study of the *actual* problems of economic order, i.e. of a study of economic disorder.

What is to count as a problem of order or a case of disorder must be judged in terms of a set of values and ideals (see Section 5.1). There is no other way if, as we have argued, there is no natural order. If an economy were to conform fully to the ideals of market order, it would not perform well from the point of view of a socialist who judges it in terms of collectivist ideals. This, however, is *not* what is meant by disorder here. The meaning of disorder we require may be indicated as follows: in our usage of the word, an ideal is a fragment of a vision of a well-ordered society. If it is a coherent vision, all the ideals derived from it would be consistent with each other and form a coherent whole. Where the identifiable ideals found in a society are not consistent with each other, either because the vision of a well-ordered society has not been articulated sufficiently to reveal the lack of consistency or because the ideals are fragments of different and incompatible visions, there is a potential for disorder which would be recognized as such by everyone who holds at least one of the identifiable ideals. This is what we shall mean by disorder. The study of economic disorder would therefore consider identifiable ideals with regard to their compatibility with each other and with various public-spirited aims and with regard to their practicability when physical obstacles and the state of technology are taken into account. Since no actual economy is ever likely to conform fully to any one coherent vision of a well-ordered society, a study of this kind may be made of any actual economy.

The study of economic disorder would encompass problems and policy issues with which economists in fact are already very much preoccupied when they are not engrossed in the structural difficulties of deterministic models. Unemployment and inflation, for example, may be regarded as problems of economic order or cases of economic disorder. What would be different about the approach proposed here? An important difference is that market order would be treated as a complex of ideals which would enter any consideration of the compatibility of all the ideals and social aspirations which may play a role in a particular setting. This cannot be done when equilibrium theory is regarded as social mechanics and market order as the actually existing market mechanism (see Section 8.4.4, especially pages 107 and 109). Though conflicts of policy objectives may well be considered, the ideals of market order are not thought of as entering the conflict simply because market order is not looked upon as a complex of ideals but as the actual and natural structure of economies. Sometimes, as in recent discussions of deregulation and privatization, market order is treated as an ideal. But then the questions of compatibility and practicability, if they are considered at all, have to be considered without much help from the most formal part of economic theory. This makes it difficult to ensure that 'any single measure of economic policy' is 'part of a policy designed to establish and maintain *economic order as a whole*', as Eucken recommended all policy should be. The 'unity of economic policy' would not be assured (see page 145 above). The study of economic disorder would not have this drawback. It could not of course establish the merits of the particular vision of a well-ordered society in terms of which 'order as a whole' and the 'unity of policy' would be judged.

Before a study of economic disorder could be undertaken, however, identifiable ideals would actually have to be identified and that means they would have to be articulated. Only if they are understood explicitly in an articulated form could the questions of compatibility and practicability be considered in anything like a rigorous way. That this articulation may be a huge and difficult task is shown by the fact that the whole of Walrasian general equilibrium may be regarded as an articulation of the ideal of allocative efficiency (Section 8.4.3). Efficiency in the context of a single producer and a single product may be readily intelligible to most people. But it is not immediately obvious what is implied when the concept and ideal of efficiency is extended to a whole economy with many producers and many products, with many consumer preferences to be catered for and with the rights to resources widely dispersed. To have set out at least one version of the implications of efficiency in this context is a considerable achievement.

The articulation of allocative efficiency in general equilibrium has two features which may be characteristic of articulation of this kind. First, the ideal is *implicitly* defined, i.e. it is exemplified in an indicated quantitative configuration (see page 100 above). Allocative efficiency is to be understood from the various cross-implications that are set out, or, in Wittgenstein's turn of phrase, the ideal is *shown* rather than *stated*. Secondly, the implicit definition incorporates other ideals, notably (as intended by Walras, see page 93 above) commutative justice, as reflected in free competition and a uniform price for each commodity. This condition makes a considerable difference to the implicit definition. Walras seemed to insist on it when he commented on Gossen's 'absolute maximum' of social utility. For Gossen, equilibrium of barter exchange occurred when, in modern terms, the marginal utility of each of the two commodities (respectively) is the same for both parties to the exchange. Walras did not object explicitly to the interpersonal utility comparison, but to the fact that the maximum 'is not the relative maximum utility of free competition' and 'does away with private property' (since the equilibrium outcome is independent of the initial distribution of endowments).[292] Gossen seemed to envisage, as Jaffé put it in commenting on Wicksell's and Baumol's misunderstanding of Walras on this point, that the endowments of the two commodities are pooled and then distributed so as to maximize the combined utility of the parties to the exchange.[293] 'From each according to his ability, to each according to his need' is an ideal of distributive justice very different from commutative justice. The former is presumably the ideal of social justice which Hayek calls a mirage, an 'atavism' based on 'primordial emotions' stemming from 'face-to-face' tribal society, which can have no coherent meaning in an open society.[294] But there may be people who can state or show what they mean by this ideal of distributive justice and the corresponding ideal of allocative efficiency. It would be different from that exemplified in Walrasian general equilibrium and presumably should guide socialist and welfare-state planners.

The point here is that the articulation of ideals may take the form of exemplification, or showing rather than stating, and that a complex of ideals rather than a single ideal is likely to be shown. There is a further point – well known in the case of the word 'justice' but less recognized in the case of 'efficiency' and even less in the case of, say, 'production' – namely that words denoting ideals may have very different connotations for different people and for the same people on different occasions and that in very many cases they may not have any logically coherent meanings at all. The purpose of articulation in the present context would be to ferret out this kind of thing, to bring it into the open. It is in terms of just such disagreement, talking at cross-purposes, inconsistency and confusion, that economic disorder, i.e. the problems of economic order, may become intelligible.

The mention above of 'production' among words denoting ideals may seem surprising. There can be little doubt, however, that 'production' is at least an emotive and evocative term, though it may not be clear what it evokes. We think that everyone should strive to be efficient because greater efficiency means more product from given resources and more product is a good thing. We judge the performance of an economy by the percentage change in GDP or GNP and a country that records a large increase is the subject of admiration and envy. The stature of a country is not raised when it is called 'less developed' and the much-desired development of such countries by and large means increasing their productive capacities. In the absence of a precise terminology, it does not really matter whether we call production an ideal or whether we merely say that production is considered desirable. We shall later refer to a social aspiration for material prosperity.

More important is the question to what extent various intuitive notions of production involve us in disagreement, talking at cross-purposes, in consistency and confusion. For that one would have to articulate intuitive notions of production, i.e. one would have to inquire into the connotations and implications of the terms 'production' and 'product'.

It would be a big task. However, to illustrate the kind of difficulties that might arise, we may start at home and comment on the explication of production in economics and on its conformity to some apparent intuitive notions of production.

For the Physiocrats little more than two centuries ago a product still had to be tangible, what we would now call a primary commodity such as wheat, timber, wool and so on. They concluded that only land had a product. Adam Smith, in his discussion of the Physiocrats,[295] found this strange but recognized only manufacturers and merchants as also productive. All work which we would now say provides services remained for him quite unproductive. Now of course production has not only been extended to all services but in a sense has become entirely a matter of factor services. What is created in production is a desired new form, shape or configuration of what already exists or simply a service which, so to say, culminates in an immediate glow of satisfaction. Production therefore is the creation of utility, the creation of something with the capacity directly or indirectly to satisfy wants. More simply, production is the creation of something useful.

The crux of the matter is how to establish what is useful. In economics with individualist utilitarian foundations, it is plain enough that consumers with the ability to pay are the ultimate arbiters of what is useful. The ideal criterion of usefulness accordingly is that a service or the product in which it is incorporated has a market price. It sets the cross-implications between, i.e. the meanings of, terms in the ideal. We may call it the market-price criterion. The practical criterion, for statistical purposes and for studies in applied economics, is that a service or its product has been exchanged for a sum of money. A service is useful and hence productive if someone has paid for it and thus created income. We may call this the income criterion. The two criteria are not the same, of course, unless the concept of a market is broadened to the point where it becomes superfluous and the guiding conception of market order is lost. A price established in a market would then be equivalent to a price established in any transaction and any exchange.

Where a central authority decides what is to be produced, it also in effect decides what is useful. 'Production' simply has different meanings (connotations, cross-implications) in this situation and in one where usefulness decisions are decentralized. But there are troublesome intermediate cases. One may imagine the arguments and counter-arguments brought up in a debate on whether agricultural surpluses distributed as taxpayer-funded foreign aid should or should not count as product in the national accounts. The balance of the argument on the side of the market-price criterion must be that it should not count as product, if for no other reason than that taxpayer-funded foreign aid is unintelligible in the ideal world being envisaged. But that would hardly satisfy those who think it wicked to say that food is not useful to starving children just because they are penniless. The income criterion is on the side of the angels in this case because surplus-producing farmers are productive by its standard. The market-price criterion has run into a conflict between an ideal of a free society and an ideal of a compassionate society. It is the kind of conflict that the study of economic disorder would watch out for.

Intuitive notions of production in any case have a public-spirited dimension which neither of the criteria of usefulness captures unless it is supplemented. Let us consider the following, for instance: at some price there is bound to be an effective demand for, say, stolen cars. Are those who labour to satisfy this demand to be regarded as producers? It is of no avail to say that car thieves do not create the cars they sell. Do miners create gold, copper, coal and so on? They merely toil like car thieves to provide a service, namely to make these things available to those who want them. It appears, at least superficially, that car thieves qualify as producers by both criteria. They provide a useful service because they have an income, or at any rate receive money, and because there usually is a market in stolen cars in which prices are established in the normal way. Intuitively, however, no one regards them as producers. Ordinary understanding makes a very definite distinction between production and robbery.

Once the distinction has been made between productive activity directed at creating something new and predatory activity directed at (or having the effect of) changing or preserving the interpersonal distribution of wealth and income, one need not stop at car thieves. Question marks appear, as we have argued already (pages 70 and 93–4 above), about the productiveness of other occupations. Would an increase in production shown by the statistical record really seem to be such if it turned out that all the additional productive activities took the form of tax avoidance advice, litigation, police work, advertising campaigns, attendance at sales conferences and activities with obvious external diseconomies? Where intuitive notions of production draw the line between productive and predatory activities, one may expect, depends on values and ideals, customs and conventions. To articulate intuitive meanings of production, one has to know a great deal about the whole society. There is nothing simple about the concept of production.

In this respect, the market-price criterion (for identifying production) probably comes much closer to intuitive notions than the income criterion. We have tried to show that the exclusion of predatory activity is at the centre of the idea of market order or at least of the liberal order of the invisible hand (Sections 6.1 and 6.2). By incorporating the idea of commutative justice, the analysis makes provision for the exclusion of predatory activity in the form of price manipulation by restrictive practices (Sections 7.1, 7.2 and 8.4.1). The ordinary understanding of a business engaging in restrictive practices, as far as one can tell, is that it combines production with an element of extortion – and pure extortion, say a Chicago-style protection racket, would definitely not be regarded as production. This may be seen from the way people would speak about it (e.g. the gang extracts protection money rather than earning an income by providing the service of protecting its clients against other protection gangs). Gains from restrictive practices are contrasted with gains from a hard day's work or honest enterprise. This kind of contrast informed the idea of market order as analysed, for instance, by Smith and Walras. The absence of other kinds of predatory activity (i.e. other than price manipulation) is shown in the idea of market order only by the general absence of predators. Smith, one may remember, qualified the economic freedom of the individual with the proviso 'as long as he does not violate the laws of justice' (page 33 above). In the classical-liberal conception of a well-ordered society, most forms of predatory activity probably would 'violate the laws of justice'. If therefore one defines product as something with a market price and understands market price in the full context of the ideal of market order, one probably comes quite close to certain aspects of intuitive notions of production.

Market price in this sense requires something like perfect competition. The fact that competitive conditions of this kind do not really prevail anywhere does not matter if the idea helps us to articulate intuitive notions of production. To draw up intelligible accounts of what people try to do in their economic life, one has to know how they understand, inter alia, production. One has to explain action 'in terms of the meaning attached to it by the actor' (page 168 above). The matter is different when one's purpose is to add up and record quantities of product because then there would be hardly anything to record. This is where the income criterion is used – add up receipts, subtract expenses and call the result quantity of product. But this procedure does not help us to articulate attitudes to predatory activity. In adding up, receipts from grossly criminal activities such as car theft are excluded but all the rest would probably be counted as product.

Unfortunately, the matter becomes even more complicated because there is another area where the income criterion is probably better than the market-price criterion, not only for recording quantities, but also for articulating intuitive notions of production. In this area, however, intuitive notions seem to differ. The issue is the following: the implications of equilibrium (market) prices consistent with commutative justice (equal values passing hands in exchange) are worked out in detail in Walras's general equilibrium. We have already taken note of the fact (pages 100–1 above and notes 190–1) that no profits from trading and arbitrage and no pure entrepreneurial profits have a place in the formal analysis. Traders, arbitrageurs and entrepreneurs have a place in the envisaged *tâtonnement* process that goes with the analysis like a pictorial appendix. There they seem to render the service of bringing the system to equilibrium. In equilibrium this service is no longer needed and therefore nothing is paid for it and it does not appear as part of the product. The formal analysis is static, merely showing the interrelationships in an optimal allocation of resources consistent with commutative justice.

This feature of static equilibrium analysis seems to be due to the way commutative justice was conceived through the centuries from at least the time of Aristotle. It may be that product was always thought of as a tangible object and that it was therefore inconceivable that traders were productive. It may be that buying low and selling high was even regarded as robbery and exploitation. The trader stood between the original producer and the final consumer of a tangible good and, if he was unproductive, the cut he took made the mediated exchange inconsistent with commutative justice. Traders may have been seen as predators living off the tangible products of others and similarly entrepreneurs who organized productive activities without actually participating in the physical execution of the work. Though it has been largely denormatized, the idea is still part of equilibrium analysis. Hicks, for instance, referred to *income effects* (a redistribution of wealth) from trading at *false prices* (disequilibrium prices). He went on to explain that the position of one of the parties trading at a false price 'is ultimately exactly the same as if' the price had not been false but he 'had been compelled to hand over' a certain sum of money to the other party.[296] If this really were the attitude, traders would hardly be seen to be making an honest living by exploiting differences in prices.

The question is whether this attitude accords with attitudes implicit in intuitive notions of production. The question concerns arbitrage profits so that other aspects may be left out of account. The transporting of goods that trade may involve, for instance, may be widely held to be productive and to be 'honest work'. But that is not the issue. The trader buys in one market and sells at a higher price in another market. Similarly, the entrepreneur sees an opportunity for combining various services on offer in such a way that total outlay is less than the potential revenue from the output. In some cases this may not even entail putting capital at risk; only 'alertness to the production possibilities already existing' and a few telephone calls.[297] The question therefore is whether arbitrage profits understood in this wide sense are taken to indicate productive contributions.

It seems, on the basis of general impressions, that intuitive notions of production are divided on this point. There are those who believe production must entail arduous labour, toil and trouble, and who consequently complain of middlemen and wheeler-dealers and of the exploitation they perpetrate. The parastatal and bureaucratic trading organizations in semi-socialist countries appear to reflect this attitude. There are also those who believe that traders and entrepreneurs render a productive service in so far as they initiate moves which enhance the variety and availability of goods and services. Implicit in this is the idea of a kind of productive public service: if man cannot produce material substance but only new forms, shapes and configurations of it, traders and entrepreneurs whose activities coordinate the activities of others and rearrange them in new ways also qualify as producers. Finally, there are those who extend the idea of a productive public service to trading on markets of every description. Speculation on asset markets, including speculation in financial assets and currencies, is always a productive activity because it creates the prices and valuations needed for spontaneous coordination and efficiency. But others will not accept this. Such trading must more than usually be orientated to what will happen in the future and, in the nature of the case, traders generally cannot know this. There may be cases of special knowledge of imminent events and intertemporal arbitrage spreads this knowledge. But such cases are rare. Those who regard speculation as productive presumably attribute to traders a sixth sense for forming correct expectations. Those who disagree see a mere groping-about in which every rumour and every ephemeral fad sends traders into a flurry and prices into a spin. To some it seems that the markets provide a daily revaluation of assets. To others it seems that the information conveyed is about as significant as the jabbering of an idiot.

These have been a few examples of the haze surrounding only one common economic term. Since other common economic terms, such as 'resource', 'capital' and 'investment', derive their meanings partly from notions of production, the haze extends to them too. The intuitive notions of production are obscure because they evoke dimly perceived values and ideals. One method, therefore, of setting about identifying ideals, provided the conceptual groundwork has been done, is to inquire into the various ways common notions such as production and efficiency are understood by all manner of people; not, however, as these notions may be brought up in intellectual discussions, but as they enter into the intents and the plans, the tactics of everyday life.

Let us for a moment suppose that we have done the conceptual analysis necessary for a precise usage of the terms 'ideal' and 'institution', for understanding the connection between them and for identifying actual ideals and institutions; and further that we have in fact identified some of them. We would then have the equipment and the raw material for a study of economic disorder. We would proceed to look for cases of incongruity, for cases of inconsistencies among ideals or among coexisting institutions based on ill-matched fragments of either the same or disparate visions of a well-ordered society. Our purpose would not be to learn to recognize situations of open confrontation or disguised hostility. Most of us can do that already. The more difficult situations are those where individuals, pursuing whatever may be their personal aims and ambitions are guided by one or two ideals in isolation which they presume to be part of a single overall order. The scene for disorder is set when people go about their daily business as though they live in a well-ordered world when in fact there is no overall order. It is this kind of situation for which a study of economic disorder would seek an intelligible account.

In a paper on economic order and economic institutions, Lachmann suggested an intelligible account of the permanent inflation of the time (1963) which amounts to something like this kind of account of economic disorder.[298] He wrote there of the *outer* institutions of a market economy (prerequisite principles corresponding more or less to what we have called the ideals of market order) and the *inner* institutions of a market economy which develop in response to circumstances and to a demand for them, such as stock exchanges and insurance companies (corresponding to what on page 45 above we called business schemes available to anyone who wishes to use them). But, Lachmann said, there are also *neutral* institutions which are neither prerequisites for nor creations of a market economy, but nevertheless are of considerable significance to it. They have to be consonant with society but not necessarily with market order (*gesellschaftskonform* rather than *marktkonform*) and are points where social pressures may break into a market economy.[299] Social pressures manifesting themselves eventually in inflation entered via the neutral institutions of collective bargaining and the norm peculiar to this century that wage rates may rise but never fall, a norm accepted by both bargaining sides. He considered this norm the decisive factor. Collective bargaining, cost-plus price fixing and obliging bankers were merely the necessary conditions for the norm to ensure that prices of industrial goods can only rise and never fall.

It becomes plain from the way Lachmann elaborated the argument, however, that he saw the coexistence of incompatible attitudes as the ultimate reason for the disorder manifesting itself as inflation. Collective bargaining is regarded as price determination by bilateral monopoly, i.e. as one possible form of the characteristic bargaining by which prices are established within the framework of a market economy. It is assumed that in all bargaining the parties accept prices other than the ones to be established as points of orientation, which for them are inexorable constraints. The attitude to collective bargaining is that it is quite normal in this regard and thus quite compatible with market order. But when collective bargaining is the order of the day in most industries, the points of orientation are in fact quite different. Both parties agree that wage rates cannot go down; the unions are concerned not to fall behind other unions in the annual round of wage demands; the employers take it for granted that profit margins may be maintained over whatever the new costs work out to, knowing that their competitors are subject to the same pressures and that by convention any temporary slack in demand may be met by reduced output and some retrenchment. Formally prices are points of orientation, in fact they are shifted by the activities of the collective bargainers themselves. Formal thinking on the subject rests on the presupposition of a price constraint without allowing for the fact that both parties in collective bargaining accept social norms on what is fair and reasonable in the setting of wage rates which are incompatible with that presupposition.[300] As Lachmann put it in a later paper in which he repeated part of the argument: 'Instead of the price system containing the area of wage bargaining within narrow limits, the autonomous price system has been destroyed in the process.'[301]

Whether this is the full story of inflation now or in the 1960s is perhaps not so important here. It is surely eminently sensible to try to make the question intelligible in such terms. In unguarded moments, when they do not feel themselves called upon to find determinants, that is probably what most economists try to do anyway. Let us in the same manner try to illustrate what a study of economic disorder might be about. Since the conceptual groundwork has not been done and we have neither the equipment nor the raw material for such a study, we shall merely suggest in broad outline how some very familiar issues might be made intelligible in terms of a lack of coherence among a few broadly stated social aspirations (identifiable ideals) in a setting in which there are also certain physical constraints to be taken into account. In such an impressionistic attempt at an intelligible account, however, the illustration of a line of approach is more important than the conclusions.

One of the most puzzling manifestations of economic disorder in our time is the dualism which seems to be becoming a feature of the economies of ever more countries. Alongside an economically active and reasonably prosperous part of the population there is another sizeable part which stands outside the active economy, which is no more part of the production process than weeds growing on the edges of a busy highway are part of road transportation. While this dualism was a feature only of so-called less-developed countries, it seemed reasonable to explain it in terms of a wildly expanding population and of various cultural and developmental factors peculiar to these countries. Perhaps this is still the correct explanation in these cases. But some other explanation also seems to be called for now that a similar dualism is manifesting itself in developed industrial countries where these conditions do not prevail and where unemployment has become so persistent and of such proportions that these countries appear to be haunted by the spectre of Adam Smith's stationary state – an immensely affluent society where craftsmen 'are continually running about the streets … offering their service, and as it were begging employment'.[302] The puzzle of unemployment is this: if at least many of the unemployed have ready hands and ready mouths, why cannot the first be set to work to feed the second? Keynes thought they could be with a little help from the State. Eucken (among others) was sceptical about the means suggested by Keynes but thought that competition policy and monetary reform would have the desired effect (see pages 131 and 143 above). Events seemed to prove Keynes right for some years but now the case must surely be considered doubtful.

Since we have to guess, we shall presume that the problem of dualism has arisen in societies that at one time had, inter alia, the following characteristics. Material prosperity is held in high esteem so that anything which is judged to extend production or to raise productivity is accorded great respectability. In this sense there is a social aspiration for material prosperity. It is generally presumed in the society that increasing material prosperity will be spread widely, though not necessarily very evenly, because everyone who so wishes is either in employment or engaged in independent enterprise. Individualist values predominate and, with some qualifications and with some voices raised in dissent, the economy is organized along free-enterprise lines. Free enterprise is interpreted to mean that everyone is allowed to do as he sees fit in conducting his business, barring, of course, outright transgressions of the criminal law and of rights under the law of contract. There is also a vague belief in the mystique of a natural order: when we are all left to do as we see fit we have free markets and when we have free markets we have the discipline of the market imposed by market prices and all our separate activities are coordinated. On occasion, the working of the system is presented in a public-spirited way as a social norm: nothing, least of all government, should stand in the way of businessmen in their task of creating more jobs and more products, for then the system creates as much material prosperity as natural limitations would allow in any system.

Quite apart from the possible presence of other factors not specially provided for (e.g. a desire for security of income or the ideals of a compassionate society), the various elements of this social arrangement are unlikely to form a coherent system. They are not consistent with each other in the sense that a course of action or an innovation, technical or institutional, deemed in the ordinary conduct of business to be respectable because, say, it advances material prosperity, may run counter to another element of the social arrangement. The various elements are not so attuned to each other that whatever conforms to one element necessarily conforms to all the others. In other words, there is a potential for economic disorder.

It is true of course that the ideal of market order was presented by Adam Smith and other writers in the classical liberal tradition as a coherent system that would promote material prosperity in conditions of personal freedom. But that was always predicated on the assumption of the central idea of market order, namely what we have called the principle of the invisible hand or control by impersonal constraint (pages 130, 132 and 139 above). There are definite prerequisites for markets that impose a discipline and for prices that coordinate and control by impersonal constraint. These prerequisites may not be met when market order is not visualized as a whole but courses of action or innovations are judged, say, by the ideal of freedom of contract or the aspiration for material prosperity considered in isolation.

Control by impersonal constraint is an ideal of freedom in the sense that no one individual should be able to restrain another individual deliberately, but not of freedom in the sense that there should be no constraints at all. As it was apparently envisaged by Smith and other writers in the classical liberal tradition, this control has two aspects which, for present purposes, we may call the *micro constraint* and the *macro constraint*. The prerequisites for these are rather different and therefore two types of conditions are required if prices are to count as market prices, if, in other words, they are to impose the discipline of the market.

The impersonal micro constraint is the constraint of competition and requires that individuals in their dealings with each other should always have other options open to them. There should always be another person with whom a party to a proposed deal could make a closely similar deal – and it must be a closely similar deal and not merely some other option. Under such conditions, all parties engaged in negotiating a deal are constrained by the fact, of which they are aware, that the other parties have alternatives. Smith, we have tried to show (page 28 above), followed a simple rule in this regard. The requisite alternatives were likely to be available only where the number of market participants was large and he mentioned many instances where he thought numbers were not large enough, even in his day of smaller firms. There is an important special case of the micro constraint. Individuals should have a choice not only between employers, but also between employment and independent enterprise. The micro constraint reflects individualist values and an emphasis on commutative justice. It is part of a vision of a well-ordered competitive economy in which everyone participates fully – an ideal of broad-based competitive enterprise rather than of enterprise as a game played by a select few in the precincts of a politburo, a Cabinet office or the boardrooms of giant concerns.

The micro constraint by itself would not coordinate the free choices of innumerable individuals. Coordination requires a macro constraint such that a decision made by one individual impinges on the choices others may make, on the alternatives open to them. To be impersonal, however, this macro constraint must be such that a decision maker does not know whom his decision constrains and how it constrains them. The macro constraint has to limit the amounts that may be spent at any one time so that market prices may put some purchases out of the reach of some individuals and changing market prices may induce individuals to change their plans in the direction of mutual compatibility, i.e. of a coordination of economic activity. All elementary economic analysis of course assumes that prices perform this function. Smith and other writers on market order, though they were aware of the role played by credit in their time, assumed that money was a commodity, the traditional gold and silver which, because their quantities cannot easily be augmented or diminished, could be a macro constraint, provided that it was not possible, as it were, to lend one's cake and have it. But in a world in which commodities may be exchanged for financial assets, i.e. for claims on others, or sold on credit in anticipation of loan repayments or other receipts, that kind of proliferation, impossible with cakes, is just the peculiarity that money acquires. Commodity money that is lent and borrowed, therefore, would be an extremely blurred macro constraint. Our modern credit-based money is not really a constraint at all. Yet if market prices are to perform their ideal function of coordinating economic activity in conditions of economic freedom (to 'function effectively as an agency of control', as Simons put it – see page 136 above), there would have to be some effective macro constraint.

Whether the conditions necessary for the efficient operation of these constraints ever did exist anywhere is beside the point here. We are concerned with the coherence of social arrangements that guide conduct and we shall argue that the conditions for the constraints may hardly be found at all where conduct is guided by one or other social aspiration (ideal, value) considered in isolation. We shall confine ourselves to the social aspiration for material prosperity.

There can be no doubt that the strides made towards greater material prosperity over the centuries were to a large extent made possible by advances in technology and the accumulation of capital. The attitude to both is therefore tied up closely with the social aspiration for material prosperity. Technical progress and capital formation are promoted at every turn and anything that may possibly stand in their way is deplored with public-spirited indignation. The person who finds a way of getting more out of a given amount of resources is treated with the respect once accorded to explorers or to generals who extended the realm. The perception that a country is not in possession of the latest technology engenders the frantic anxiety of one who knows he is losing a race. But when a matter is judged by one aspiration in isolation, rather than as part of a coherent system, problems are apt to arise in other respects. The attitude to technological advances and the accumulation of capital, by conferring high social standing on certain ordinary gain-orientated activities, has no doubt contributed much to raising the standard of living of almost everyone. But it has also created what we may call an economic oligarchy which is not conducive to the efficient operation of the micro constraint.

Schumpeter observed that periodic waves of innovation and mechanization are followed each time by 'an avalanche of consumers' goods that permanently deepens and widens the stream of real income' and 'progressively raises the standard of life of the masses', that 'the modern standard of life of the masses evolved during the period of relatively unfettered "big business"'.[303] But he also observed: 'The capitalist process, by substituting a mere parcel of shares for the walls of and the machines in a factory, takes the life out of the idea of property' (see page 37 above). Large concerns are necessary because through them society reaps the benefits of economies of scale and because many production processes are simply not feasible on a small scale. But large concerns need large amounts of capital. The spontaneous evolution of a luxuriance of institutions by which the finance for these concentrations of capital is raised in intricate ways has made large concerns possible and is widely regarded as a necessary part of economic progress. Financial intermediaries are necessary because they channel funds from small savers to large concerns and because they allow the man in the street to share in the economic development started by entrepreneurs who have the necessary ability, temperament, organizations and connections to get things done.

Specialization in enterprise, as in other spheres, leads to efficiency and efficiency leads to material prosperity. But the same spontaneous evolution has also led to the so-called divorce of ownership and control.

Perhaps it is better to distinguish between the *control of capital*, i.e. the right to make decisions about the creation and applications of capital equipment and other 'means of production', and *beneficiary rights*, i.e. the rights to receive a share of profits, a periodic interest payment, a pension, an annuity, the proceeds of a life assurance policy and so forth. The institutions which divide the ordinary idea of ownership in this way make possible an economic oligarchy in which the control of capital is vested in ever-fewer hands while the beneficiary rights are spread widely. The controllers of capital, i.e. the oligarchs, may have very modest and in some cases no beneficiary rights, directly or indirectly through loans, in the capital they control. Once these institutions become predominant, the further spontaneous evolution of an economic oligarchy can proceed easily by acquisition and merger, by what Eucken called the bringing of many works under unified control (page 144 above). When such moves are undertaken the aspiration for material prosperity usually is also invoked. It is a case of rationalization, of making better use of scarce management talents, of the need to remain efficient and so on. Of course, people are also making a living and building up careers. Furthermore, it may be, as Knight suggested, that business often takes on the character of a game in which the winner's prize is 'power and prestige'.[304] But Knight, as we saw (page 118 above), also pointed out that action cannot easily be traced to a single motive, and, in any case, sincerity is not the issue. The aspiration for material prosperity makes such exercises possible because it makes them respectable in a way in which playing games with the means to other people's livelihood would not.

Here is one area where the aspiration for material prosperity considered in isolation runs counter to individualist values and the ideal of broad-based competitive enterprise. Conditions arise which do not favour the operation of the micro constraint. Advances in technology and the accumulation of capital affect the options open to ordinary people. In so far as production processes increasingly require highly specialized knowledge and skills, the number of options open to them is reduced, not necessarily because they have no skills but because it is difficult to be skilled at more than one or two tasks. In so far as production processes require operatives without any skills whatsoever, the number of options open to them is actually increased, but only at what is commonly regarded as the lowest level of economic activity. When goods and even services once produced on a small scale are increasingly mass produced at low unit costs by specialized machinery, and when the specialized machinery itself requires an ever-greater capital outlay, independent enterprise as an alternative to employment becomes ever-more remote.

As a consumer the ordinary person enters into market relations, even if at fixed prices. As a producer his economic initiative in most cases is confined to finding himself a place within the command hierarchy of some organization. Thereafter, his productive activity is laid out for him by the particular oligarchs he falls under, while his personal interest and ambitions are orientated towards the politics of the command hierarchy and the chance of rising through the ranks to become an oligarch himself. (Smith had reservations about the nascent joint-stock company of his time on grounds similar to these – see page 36 above.) For purposes of understanding the problems of economic order in a world in which control of capital is vested in ever-fewer hands, rather too sharp a distinction is made between big business and government, between the private and the public sector, between private and public ownership and between the capacity and the legal right to coerce and lay down rules. From the point of view of the ordinary person, decisions that affect him and his beneficiary rights are made in remote quarters and whether these quarters are officially located in the private or the public sector can in most cases make little practical difference.

Whether the majority would have the inclination for independent enterprise if it were easier, or whether it ever was easier, is beside the point here. The point is that the interplay of attitudes does not form a coherent whole. On the one hand, the conduct of affairs is guided by an ideal of economic order that presupposes broad-based enterprise. On the other hand, ordinary people often see themselves in the position of passive onlookers who wait for the initiative of those in positions of economic and political power rather as farmers may wait for rain. The contrast between Smith's vision of market order and present attitudes is brought out clearly when one looks at the remark he made immediately after he used the invisible-hand expression. 'What is the species of domestic industry which his capital can employ, and of which the produce is likely to be of the greatest value, every individual, it is evident, can, in his local situation judge much better than any statesman or lawgiver can do for him.'[305]

The present attitude is almost the antithesis of this: the best that the man in the street can do with spare funds in his local situation is to pass them on immediately to someone more qualified than he is to control capital.

The role of the aspiration for material prosperity in the evolution of a high-technology economy and of an economic oligarchy of big business and government, with the restrictions they place on the options open to ordinary people, i.e. on the working of the micro constraint, is only one factor one might consider for an intelligible account of the dualism that has appeared in many countries. One might also look at the question of credit. With regard to material prosperity and the creation of employment opportunities, there is much to be said for credit. It would be very unfortunate if an enterprising scheme backed by the necessary skills and talents were hampered by a lack of finance or high interest rates. In an economy in which many see themselves as passive onlookers, it would be a good thing if individuals who are impecunious but full of initiative could say to every Shylock that they have the option ultimately of the open credit window. But credit weakens the macro constraint which, as a necessary condition for the coordinating function of prices, is a necessary part of the free-market ideal.[306] The monetary authorities are supposed to be the guardians of this aspect of a free-market economy but the fact that their (in any case limited) control is discretionary implies that they are expected to bear various social interests in mind.

Rising prices can force consumers and the controllers of capital to change their plans only if their funds are limited and credit makes the limitation on funds flexible. Rising interest rates similarly can force them to change their minds only if the limitation on funds is not flexible. As a monetary policy measure for enforcing a macro constraint, they seem strangely to presuppose that the macro constraint is already in force. The function of the macro constraint is to make some courses of action impossible. In many cases, it should make it impossible for a manufacturer to adopt the latest technology and to mechanize and automate his production process accordingly. The macro constraint, according to the ideal, should force him to employ the unemployed instead. But credit lets him off the hook and ordinary people, whom the same advanced technology is steadily reducing to passive onlookers, can do nothing but look on passively.

What the absence of a macro constraint amounts to (in the limit) is that each economically active person can more or less go his own way without being affected by what others are doing. Eventually each in his own way will run into physical constraints, i.e. a scarcity of resources. But it would be pure chance if everyone did so at the same time and to the same extent. The pressure on resources, where it occurs, may often be reflected in rising prices, but a person who is determined enough to stick to his plans can borrow more to pay the higher prices, knowing he has enough customers who are equally determined to stick to their plans. Since this is unlikely to increase the quantity of scarce resources, a competitive bidding for resources may develop, but not necessarily for all resources; not, for instance, for all human resources. With little else to control it, the volume of credit, it seems, comes to be ruled by the expectations of borrowers, by their bouts of enthusiasm and depression. The economy becomes subject to waves of optimism and pessimism.

Eucken presumably had considerations of this kind in mind when he repeatedly stressed the need for monetary reform and considered 'the linking up of money and credit' to be an inadequate monetary system (pages 131 and 143 above); and Simons as well when he called quite simply for the abolition of private fractional-reserve banking (pages 37 and 136 above). Simons was probably correct that it is not possible to attain the ideal of market order with banking systems as they are found in most western countries. But that does not mean that with their well-nigh unimaginable abolition a macro constraint would automatically appear. If people want to give each other credit, the absence of banks need not stop them. In any case, there is the question of just what would be the *right* quantity of money and credit for a wholesome combination of coordination by prices, broad-based enterprise, growth of material prosperity, full employment and perhaps an equitable distribution of wealth and income. There does not appear to be an answer that has found wide acceptance. It is not even clear whether the question is posed in a sensible way. What is at issue is an impersonal constraint. When the classical writers took it for granted that money consisted of precious metals distinct from credit, the quantity of money was significant as a constraint because it was subject to physical limitations. But is there any significance in a quantity of credit which changes at the stroke of a pen or on a mere say-so? Instead of posing questions about the right quantity of credit money, it seems one should be asking how economic activity may be constrained impersonally so that a fair degree of coordination by prices is ensured and yet allowance is made for various other social interests.

It may be that money and credit were often kept distinct in the minds of writers on market order by the presupposition of a macro constraint in the form of full and immediate convertibility and a prudence on the part of lenders, a prudence born of mistrust. But such mistrust would have to be reinforced from time to time by bankruptcies and financial losses. These would create disruptions which would obviously run counter to so many interests, including that in material prosperity, that all sorts of institutions would be likely to arise, as in fact they have, which diminish the influence of mistrust in financial institutions as a form of control. We saw (page 36 above) that Adam Smith suggested a minor institutional compromise in this regard. As a form of the macro constraint, prudence born of mistrust is not in any way attuned to social interests other than that in coordination by prices. Suggestions about the appropriate kind of control (or the right quantity of money), e.g. how far it should be by impersonal constraint and how far by ad hoc administrative and political decision, may be expected to differ according to the particular combination of social intersets, aspirations and ideals which the person making the suggestion thinks should be taken into account.

Let us at this point introduce two further social aspirations which are quite likely to be found in the kind of society we have been describing. They are implied in the first sentence of Keynes's concluding notes on the social philosophy towards which the *General Theory* might lead: 'The outstanding faults of the economic society in which we live are its failure to provide for full employment and its arbitrary and inequitable distribution of wealth and incomes.'[307] One may take it that for Keynes a well-ordered society, or in his case a well-run society,[308] would not fail in these respects. The appropriate form of coordination and control Keynes had in mind is geared to serve the aspiration for full employment. But he thought it would also serve, as a kind of by-product, the aspiration for a more equitable distribution of wealth and income. Apart from having shown that savings out of the 'superfluity' of the rich were not needed in conditions where unemployment prevailed, he had also shown that 'we might aim in practice (there being nothing in this which is unattainable) at an increase in the volume of capital until it ceases to be scarce, so that the functionless investor will no longer receive a bonus'. Keynes referred to this aim rather felicitously as 'the euthanasia of the rentier' and more harshly as 'the euthanasia of the cumulative oppressive power of the capitalist to exploit the scarcity-value of capital'.[309] The same form of control which would ensure full employment, and by the same token would be in the interests of material prosperity, would 'within a single generation' or 'within one or two generations' make 'capital-goods so abundant that the marginal efficiency of capital is zero'.[310] Interest payments would then be a thing of the past and that of course would make the rich less rich.

The reasoning is something like the following: everything is produced by labour aided by capital equipment and natural resources. The 'only reason why an asset offers a prospect of yielding during its life services having an aggregate value greater than its initial supply price is because it is *scarce*'[311] and capital assets remain scarce because psychological and institutional factors prevent the rate of interest from falling to zero. But where the State provided appropriate inducements to invest, capital would eventually cease to be scarce. The expected return (not discounted) on a capital asset over its life would just cover the labour costs incurred in its production, the costs of entrepreneurial skill and supervision and an allowance for risk.[312] One may still wonder why the scarcity of capital should vanish so quickly. In his last mention of the matter in the *General Theory*, Keynes said: 'I feel sure that the demand for capital is strictly limited in the sense that it would not be difficult to increase the stock of capital up to a point where its marginal efficiency had fallen to a very low figure.'[313]

Keynes was interested in the short run and for the short run it is entirely reasonable to presume that labour and capital equipment are more or less *complementary* inputs rather than *substitutes*. The demand for capital is then strictly limited. A stage would soon be reached where in full employment the production of more capital equipment would be pointless since there would be no one to operate the equipment and therefore no one would be prepared to pay for the finance to produce it. But is it reasonable to extend this thinking to the longer period of time over which the euthanasia of the rentier is to take place? Keynes did provide some discussion of the matter, but by the way he expressed himself – 'I should guess that', 'If I am right in supposing' and 'I feel sure that' – he seemed to acknowledge that it was at least debatable.[314]

An observer of the current scene surely may conclude that capital and labour are not always complementary. Robots assembling motor cars, computers cutting out the typesetter between the writer and the printing press, and a host of other cases surely justify the conclusion that newly created capital equipment more often than not is a substitute for labour. Furthermore, it is also just what one would expect. The major part of investment is in the hands of comparatively few controllers of capital whose own employment is not easily automated. Credit, with some recent exceptions, is intentionally made cheap – where there is high inflation it may in effect cost nothing – whereas labour has to be paid what by general estimation is a decent wage and unionized labour may often be a nuisance and worse. The most profitable course under these circumstances is to substitute uncomplaining equipment for workers. For the developers of new technology the most profitable course then is to cater for the demand for equipment that replaces labour. It is in both cases the correct thing to do in an economy taken to be ordered on free-market lines. One has to say 'taken to be' because market order would require an effective macro constraint which would make the substitution of capital equipment for labour more difficult. By the same token it would also hinder the drive for progress and so has more or less been done away with.

The logic of Keynes's prescription remains intact when labour and capital equipment are substitutes rather than complements, but a serious complication arises. Economics has a long tradition of allaying Luddite fears with the assurance that displaced labour will be re-employed somewhere else, so that everyone benefits from the greater productivity achieved with labour-saving equipment. Even in a world in which robots and computers assemble motor cars and are themselves possibly made by more robots and computers, there is still a need somewhere along the line for the human services of those in one or other occupation. Every boom shows up, by the mad tussle and bidding for certain workers, which occupations they are at that stage, though with technical progress going on apace, they may be different occupations in every-successive boom. If all those other than the oligarchs and their lieutenants could somehow keep on changing occupations and manage to jockey themselves into occupations currently in demand and if government provided the right Keynesian inducements to invest, then indeed cornucopia could be ours.

Progress would be far more dazzling than would have been possible under market order, for there everyone would from time to time be compelled to change plans and adjustment would be widespread and slow. But in a world of oligarchs, passive onlookers and credit money such coordination worked very poorly. It has been replaced, it appears, by a system in which the oligarchs are relieved of the burden of adjustment, which has been shifted into an area where adjustment is least likely to be forthcoming. The controllers of capital may concentrate on forging ahead and creating progress unhindered by a lack of finance, while all the rest, since few have the option of making use of such skills as they have in independent enterprise, are expected to scramble and keep up with the pace as best as they can, even if it means changing occupations and skills several times in the course of a working life. Since not even the exigencies of deprivation and destitution seem capable of provoking that kind of adjustment, the ideals of a compassionate society come into play, especially where affluence makes compassion affordable. Social security and other welfare benefits take the edge off the need to adjust and the effort is hardly made anymore. The situation is bearable but not pleasant. Here at last ordinary people have a role to play, at least in some countries, and they play it with abandon. They may vote for someone who promises to keep prices down and the next time around for someone who promises to create jobs. The economy gets periodic shots in the arm in the form of inducements to invest and above all low interest rates. They start the mad tussle and bidding for some workers, draw in a few marginal onlookers and create hardly a stir among the rest. And that is our account of dualism: while some are engaged in feverish activity, others are languishing in limbo.

There are some who will say that Keynes did not go far enough. The 'forces of production' have outrun the 'relations of production' and market order has outserved its usefulness. The interests of material prosperity, full employment and equitable incomes would be better served if a Caesar came to rule with a retinue of planners, provided he shared these aspirations. But however it is explained away, the evidence seems to be unfavourable. The Caesars who appear at present to be approaching from the direction of Moscow have not, even by their own standards, done too well at home. In any case, present western societies are far more socialistic than the society of capital concentration Marx probably had in mind, the society of a rentier class Keynes must have known in his younger days and the stationary state Smith described. The beneficiary rights held through pension funds, life assurance policies, deposits of various kinds, mutual funds and small share portfolios must account for a substantial part of the total. In most countries, moreover, those who hold no beneficiary rights through any of these channels nevertheless draw their beneficiary payments, their share of the product, through social security allocations, free or subsidized food, education and health services, and in the form of other social welfare benefits, not to mention what is for many a free infrastructure. We are all rentiers now. This observation also has a bearing on recent reassertions of individualist values. It seems that the present state of western societies is so far removed from an individualist market order that its mere reassertion as an ideal can make little difference.

One may believe that, for the sake of the good health of the entire society, we should all be thrown in at the deep end and left to sink or swim. But in the event we can neither sink nor swim because there is no water in the pool.

10.3.4. Ideal order and actual disorder

The account we have given of these familiar issues was based on impressions and even these were exaggerated so that the point could be made. The main purpose, however, was not to make this point but to illustrate the principle of a study of economic disorder. We still have to say something about the rationale of looking for economic disorder rather than for economic order. Let us lead into the question as follows.

Shackle has said that in the *General Theory* Keynes enunciated an economics of disorder which was 'not intellectually acceptable' to those trained in the economics of order. 'A theory of unemployment is, necessarily, inescapably, a theory of disorder. The disorder in question is the basic disorder of uncertain expectation, the essential disorder of the real, as contrasted with the conventionally pretended, human condition.' In stating the grounds for unemployment, Keynes had denied 'the orderliness of economic society and economic life, and to deny this life the attribute of orderliness was to seem to deny the study of it the attributes of science'.[315]

Shackle had in mind only the disorder emanating from uncertainty and ignorance of the future. But Keynes seemed to extend this kind of disorder to the kind we have been concerned with. Speculation on Wall Street, for example, was held up against the conventionally pretended function and 'proper social purpose' of capital markets. 'When the capital development of a country becomes a by-product of the activities of a casino, the job is likely to be ill-done.'[316] One might say therefore that the economists Keynes was arguing against were really describing an ideal of economic order while he was trying to describe the 'essential disorder' of reality, though none of the parties appear to have seen it that way.

There are now so many Keynes interpretations that one would have to be brave to say this is the correct one. In so far as Keynes presented a model and in so far as there are Keynesian models, another type of interpretation is possible. According to it, Keynes started from the premise that scientific study does indeed discern if not orderliness, then at least coherent systems. The classical economists simply had not discovered the true system of the economy, but it was possible to construct models which give us a much truer picture of the actual system of the economy.

These two types of interpretation differ in that they ascribe to Keynes different presuppositions about the nature of economic order. The difference between them is fundamental. Ultimately we have been concerned throughout this study with two contrary premises on which thought about economic order is based. There is what we may call the *subjective premise*. It is something like the following. Human beings manifestly are able to think up systems of ideas of varying degrees of coherence. In so far as they manage to order their affairs, albeit only tacitly, according to one or a few coherent systems of ideas, one may expect to find a degree of order in social and economic affairs and such order usually becomes institutionalized. But social and economic order goes no further than that. Since the systems of ideas human beings think up are not always coherent, since there are rival systems and since new ones appear from time to time, the actual state of affairs is not likely to be very orderly. There is also the *objective premise*. According to it, there is an order, or at least a coherent system, in social and economic affairs irrespective of what human beings may be thinking about.

The idea of the natural order is based on the objective premise but is obscure and difficult because a distinction is made between man and nature, so that man may obstruct and break the natural order. The idea of spontaneous order is difficult because it appears to be based on the subjective premise but somehow seems to end up as a version of the objective premise.[317] The simplest version of the objective premise is that there is system in everything because everything operates according to law and therefore the economy, like everything else, makes up a coherent system. This is no doubt an ancient presupposition but has probably been reinforced over the past three centuries by the remarkable findings in astronomy and celestial mechanics. Laplace captured the spirit of the *système du monde* in a famous passage.

> Given for one Instant an intelligence which could comprehend all the forces by which nature is animated and the respective situation of the beings who compose it … it would embrace in the same formula the movements of the greatest bodies of the universe and those of the lightest atom; for it, nothing would be uncertain and the future, as the past, would be present to its eyes. The human mind offers, in the perfection which it has been able to give to astronomy, a feeble idea of this intelligence. Its discoveries in mechanics and geometry, added to that of universal gravity, have enabled it to comprehend in the same analytical expression the past and future states of the system of the world. Applying the same method to some other objects of its knowledge, it has succeeded in referring to general laws observed phenomena and in foreseeing those which given circumstances ought to produce.

> The regularity which astronomy shows us in the movements of the comets doubtless exists also in all phenomena.[318]

It would seem that this passage by Laplace expresses the spirit in which model construction is pursued in economics. It articulates the normally unarticulated premise on which economic models are based. Economic models are meant to be analytical expressions of the system of the economy. It is not an unduly restrictive presupposition. But it does, as an article of faith, exclude one possibility a priori, namely the possibility that there is no coherent system in social and economic affairs. It excludes from possible consideration what to Shackle and others is the 'essential disorder' in human affairs.

If one's purpose truly is to find out, analyse and understand, it seems that one should try not to exclude any possibilities simply as an article of faith. In this respect the subjective premise seems to be the better basis for inquiry. It presumes less, and incoherence as well as complete coherence and order in human affairs are compatible with it. However, what is the function of a coherent system of ideas, i.e. of theory, when the subjective premise is the basis of inquiry? As argued throughout this study and as seems to follow from the subjective premise, the situation is the following.

Theory has the function of articulating the generally ill-articulated guiding conceptions by which people try to impose some order on social and economic affairs. In performing this function, theory is clearly in the service of various sets of values and, when inconsistencies are laid bare, the theorist may find himself at least posing questions about what ought to be. The theorist may prefer the passive role of merely describing what is the case. On the basis of the subjective premise, however, he cannot simply turn a guiding conception into a description, as appears to have happened in the case of equilibrium theory, because that presumes that there is only one, and moreover a successfully applied, guiding conception and excludes disorder from possible consideration.

On the other hand, analysis can proceed only by systematizing. We cannot, it seems, grasp pure confusion and chaos. To establish and ascertain what is the case, we need a system of ideas. Theory accordingly may be used as a heuristic device, as we called it earlier. Incoherence becomes apparent as a deviation from a coherent system of ideas. But aberrations are not necessarily intelligible. For an intelligible account of economic disorder, the separation in analysis of distinct guiding conceptions incorporating ideals becomes significant exactly because all ideals play in the same arena, because they are found cheek by jowl in the same world, a world, moreover, in which there are also ineluctable physical constraints. Incoherence is to be grasped by the interplay of coherent systems of ideas.

It may be that one of the features which apparently makes Marxian analysis intellectually attractive to many people is that it, like its Hegelian parent, offers a study of social disorder based on a form of the objective premise. There is the sanctuary of a monumental and rather ponderous metaphysical system, the comfort and assurance of a system apparently more real than the mere systems of ideas men think up. At the same time, the analysis of 'contradictions' seems to get to the heart of the essential disorder of which we are all vaguely aware. The disorder in human affairs always assumes the guise of class conflict, a slant and bias imparted by the metaphysical system. Nevertheless, despite the potential austerity of a view of historical forces sweeping mankind along on their inevitable course, Marxian analysis manages to capture the human interest and vitality also to be found in the *Wealth of Nations*.

Similarly, the free-market dogmatist has the confidence gained from the assurance of a natural or spontaneous order and in his case the disorder in economic affairs always assumes the guise of government intervention, a bias imparted by the mystique of his metaphysics. For some this also has human interest and vitality, that, in fact, which conventional opinion ascribes to Smith's book. But equilibrium theory, which also may claim a fairly direct descent from Adam Smith, has a bias imparted to it by its particular version of the *système du monde* which has all but removed the last vestiges of the human interest and vitality with which the whole story started.

In this respect equilibrium theory fails modern society. In the remarks with which he concluded the *General Theory*, it may be remembered, Keynes said that 'the ideas of economists and social philosophers, both when they are right and when they are wrong, are more powerful than is commonly understood', that 'the world is ruled by little else', but that 'there are not many who are influenced by new theories after they are twenty-five or thirty years of age'.[319] If Keynes was right, the impressions which theories make on the earnest and idealistic among students – it is they who will propagate ideas – will have an overriding influence on the shape of the society into which we are steadily moving. But people at that age have perhaps not lived long enough to realize that the state of social conflict is probably much as it has always been. To them it must seem that the world is full of burning questions and to them it must also seem that all the equilibrium theorists are fiddling like Nero. They come to humour equilibrium theory as stuff for passing examinations while they regard the Marxian analysis as the real stuff. When they reach this point, in all probability they are pounced upon by political predators dressed up as economic holy men. But political predators have it almost all their own way. Apart from some free-market dogmatists, there are very few in the ranks of economic theorists to gainsay them. The equilibrium theorist has quite voluntarily withdrawn from the arena of theory where the blood and guts of social life is discussed. No doubt he is able to make an occasional remark, like any intelligent bystander – but no more than that, because his chosen job is to work on Pareto's analogue of celestial mechanics.

Notes

N.B. Italics in a quotation are in the original unless otherwise indicated.

[1] Friedman 1980, pp 330–59.
[2] Attitudes to free enterprise in free markets may of course also be characterized in other ways. A romantic attitude seems to be very common. The successful entrepreneur is an admired figure rather like the successful warrior of an earlier age.
[3] Rothbard 1970, p 45.
[4] *An Inquiry into the Nature and Causes of the Wealth of Nations* (hereafter W.N.) 437–8.
[5] Ferguson 1767, pp 204–5.
[6] W.N. 339–40.
[7] W.N. 529–30.
[8] W.N. 539.
[9] W.N. 684.
[10] W.N. 128.
[11] W.N. 66–7.
[12] W.N. 98.
[13] W.N. 492.
[14] W.N. 142.
[15] W.N. 342.
[16] W.N. 620.
[17] W.N. 745.
[18] W.N. 668.
[19] W.N. 734–5. various writers have commented on this passage. See, for example, Rosenberg 1965 and Weiss 1976, especially pp 106–7. Weiss specifically compares Smith's and Marx's views on the matter.
[20] Schumpeter 1954, p 107. Schumpeter discusses many aspects of natural law. See especially pp 107–42.
[21] Locke 1690, Book II, Chapter V, 'Of Property', pp 129–41. For example: 'Thus this law of reason makes the deer that Indian's who hath killed it …' (p 131).
[22] W.N. 47.
[23] Robbins 1952, p 47.
[24] Robbins 1952, pp 34–5.
[25] W.N. 642.
[26] Smith 1759, pp 184–5.
[27] W.N. 651.
[28] Stewart 1793, pp 67–8.
[29] On this see, for instance, Chalk 1951.
[30] See Rosenberg 1960. Rosenberg argues that Smith was concerned with the welfare implications of different kinds of institutional arrangements.

31 Stewart 1793, p 12.
32 Viner 1928, pp 120, 126 and 138. Viner devoted the entire paper to the differences in the respects mentioned between Smith's two major works.
33 W.N. 128–9.
34 W.N. 126 and 428–9.
35 W.N. 67.
36 W.N. 308. The paper money issue is discussed on pp 306–13.
37 W.N. 308.
38 W.N. 713–16.
39 W.N. 605. 'It is a very singular government in which every member of the administration wishes to get out of the country, and consequently to have done with the government, as soon as he can, and to whose interest, the day after he has left it and carried his whole fortune with him, it is perfectly indifferent though the whole country was swallowed up by an earthquake.'
40 W.N. 710. 'It gives him a share, though not in the plunder, yet in the appointment of the plunderers of India.'
41 The tract dates from 1934 and appears in Simons 1948, pp 40–77. See especially pp 42 and 56–60.
42 Schumpeter 1942, p 142.
43 W.N. 605–6.
44 See, for instance, 'Ludwig van Mises and the Market Process' in Lachmann 1977, pp 181–93.
45 W.N. 553–5.
46 Smith 1756, p 251.
47 W. N. 47.
48 W.N. 47–9.
49 W.N. 99. Similar expressions without reference to a 'natural course' appear on pp 56 and 62.
50 W.N. 356–60.
51 W.N. 128.
52 W.N. 359.
53 W.N. 362–5 and 392–4.
54 W.N. 71–3.
55 W.N. 95.
56 Buchanan 1976, p 274.
57 Robbins 1952, pp 46–8 and 176–8.
58 Robbins 1952, pp 2 and 48.
59 Robbins 1952, p 48.
60 Robbins 1952, pp 56–7.
61 Buchanan 1976, p 272. 'Is Rothbard the modern analogue to Adam Smith? Little or no exegesis is required to answer such a question emphatically in the negative' (p. 273).
62 Rothbard 1970, p 196.
63 Rothbard 1970, p 180.
64 Rothbard 1970, p 1. See also pp 176–7 and 197.
65 Rothbard 1970, p 6.
66 Rothbard 1970, Chapter 1 is devoted to explaining this scheme.
67 Rothbard 1970, p 4.
68 Rothbard 1970, p 5.
69 Rothbard 1970, pp 181 and 197.

70 *Leviathan*, Part I, Chapter 13.

71 Friedman 1980, pp 44–5. Scientific knowledge and the structure of scientific disciplines is given as another example.

72 Hayek has intimated that he borrowed the term 'rule of conduct' from David Hume.

73 Ryle 1949, pp 25–61.

74 Polanyi 1958, Part 2, pp 69–245.

75 'Rules, Perception and Intelligibility' in Hayek 1967, pp 43–65. See especially pp 45–6.

76 For instance, Hayek 1967, pp 60–3, Hayek 1973, pp 17–19 and 29–31 and Hayek 1979, pp 156–8.

77 'The Result of Human Action but not of Human Design' in Hayek 1967, pp 96–105; quote on p 97. The title of this article is an adaptation of an expression used by Adam Ferguson (see note 80 below).

78 Mandeville 1714 is a witty elaboration of the theme in question here and was influential in the history of economic thought. See also Hayek's essay 'Dr Bernard Mandeville' in Hayek 1984, pp 176–94.

79 See Hayek 1949, pp 7–8; Hayek 1967, pp 76–8 and 99–105; Hayek 1984, p 319. Hayek says that the idea also came to economics via Menger and, through him, from Savigny's historical approach to jurisprudence. See Menger 1883, pp 139–83.

80 Ferguson 1767, p 205. After the last word quoted here ('design'), Ferguson made a laconic footnote reference to 'De Retz Memoirs'. Cardinal de Retz was an aristocrat involved in various rebellions against the French monarchy and the dirigisme of its ministers. He lived from 1613 to 1679.

81 This is a theme in many of Hayek's writings. Its most uncompromising exposition is to be found in the Epilogue to Volume 3 of Law, Legislation and Liberty (Hayek 1979, pp 153–176).

82 Hayek 1973, pp 22–4.

83 Hayek 1973, p 11.

84 The terms are used in many of Hayek's writings and in nearly all his more recent writings. For expositions of constructivism, see Hayek 1973, pp 5–34 and 'Individualism: True and False' in Hayek 1949, pp 1–32 or Hayek 1984, pp 131–59.

85 Hayek 1973, p 17; Hayek 1979, p 156.

86 Hayek 1973, p 18.

87 Hayek 1979, p 157.

88 Hayek 1973, p 17.

89 Hayek 1973, pp 25–6.

90 Buchanan and Tullock 1962, p 306.

91 Hayek 1973, p 41.

92 Hayek 1973, p 45.

93 Hayek 1973, p 51.

94 Hayek 1976, p 128.

95 Eucken 1951, p 96.

96 Eucken 1951, p 27.

97 Eucken 1940, pp 34–44.

98 Hayek 1979, pp 159–61. See also 'Notes on the Evolution of Systems of Rules of Conduct' in Hayek 1967, pp 66–81.

99 Hayek 1976, pp 133–5 and Hayek 1979, pp 165–8.

100 Hayek 1979, p 160.

101 Hayek 1973, p 65.
102 Hayek ends the Epilogue to Volume 3 of *Law, Legislation and Liberty* (1979, p 176) with the words: 'In concluding this epilogue I am becoming increasingly aware that it ought not to be that but rather a new beginning. But I hardly dare hope that for me it can be so.' Characteristic of the 'new beginning' are: (a) 'The Origins and Effects of Our Morals : A Problem for Science' (Hayek 1984, pp 318–30), (b) *Evolution und Spontane Ordnung* (Hayek 1983a), (c) 'The Rules of Morality are not the Conclusions of Our Reason', a lecture delivered at the 12th International Conference on the Unity of the Sciences in 1983. The present writer is very grateful to Prof Lachmann for making this material available to him. Hayek's forthcoming book *The Fatal Conceit* will presumably set out the new ideas more fully.
103 Hayek 1979, p 176.
104 Hayek 1984, p 325. See note 102 above for the title of this lecture.
105 'Economics and Knowledge' in Hayek 1949, pp 33–56 (*Economica* 4 n.s. 1937, pp 33–54); 'The Use of Knowledge in Society' in Hayek 1949, pp 77–91 (*American Economic Review* 35 September 1945, pp 519–30).
106 'Competition as a Discovery Procedure' in Hayek 1984, pp 254–65. The paper was previously published in German (Freiburger Studien, Tübingen) in 1969.
107 Hayek 1973, p 45.
108 Hayek 1984, pp 324–5.
109 This is the point made in the paper 'The Origins and Effects of our Morals: A Problem for Science' (Hayek, 1984). It is spelt out even more explicitly in the other two papers mentioned in note 102 above.
110 Hayek 1984, pp 322ff *passim*.
111 Hayek 1983a, pp 23 and 29. See note 102 above.
112 Hayek 1979, pp 169–75.
113 Hayek 1984, p 326.
114 Hahn 1981, p 123.
115 Bastiat 1848, pp 129–30.
116 Bastiat 1848, p 129.
117 W.N. 420 and 429.
118 W.N. 126.
119 W.N. 612.
120 W.N. 250.
121 W.N. 125.
122 W.N. 95.
123 W.N. 576–7.
124 W.N. 423.
125 W.N. 421.
126 W.N. 456. 'By advantage or gain, I understand, not the increase of the quantity of gold and silver, but that of the exchangeable value of the annual produce of the land and labour of the country, or the increase of the annual revenue of its inhabitants.'
127 Commons 1924, pp 225ff; Commons 1934, pp 27–40. Commons argued Locke's treatises on government (Locke 1690) incorporated the same idea.
128 Ricardo 1817, p 184 (Chapter 20).
129 Mill 1848, p 141 (Book IV, Chapter VII, para 7).
130 W.N. 336.
131 W.N. 532.
132 W.N. 249–50.

[133] W.N. 250.

[134] W.N. 602–3.

[135] W.N. 249.

[136] W.N. 463.

[137] W.N. 402.

[138] W.N. 461.

[139] W.N. 250.

[140] W.N. 438.

[141] W.N. 438.

[142] Article on individualism in the Micropaedia.

[143] Hollis and Nell 1975, Chapters 8 and 9 *passim*. The quotations are from pp 210, 216 and 259.

[144] Schumpeter 1954, pp 188–9.

[145] Hollander 1973, pp 117–24 and 134–43.

[146] Schumpeter 1954, pp 60–1, 93–9; Hollander 1973, pp 27–51.

[147] Walras was as eager as Jevons to promote mathematical analysis in economics. But it will be argued below that the ultimate purpose Walras had in mind for the mathematical analysis of interrelated markets was the one stated here. His paper of 1873 presaging the *Eléments* was entitled 'Principe d'une théorie mathématique de l'échange'. Jaffé (1971, p 115) has said of it: 'The paper opened with a statement of the relation of pure economics to applied economics, pointing out that before we can weigh the relative merits of *laissez-faire, laissez-passer* on grounds of efficiency or justice, we must first investigate "the natural and necessary" consequences of free competition in exchange and production.' See also Jaffé 1980.

[148] Jaffé 1971, especially pp 121–32; Jaffé 1976, pp 513–16.

[149] According to Jaffé (1977b), Walras did not see it this way. 'Why did Léon Walras stubbornly refuse to open his eyes to so many resemblances between himself and Adam Smith? The only explanation I can offer lies in his fanatical anglophobia … for the whole Walras family everything across the Channel betokened "perfidious Albion".'

[150] Walras 1874/7, para 221, p 255. As Walras sets them out in this place, the conditions for (individual) utility maximization could also serve as the conditions for Smith's natural prices.

[151] Walras 1874 /7, para 222, pp 255–6.

[152] Walras 1874/7, para 223, pp 256–7.

[153] Jaffé (1977a, p 371) quotes Baumol as noting this difficulty and Baumol remarked that Wicksell did also. It appears from certain remarks made by Walras and from his comments on some analysis by Gossen that the 'certain conditions' with which Walras always qualified the maximization of individual utilities are those of commutative justice or justice in exchange. (Jaffé 1977a is devoted to this issue, Jaffé 1980 takes it further.) This restricts the analysis by definition to market order or at least to just or natural prices (see p 46 of the text) and Walras's general equilibrium analysis is thus still in the same tradition as that of the Scholastics and Smith. But more of this later (Section 8.4.1). See also note 150 above.

[154] Walras 1874 /7, paras 3–5, pp 51–4. See also Jaffé 1977b, pp 21–3.

[155] Walras 1874/7, paras 6–8, pp 54–6.

[156] Walras 1874/7, para 30, pp 70–2.

[157] Walras 1874/7, para 9, p 56.

[158] Schumpeter 1949, pp 119–20.

[159] Schumpeter 1949, p 119.

160 Schumpeter 1949, p 130.

161 Pareto 1900 and Pareto 1901. Croce's general point was that the term 'economic action' implied a value such as whether something had been done correctly or not. It was open to approbation or disapprobation. Croce of course was not a positivist.

162 Pareto 1900, pp 182–3.

163 Pareto 1900, p 184.

164 Pareto 1900, p 187.

165 Pareto 1901, p 203.

166 Pareto 1901, p 204.

167 Pareto 1901, p 205.

168 Pareto 1901, p 206.

169 Pareto 1901, p 207.

170 Friedman 1953; Lipsey 1963.

171 This is how Walras saw the matter. (See p 48 of the text or, for instance, para 30 of the *Eléments* where Walras said that the pure theory of economics must precede applied economics.) However, the pure analysis of free competition is nevertheless the analysis of an ideal situation, in which, for instance, commutative justice prevails (see note 153 above). Jaffé (1980, p 530), commenting on Morishima's interpretation of Walras, said that Morishima 'got off on the wrong foot' in supposing that the ultimate aim of the *Eléments* 'was to construct a model, by the use of which we can examine how the capitalist system works'. Jaffé continued: 'That, I contend, was not the aim of the *Eléments*, either ultimate or immediate … The *Eléments* was intended to be and is, in all but the name, a realistic utopia, i.e. a delineation of a state of affairs nowhere to be found in the actual world, independent of time and place, ideally perfect in certain respects, and yet composed of realistic psychological and material ingredients.' Morishima (1980) disagreed, saying that Walras used the method of successive approximations (1980, p 552). This is also a 'realist' method (see p 89). That Walras's thought was ambiguous in this regard will be noted presently (p 97).

172 Lucas 1981, p 288.

173 W.N. 397.

174 For instance, Mises 1949, pp 13–14.

175 Hahn 1981, p 126.

176 Jaffé 1980, p 532. See also notes 153 and 171 above.

177 See Schumpeter 1954, pp 60–2, 93–4 and 112. Kirzner 1979, pp 209–11.

178 Jaffé 1980, pp 532–3. Original French on p 549.

179 Jaffé 1977a, p 380.

180 Walker 1984, p 446.

181 Jaffé 1980, pp 530 and 533.

182 Walras 1874/7, para 41, pp 83–4.

183 Walras 1874/7, paras 125–30, pp 169–72. See also Jaffé 1967.

184 Walras 1874 /7, p 37 and para 207, p 242. Walras 1874 /7 F, p VIII and para 207, pp 214–15.

185 Jaffé 1980, p 533.

186 W.N. 220–2. See also W.N. 148–9.

187 For instance, W.N. 466, 471 and 489.

188 W.N. 482–3. A similar statement appears at W.N. 473.

189 For instance, W.N. 238, 508, 576 and 785. '… a government which afforded to industry the only encouragement which it requires, some tolerable security that it shall enjoy the fruits of its own labour'. 'That security which the laws in Great

Britain give to every man that he shall enjoy the fruits of his own labour, is alone sufficient to make any country flourish …'

[190] See Jaffé 1980, pp 533–7. The exclusion of the entrepreneur from the formal equilibrium analysis seems to be due to the idea of commutative justice that has come down the centuries. Justice in exchange, we have noted, implies a definition of production. Entrepreneurial activity and the dealing it involves were not regarded as productive in the traditional view. Profits made by such activity would therefore violate the principle of equal values in exchange. In other words, entrepreneurs in the traditional view were something like wheeler-dealers engaging in what amounts to predatory activity.

[191] Walras 1874/7, para 188, p 225. '… with exchange and production in a state of equilibrium we may abstract, if not from *numéraire*, at least from money, provided that the land-owners, labourers and capitalists receive from the entrepreneurs a certain quantity of products in the form of rent, wages and interest in exchange for a certain quantity of productive services in the form of land-services, labour and capital-services. Assuming equilibrium, we may even go so far as to abstract from entrepreneurs and simply consider the productive services as being, in a certain sense, exchanged directly for one another, instead of being exchanged first against products, and then against productive services.' Unlike entrepreneurial activity, the demand for money does enter the equations of Walras's full general-equilibrium system and the interesting question is how Walras managed to deal with money at all in a static framework that did not allow for uncertainty. Jaffé (1980, pp 543–5) said he did it by assimilating money with circulating capital. The *encaisse désirée* provides a *service d'approvisionnement* in a spot cash economy in which receipts and payments are not synchronized so that money has to be held even though the dates of payments are perfectly known. This involves only a 'barren time' in which the data of the problem do not change and the analysis remains essentially timeless (Jaffé 1980, p 535). One may also consider Walras's monetary analysis important irrespective of how consistent it is with the general-equilibrium system. For instance, Marget (1935, pp 158–63), commenting on an early paper by Hicks in which the problem was raised, said that Walras might well have left money out of his equations on the grounds that there would be no demand for it. He continued: 'To his glory, he did nothing of the kind' and thus left powerful analytical techniques to posterity. In other words, bits and pieces of analytical technique pertaining to the vision accompanying the theory may be considered more important than the theory itself.

[192] For instance, Shackle 1972, pp 229–40.

[193] For instance, Simon 1978.

[194] Shackle's critique of rational determinacy (see note 192 above) is pertinent in this regard. It has been a theme in many of Shackle's writings over many years. Shackle 1958 and 1976 are good examples. Shackle 1972 contains perhaps the fullest discussion of the issue. Lachmann has often pursued a similar theme and many parts of his writings are relevant in this regard. See, for instance, Lachmann 1956, pp 20–34 and 1977, pp 65–93, 112–29 and 149–65.

[195] Robertson 1963, p 14.

[196] Lipsey 1963, pp 17–8, 19 and 26.

[197] In a commentary on a book by Stammler, Max Weber analysed very fully the various nuances of meaning that may be attached to terms such as *rule* and *regularity*. He used a very extensive analogy to the German card game Skat to make many of his points. See Weber 1907, pp 322–59.

[198] There is a short note on the dual sense of individualism as a method of analysis and as a norm for organizing society in Buchanan and Tullock 1962, pp 315–17. See also pp 3–39.

[199] Rothbard 1970, p 218.

[200] Rothbard 1970, p 196 and 1962, pp 880–1. The wording in the latter is slightly different.

[201] The social contract, however, is not usually understood in quite so literal a sense. Often it is merely a theoretical construct that serves certain heuristic purposes. See Buchanan and Tullock 1962, pp 305–22.

[202] 'Ethics and the Economic Interpretation' in Knight 1935, pp 19–40. See especially pp 33–4. Buchanan 1979, p 100.

[203] Hayek 1984, p 324.

[204] Hayek 1967, p 67.

[205] Polanyi 1958. See especially the chapter on 'Articulation', pp 69–131.

[206] Buchanan 1979, p 203.

[207] A fairly recent overview of Stoicism may be found in Sandbach 1975.

[208] Schumpeter 1954, p 112.

[209] Locke 1690, p 131.

[210] Rothbard 1970, p 174.

[211] Rothbard 1970, p 176.

[212] Rothbard 1970, p 1. Locke (1690, p 130) stated the basis of property as follows: 'Though the earth and all inferior creatures be common to all men, yet every man has a "property" in his own "person" … The "labour" of his body and the "work" of his hands, we may say, are properly his. Whatsoever, then, he removes out of the state that Nature hath provided and left it in, he hath mixed his labour with it, and joined to it something that is his own, and thereby makes it his property.'

[213] Rothbard 1970, p 172.

[214] Rothbard 1970, pp 168–71.

[215] Rothbard 1970, p 170.

[216] Hayek 1973, pp 20–1 and 82–5; 1976, pp 40–1 and 59–60.

[217] Hayek 1976, pp 59–60.

[218] Buchanan 1979, pp 274–5. Dr Pangloss is a character in *Candide* to whom Voltaire gave this kind of outlook.

[219] Hayek 1984, pp 353–6.

[220] Hayek 1984, p 354. That there is something strange about Hayek's apparent contention that spontaneous cultural evolution leads to a liberal order has been pointed out by various commentators. Gray (1980, p 120), for instance, set out to show inter alia 'that nothing in Hayek's argument supports the belief that a spontaneous order or cosmos in society must conform with the moral and political principles of classical liberalism'.

[221] Hayek 1984, p 330.

[222] This perception was articulated not at all vaguely by Schumpeter (1942, Part II), though he denied that there ever was a golden age of perfect competition.

[223] Hayek 1979, pp 56–9 and 105–27.

[224] He has written a paper under that title. Hayek 1984, pp 361–81.

[225] Hayek 1960, Postscript entitled 'Why I Am Not a Conservative', pp 397–411.

[226] Hayek 1984, pp 326 and 329.

[227] Hayek 1973, pp 55–6. He speaks there of 'the short formula by which I have repeatedly described the condition of freedom, namely a state in which each can use his knowledge for his purposes'.

228 See Hayek 1973, pp 35–84, especially pp 48–52; and 1984, pp 365–7.

229 Eucken 1951, pp 56–82, especially pp 64–8; Simons 1948, pp 53–6, 73–7 and 107–20. Simons seemed to object mainly to the idea that stabilization policy could take the place of the institutional reforms he thought were necessary.

230 Keynes 1936, p 379.

231 Eucken 1951, pp 65–6.

232 Friedman 1980, pp 47 and 50.

233 Menger 1883. The Third Book, pp 139–83, is devoted to the issue.

234 Eucken 1951, pp 31 and 84.

235 Hayek 1984, p 365.

236 Simons 1948, p 42.

237 Simons 1948, pp 1–4.

238 Simons 1948, pp 4, 27, 29–33 and 37.

239 Simons 1948, p 23.

240 Hayek 1973, pp 64–5.

241 Schumpeter 1942, p 308.

242 The profile will be based mainly on Eucken 1951. Eucken 1940 is about a method of institutional analysis which is applied to the question of economic policy in the later tract.

243 Eucken 1951, p 27.

244 Eucken 1940, see especially pp 34–44 and 117–273.

245 Eucken 1951, p 88.

246 Eucken 1951, p 95.

247 Eucken 1951, p 93.

248 Eucken 1951, p 29.

249 Eucken 1951, p 31.

250 Eucken 1951, p 31.

251 Eucken 1951, p 37.

252 Eucken 1951, p 95.

253 The quotations relating to full-employment policy were taken from Eucken 1951, pp 63, 65, 66–8 and 79–80.

254 Eucken 1951, pp 41–55. Quotation from p 49.

255 Simons 1948, p 38.

256 Eucken 1951, pp 54–5.

257 Eucken 1951, pp 94–5.

258 Eucken 1951, p 38.

259 Buchanan 1979, p 178.

260 Buchanan 1979, pp 178–9.

261 Buchanan 1979, pp 179 and 181.

262 Buchanan 1979, p 110. Hayek (1984, p 328) has this to say on the kind of sentiment expressed by Buchanan: 'The Fatal Conceit, which is the subject of the book on which I am working, is devoted precisely to refute the erroneous belief that *Man Bas Made Himself*'.

263 W.N. 507.

264 Jaffé 1980 and Morishima 1980. See also note 171 above and page 66 of the text.

265 The work of Thomas S Kuhn in particular has brought this aspect of science to the forefront of discussion. See Kuhn 1962, especially pp 176–98. The term 'growth of knowledge', however, is rather inappropriate in the case of Kuhn.

266 The term *wertfrei* seems to have become well known through its use by Max Weber. Weber 1904, written when Max Weber became one of the publishers

of the Archiv für Sozialwissenschaft und Sozialpolitik, sets out his views on the matter. Weber 1917 also deals with the topic, but is less relevant in the present context.

267 See Menger 1883, Book I, Chapters 1–3 and Appendixes III and IX; Walras 1874/7, Lessons 2–4.

268 Walras 1874/7, pp 71–2.

269 Mill 1843, Book VI, p 833.

270 Samuelson 1947, pp 8–9.

271 See, for instance, Lachmann 1977, pp 34, 156–7, 181–3 and 112–29. The present writer's discussion of the matter is Mittermaier 1986.

272 If the methods of neoclassical economics are not to be accepted uncritically, then this, it seems to the writer, is the strongest argument for them. It cannot really be refuted on logical grounds. The writer, however, is not aware of any publication in which the argument has been used. Hayek (1952, Chapter II) has dealt with the way science changes concepts. For example, '… what men know or think about the external world or about themselves, their concepts and even the subjective qualities of their sense perceptions are to Science never ultimate reality, data to be accepted … The concepts which men actually employ, the way in which they see nature, is to the scientist necessarily a provisional affair and his task is to change this picture, to change the concepts in use so as to be able to make more definite and more certain our statements about the new classes of events' [p 22.]. The picture which man has actually formed of the world and which guides him well enough in his daily life, his perceptions and concepts, are for Science not an object of study but an imperfect instrument to be improved' (p 23).

273 Mittermaier 1986.

274 Hayek 1952, p 31. The sentence immediately prior to the quotation reads: 'And it is probably no exaggeration to say that every important advance in economic theory during the last hundred years was a further step in the consistent application of subjectivism.' See also his article 'The Facts of the Social Sciences' in Hayek 1949, pp 57–76.

275 Hayek 1949, p 65.

276 The relation between language and scientific knowledge has been much investigated since the work of Wittgenstein and more recently Kuhn. A good survey of the new approach may be found in Phillips 1977, especially, for the present context, pp 74–92. Nagel 1945 deals with similar issues in the perspective of an older tradition.

277 Collingwood 1945, p 3.

278 Eratosthenes of Cyrene (c. 275–195 BC) who was the librarian of the great library in Alexandria. The method involved measuring the angle of shadows cast by sunlight at points some 800 km apart. The atomic theory was postulated by Leucippus and his pupil Democritus. They lived in the 5th and 4th centuries BC.

279 Cassirer 1910 describes in great detail the gradual change-over in the physical sciences from concepts of substance to functional or relational formulations.

280 Nagel (1945) mentions a number of examples of how physical theories were developed when specialized usages for ordinary words such as 'force' and 'energy' were specified. 'But perhaps the by now classical illustration of the rôle of explicitly formulated rules of usage in the development of physical theories is provided by relativity theory.' The ordinary word 'simultaneous' was applied 'to cover the temporal relations of events occurring under highly complex conditions. And shortly after the turn of the present century it was recognized that for this extended

application, the word was not defined at all, since it has no specified usage. The rest is well-known history, rules of usage for this word were carefully instituted and the physical theory of relativity was developed' (pp 61–2).

[281] Lachmann 1943, p 14.

[282] Lachmann 1970, pp 31 and 36.

[283] See Lachmann 1970, 'The Method of Interpretation', pp 17–48. The denotation of the word 'hermeneutics' has recently been extended to cover this method.

[284] In the case of Menger the matter is bedevilled by the fact that his Aristotelian presuppositions did not allow him to speak of conceptual schemes but rather of phenomenal forms (*Erscheinungsformen*). But these amount to concepts. In the Foreword to the *Grundsätze*, for instance, he said that reference to human free will may well be used to contest the 'Gesetzmässigkeit' (which may have a meaning of conformity to theoretical principles) of economic action ('wirtshaftliche Handlungen'), but never of the phenomena. It is the latter which are the objects of inquiry in economic theory (Menger 1871, p xlvii). He dedicated the *Grundsätze* to Roscher and ended the Foreword with a friendly greeting from Austria to the German historical economists to whose movement, he said, his attempted reform of the principles of economics belonged and on whose work it had been based (Menger 1871, pp xli and xlviii). His later altercations with these economists removed the friendliness but not the point he was making. In the *Untersuchungen* he said that historical inquiry was conducted by means of an understanding of phenomenal forms and even justified his position with a reference to Adam Smith's 'The History of Astronomy' (Menger 1883, pp 18–24). In this he was mistaken because Smith's stance there is that of David Hume rather than of Menger's version of Aristotle.

[285] Mises 1949 is really a long elaboration of this point.

[286] Hayek 1952, Chapter IV. The point about general equilibrium is made on p 43. See also Hayek 1967, 'The Theory of Complex Phenomena', pp 22–42.

[287] For a discussion of this, see Nagel 1961, pp 174–202. The question is raised briefly in Mittermaier 1986, p 245.

[288] Nagel 1945, p 62.

[289] Stigler and Becker 1977, p 76.

[290] Stigler and Becker 1977, p 89.

[291] The one-world-only assumption (which is made in all historical inquiry) is of course quite different from the point made earlier (pp 131–2 of the text) about subjective and physical domains of thought between which there are no cross-implications. Economic explanations usually involve concepts and words from both domains since economic affairs are conducted by physical beings in a single physical world. This is in fact what makes economic explanation so much more difficult than a purely physical explanation.

[292] Walras 1874/7, Lesson 16, para 162.

[293] Jaffé 1977a, p 385.

[294] The subheading of Hayek 1976 is 'The Mirage of Social Justice'. The quoted words are from Hayek 1979, pp 164–5.

[295] W.N., Book IV, Chapter IX. See especially pp 630 and 639.

[296] Hicks 1939, p 128.

[297] The quotation is from Kirzner 1979, p 215. Kirzner considers the entrepreneurial role understood in an arbitrage sense in relation to Nozick's entitlement theory of justice (pp 200–24). The question is similar to that raised in the text, except that we are concerned with what is considered just and Kirzner with what is

just. The entrepreneurial function may of course be regarded in other than an arbitrage sense.

[298] Lachmann 1963.

[299] Lachmann 1963, pp 66–9.

[300] Lachmann 1963, pp 69–75.

[301] Lachmann 1977, p 297.

[302] W.N. 72.

[303] Schumpeter 1942, pp 68 and 81.

[304] Knight 1935, pp 58–66. Quoted words on p 61.

[305] W.N. 423. See also pp 62 and 99 above.

[306] The macro constraint is of course a constraint and not a stimulus. It cannot by itself coordinate economic activity in the sense of bringing idle resources into production.

[307] Keynes 1936, p 372.

[308] Keynes speaks, for instance, of a 'properly run community' (1936, p 220).

[309] Keynes 1936, pp 372–3 and 376.

[310] Keynes 1936, pp 220–1 and 377.

[311] Keynes 1936, p 213. 'I sympathise, therefore, with the pre-classical doctrine that everything is produced by labour, aided by …' (p 213).

[312] Keynes 1936, pp 221 and 375.

[313] Keynes 1936, p 375.

[314] Keynes 1936, p 214: 'Some, probably most, lengthy processes would be physically very inefficient, for there are such things as spoiling or wasting with time. With a given labour force there *is* a definite limit to the quantity of labour embodied in roundabout processes which can be used to advantage. Apart from other considerations, there must be a due proportion between the amount of labour employed in making machines and the amount which will be employed in using them. The ultimate quantity of value will not increase indefinitely, relatively to the quantity of labour employed, as the processes adopted become more and more roundabout, even if their physical efficiency is still increasing.' The words quoted are from pp 220–1 and 375.

[315] Shackle 1967, pp 133–4.

[316] Keynes 1936, p 159.

[317] That institutions may and usually do arise without having been planned or designed by anyone is of course beyond question. What has been disputed in this study is that such institutions considered as a whole necessarily form a coherent system, as it would be asserted in the objective premise. It is also beyond question that adaptations and accommodations are made, again without an overall plan or design, in a process of social interaction (Section 4.3.2. above) in response to perceived disorder, among other reasons. Only the habit of thinking in terms of long-run equilibrium can make this into the objective premise by postulating a state in which all adaptations and accommodations have been made. But in the long run we are all dead and so we experience only the disorder. However, what was brought out in the course of this study is that the idea of spontaneous order may also be made to approximate the idea of the natural order by the ploy of ascribing whatever is considered sound to spontaneity and whatever is considered unfortunate to the foolishness of man.

[318] Laplace 1814 pp 4 and 6. Laplace was making the point that the gap which nevertheless exists between the human mind and the vast intelligence referred to makes a theory of probability essential.

[319] Keynes 1936, pp 383–4.

Bibliography of Works Cited

N.B. Works are identified by the year of first publication. (This has been done to avoid anachronisms.) The year of publication of the edition or imprint actually used is shown subsequently.

Bastiat, F. 1848. 'The Physiology of Plunder' in *Economic Sophisms*, pp 129–46. Translated and edited by A. Goddard. Princeton: van Nostrand, 1964.

Buchanan, J.M. 1976. 'Public Goods and Natural Liberty' in *The Market and the State: Essays in Honour of Adam Smith*, pp 271–86. Edited by T. Wilson and A.S. Skinner. Oxford University Press, 1976.

———. 1979. *What Should Economists Do?* Indianapolis: Liberty Press, 1979.

Buchanan, J. and Tullock, G. 1962. *The Calculus of Consent: Logical Foundations of Constitutional Democracy*. The University of Michigan Press, Ann Arbor Paperbacks, 1965.

Cassirer, E. 1910. *Substance and Function*. Translated by W.C. and M.C. Swabey from 'Substanzbegriff und Funktionsbegriff' in 1923. New York: Dover, 1953. (Bound in one volume with a translation of Cassirer's 'Zur Einstein'schen Relativitätstheorie', 1921.)

Chalk, A.F. 1951. 'Natural Law and the Rise of Economic Individualism in England'. *The Journal of Political Economy* 59 (Aug. 1951) 330–47.

Collingwood, R.G. 1945. *The Idea of Nature*. Oxford: Clarendon, 1945.

Commons, J. 1924. *Legal Foundations of Capitalism*. New York: Macmillan, 1924.

———. 1934. *Institutional Economics: Its Place in Political Economy*. Vol I. University of Wisconsin Press, 1961.

Eucken, W. 1940. *The Foundations of Economics: History and Theory in the Analysis of Economic Reality*. Translated from the 6th German edition by T.W. Hutchison. London: William Hodge, 1950.

———. 1951. *This Unsuccessful Age or The Pains of Economic Progress*. London: William Hodge, 1951.

Ferguson, A. 1767. *An Essay on the History of Civil Society*, 7th edition. Edinburgh: Bell & Bradfute, 1814.

Friedman, M. 1953. 'The Methodology of Positive Economics' in *Essays in Positive Economics*, pp 3–43. University of Chicago Press, 1953.

Friedman, M. and Friedman, R. 1980. *Free to Choose: A Personal Statement*. Harmondsworth: Penguin Books, 1980.

Gray, J.N. 1980. 'F.A. Hayek on Liberty and Tradition'. *The Journal of Libertarian Studies* 4 (Spring 1980) 119–37.

Hahn, F. 1981. 'General Equilibrium Theory' in *The Crisis in Economic Theory*, pp 123–38. Edited by D. Bell and I. Kristol. New York: Basic Books, 1981.

Hayek, F.A. 1949. *Individualism and Economic Order*. London: Routledge & Kegan Paul, 1949.

———. 1952. *The Counter-Revolution of Science: Studies on the Abuse of Reason*. London: Allen & Unwin and Glencoe, Illinois: The Free Press,, 1952. First published as two series of articles in *Economica* between 1941 and 1945.

———. 1960. *The Constitution of Liberty*. London: Routledge & Kegan Paul, 1960.

———. 1967. *Studies in Philosophy, Politics and Economics*. London: Routledge & Kegan Paul, 1967.

———. 1973. *Rules and Order*: Volume I of *Law, Legislation and Liberty: A New Statement of the Liberal Principles of Justice and Political Economy*. The University of Chicago Press, 1973.

———. 1976. *The Mirage of Social Justice*: Volume 2 of *Law, Legislation and Liberty: A New Statement of the Liberal Principles of Justice and Political Economy*. The University of Chicago Press, 1976.

———. 1979. *The Political Order of a Free People*: Volume 3 of *Law, Legislation and Liberty: A New Statement of the Liberal Principles of Justice and Political Economy*. The University of Chicago Press, 1979.

———. 1983a. *Evolution und Spontane Ordnung*. Lecture delivered in Zürich on 5 July 1983 at the invitation of, and published on behalf of, Bank Hoffman AG, Talstrasse 27 8001, Zürich.

———. 1983b. 'The Rules of Morality Are Not the Conclusions of Our Reason'. Twelfth International Conference on the Unity of the Sciences. 25 November, 1983, The Chicago Marriott Hotel.

———. 1984. *The Essence of Hayek*. Edited by C. Nishiyama and K.R. Leube. Stanford: Hoover Institution Press, 1984.

———. 1988. *The Fatal Conceit: The Errors of Socialsim*. *The Collected Works of Friedrich August Hayek*. *Volume I*. London: Routledge, edited by W.W. Bartley III.

Hicks, J.R. 1939. *Value and Capital: An Inquiry into Some Fundamental Principles of Economic Theory*. 2nd edition. Oxford: Clarendon, 1965.

Hollander, S. 1973. *The Economics of Adam Smith*. London: Heinemann, 1973.

Hollis, M. and Nell, E. 1975. *Rational Economic Man: A Philosophical Critique of Neo-Classical Economics*. Cambridge University Press, 1975.

Jaffé, W. 1967. 'Walras' Theory of Tâtonnement: A Critique of Recent Interpretations'. *Journal of Political Economy* 75 (Feb. 1967) 1–19.

———. 1971. 'Léon Walras's Role in the "Marginal Revolution" of the 1870s' in *The Marginal Revolution in Economics: Interpretation and Evaluation*. Papers presented at a conference held at the Villa Serbellione, Bellagio, Italy, 22–28 August 1971, pp 113–39. Edited by R.D. Collison Black, A.W. Coats and C.D.W. Goodwin. Durham: Duke University Press, 1973.

———. 1976. 'Menger, Jevons and Walras De-homogenized'. *Economic Inquiry* 14 (Dec. 1976) 511–24.

———. 1977a. 'The Normative Bias of the Walrasian Model: Walras versus Gossen'. *The Quarterly Journal of Economics* 91 (Aug. 1977) 371–87.

———. 1977b. 'A Centenarian on a Bicentenarian: Léon Walras's Eléments on Adam Smith's Wealth of Nations'. *The Canadian Journal of Economics* 10 (Feb.–Nov. 1977) 19–33.

———. 1980. 'Walras's Economics as Others See It'. *Journal of Economic Literature* 18 (June 1980) 528–49.

Keynes, J.M. 1936. *The General Theory of Employment Interest and Money*. London: Macmillan, 1957.

Kirzner, I.M. 1979. *Perception, Opportunity, and Profit: Studies in the Theory of Entrepreneurship*. University of Chicago Press, 1979.

Knight, F.H. 1935. *The Ethics of Competition and Other Essays*. London: Allen & Unwin, 1935.

Kuhn, T.S. 1962. *The Structure of Scientific Revolutions*, 2nd edition, with a Postscript – 1969. University of Chicago Press, 1970.

Lachmann, L.M. 1943. 'The Rôle of Expectations in Economics as a Social Science'. *Economica* N.S. 10 (Feb. 1943) 12–23. Also in Lachmann 1977, pp 65–80.

———. 1956. *Capital and Its Structure*, 2nd edition. Kansas City: Sheed Andrews and McMeel, 1978.

———. 1963. 'Wirtschaftsordnung und Wirtschaftliche Institutionen'. *Ordo* 14 (1963) 63–77.

———. 1970. *The Legacy of Max Weber*. London: Heinemann, 1970.

———. 1977. *Capital, Expectations, and the Market Process: Essays on the Theory of the Market Economy*. Edited by W.E. Grinder. Kansas City: Sheed Andrews and McMeel, 1977.

Laplace, P.S. 1814. *A Philosophical Essay on Probabilities*. Translated by F.W. Truscott and F.L. Emory. New York: Dover, 1951.

Lipsey, R.G. 1963. *An Introduction to Positive Economics*, 6th edition, paperback. London: Weidenfeld & Nicolson, 1983.

Locke, J. 1690. *Two Treatises of Civil Government*. London: Everyman's Library, 1970.

Lucas, R.E. 1981. *Studies in Business-Cycle Theory*. Oxford: Blackwell, 1981.

Mandeville, B. 1714. *The Fable of the Bees or Private Vices, Publick Benefits*. Edited by P. Harth. Harmondsworth: Penguin Books, 1970.

Marget, A.W. 1935. 'The Monetary Aspects of the Walrasian System'. *The Journal of Political Economy* 43 (Apr. 1935) 145–86.

Menger, C. 1871. *Grundsätze der Volkswirthschaftslehre. The Collected Works of Carl Menger, Vol. I*. London School of Economics Reprints No. 17, 1934.

———. 1883. *Untersuchungen über die Methode der Socialwissenschaften, und der Politischen Oekonomie insbesondere. The Collected Works of Carl Menger, Vol. II*. London School of Economics Reprints No. 18, 1933.

Mill, J.S. 1843. *A System of Logic*. Edited by J.M. Robson, University of Toronto Press, 1974.

———. 1848. *Principles of Political Economy with Some of Their Applications to Social Philosophy. Books IV and V*. Edited by D. Winch. Harmondsworth: Penguin Books, 1970.

Mises, L. von 1949. *Human Action: A Treatise on Economics*. Yale University Press, 1949.

Mittermaier, K. 1986. 'Mechanomorphism' in *Subjectivism, Intelligibility and Economic Understanding: Essays in Honor of Ludwig M. Lachmann on his Eightieth Birthday*, pp 236–51. Edited by I.M. Kirzner. New York University Press, 1986.

Morishima, M. 1980. 'W. Jaffé on Léon Walras: A Comment'. *Journal of Economic Literature* 18 (June 1980) 550–8.

Nagel, E. 1945. 'Some Reflections on the Use of Language in the Natural Sciences' in *Teleology Revisited and Other Essays in the Philosophy and History of Science*. New York: Columbia University Press, 1979. Read at a symposium of the New School for Social Research and published in the *Journal of Philosophy* in 1945.

———. 1961. *The Structure of Science: Problems in the Logic of Scientific Explanation*. London: Routledge & Kegan Paul, 1979.

Pareto, V. 1900. 'On the Economic Phenomenon' in *International Economic Papers* No. 3, pp 180–96. London: Macmillan, 1953. Translated by F. Priuli. First published in *Giornale degli Economisti*, 1900.

———. 1901. 'On the Economic Principle' in *International Economic Papers* No. 3, pp 203–7. London: Macmillan, 1953. Translated by F. Priuli. First published in *Giornale degli Economisti*, 1901.

Phillips, D.L. 1977. *Wittgenstein and Scientific Knowledge: A Sociological Perspective*. London: Macmillan, 1977.

Polanyi, M. 1958. *Personal Knowledge: Towards a Post-Critical Philosophy*. London: Routledge & Kegan Paul, 1958.

Ricardo, D. 1817. *The Principles of Political Economy and Taxation*. London: Everyman's Library, 1965.

Robbins, L. 1952. 'The Theory of Economic Policy' in *English Classical Political Economy*. London: Macmillan, 1952.

Robertson, D.H. 1963. *Lectures on Economic Principles*. London: Collins, The Fontana Library, 1963.

Rosenberg, N. 1960. 'Some Institutional Aspects of the Wealth of Nations'. *The Journal of Political Economy* 68 (Dec. 1960) 557–70.

Rosenberg, N. 1965. 'Adam Smith on the Division of Labour: Two views or One'. *Economica* 32 (May 1965) 127–40.

Rothbard, M.N. 1962. *Man, Economy, and State: A Treatise on Economic Principles*, Vol. II. New York: van Nostrand, 1962.

———. 1970. *Power and Market: Government and the Economy*. Institute for Humane Studies, 1970.

Ryle, G. 1949. *The Concept of Mind*. London: Hutchison, 1949.

Samuelson, P.A. 1947. *Foundations of Economic Analysis*. Cambridge: Harvard University Press, 1963.

Sandbach, F.H. 1975. *The Stoics*. London: Chatto & Windus, 1975.

Schumpeter, J.A. 1942. *Capitalism, Socialism and Democracy*, 5th edition. London: Allen & Unwin, 1976.

———. 1949 'Vilfredo Pareto' in *Ten Great Economists from Marx to Keynes*, pp 110–42. London: Allen & Unwin, 1952. First published in the *Quarterly Journal of Economics*, May 1949.

———. 1954. *History of Economic Analysis*. Edited from manuscript by E.B. Schumpeter. London: Allen & Unwin, 1972.

Shackle, G.L.S. 1958. *Time in Economics*. De Vries Lecture. Amsterdam: North Holland, 1958.

———. 1967. *The Years of High Theory: Invention and Tradition in Economic Thought 1926–1939*. Cambridge University Press, 1967.

———. 1972. *Epistemics & Economics: A Critique of Economic Doctrines*. Cambridge University Press, 1972.

———. 1976. *Time and Choice*, Keynes Lecture in Economics 1976. London: The British Academy, 1976. From the Proceedings of the British Academy, Vol. 62, 1976.

Simon, H.A. 1978. 'Rationality as Process and as Product of Thought'. Ely Lecture. American Economic Association, Papers and Proceedings, May 1978, pp 1–16.

Simons, H. 1948. *Economic Policy for a Free Society*. University of Chicago Press, 1948.

Smith, A. 1756. 'Letter to the Edinburgh Review' in *Adam Smith: Essays on Philosophical Subjects*, pp 242–54. Edited by W.P.D. Wightman and J.C. Bryce. Oxford University Press, 1980.

———. 1759. *The Theory of Moral Sentiments*. Edited by D.D. Raphael and A.L. Macfie. Oxford University Press, 1976.

———. 1776. *An Inquiry into the Nature and Causes of the Wealth of Nations*. Edited by Edwin Cannan. New York: The Modern Library, 1937.

Stewart, D. 1793. 'Account of the Life and Writings of Adam Smith LL.D'. in *The Collected Works of Dugald Stewart Esq. F.R.SS.*, Vol X, pp 5–98. Edited by Sir W. Hamilton. Reprint of 1858 edition by Gregg International Publishers, 1971.

Stigler, G.J. and Becker, G.S. 1977. 'De Gustibus Non Est Disputandum'. *American Economic Review* 67 (March 1977) 76–90.

Viner, J. 1928. 'Adam Smith and Laissez-Faire' in *Adam Smith, 1776–1926: Lectures to Commemorate the Sesquicentennial of the Publication of 'The Wealth of Nations'*, pp 116–55. New York: Augustus Kelly, 1966.

Walker, D.A. 1984. 'Is Walras's Theory of General Equilibrium a Normative Scheme?' *History of Political Economy* 16:3 (1984) 445–69.

Walras, L. 1874/7. *Elements of Pure Economics or The Theory of Social Wealth*. Translated by W. Jaffé from the Edition Définitive 1926. London: Allen & Unwin, 1954.

———. 1874/7F. *Eléments D'Economie Politique Pure ou Théorie de la Richesse Sociale*. Edition Définitive. Lausanne: Rouge, 1926.

Weber, M. 1904. 'Die "Objektivität" sozialwissenschaftlicher und sozialpolitischer Erkenntnis' in Weber 1951, pp 146–214.

———. 1907. 'R. Starrrnlers "Ueberwindung" der materialistischen Geschichtsauffassung' in Weber 1951, pp 291–359.

———. 1917. 'Der Sinn der "Wertfreiheit" der soziologischen und ökonomischen Wissenschaften' in Weber 1951, pp 475–526.

———. 1951. *Gesammelte Aufsätze zur Wissenschaftslehre*, 2nd edition. Edited by J. Winckelmann. Tübingen: Mohr, 1951.

Weiss, D.D. 1976. 'Marx versus Smith on the Division of Labor'. *Monthly Review* 28:3 (July–Aug. 1976) 104–18.

W.N. See Smith, A. 1776.

Karl Mittermaier's Pursuit of Classical Liberal Coherence

Daniel B. Klein

> But there was a time not so long ago when the ideal of
> market order as the principle of the overall economic order of
> society must have seemed very new-fangled indeed. Dogmatic
> antirationalism would have had to dismiss the *Wealth of Nations*
> as constructivist folly, as the product of the fatal conceit of a
> cloistered academic who could not appreciate the inherent
> wisdom of feudal institutions or of whatever was considered
> traditional. If the advent of the ideal of market order was
> sound cultural evolution, then why does not the same apply,
> for instance, to the strides made by social-democratic ideals
> in this century?
>
> Karl Mittermaier (this volume, 127)

Karl Mittermaier was a classical liberal economist at the University of
Witwatersrand in Johannesburg. He completed a mature work in 1987,
titled *The Hand Behind the Invisible Hand: Dogmatic and Pragmatic Views
on Free Markets and the State of Economic Theory*. It was his PhD thesis at
Witswatersrand – he received his degree at the age of 49. Born in 1938,
Mittermaier was a beloved teacher and colleague but published little; he
died in 2016. I learned of him only after his colleagues contacted me after
his death. I am grateful to them for the opportunity to participate in this
volume's presentation of *The Hand Behind the Invisible Hand*.

I get the feeling that Mittermaier was one who felt his work was never
quite 'there' and so was never keen on publishing it. His colleague Chris
Torr tells a story of his having had a piece accepted by the *Cambridge*

Journal of Economics, a few minor changes to be made, yet never sending in the final version. 'Karl is the only economist I know who put his manuscript back into the bottom draw after it had been accepted for publication' (Torr 2016). After many years and Mittermaier's passing, his colleagues completed the process and the paper appeared, on Menger's Aristotelianism (Mittermaier 2017).

Mittermaier (this volume, 85) writes that formerly economics' 'association with the art of a statesman was very close, and equilibrium theory and its antecedents in particular were closely tied to the advocacy of economic liberalism and even to the ethical question of what constitutes a fair price'. He emphasizes the moral, cultural and institutional preconditions of a liberal market order, and he says that some of the preconditions depend on people feeling that they have reason to embrace such classical liberal principles. The preconditions, then, depend in part on the perception of coherence and appeal of the liberal order.

The pages of Mittermaier radiate a mind and a spirit to like and admire. We visit with a candid, thoughtful, learned man in calm pursuit of classical liberal coherence. Like the pursuit of happiness, that pursuit has always been one of we're not sure what, exactly. In pursuing liberal coherence, we pursue gains in coherence that are hard to anticipate, but perhaps we know them when we see them.

Mittermaier (this volume, 23) speaks of a liberal revival. '[T]here is evidence of a reawakening of free-market sentiment and of a readiness to "leave to the market" what was previously left to the discretion of politicians and bureaucrats.' He asks: 'Who would have believed twenty years ago that politicians who made a return to free-market principles and a reduction in the scope of government their main election plank would find favour among voters in a number of countries?' He paraphrases Milton and Rose Friedman: 'The tide of public opinion is turning against big government.'

The decades since 1986 have been ones of transition and institutional analysis. Much attention has been brought to things that lie *behind* the market's corrective mechanisms. By 'things' I mean the rules, laws, institutions, traditions, focal points, conventions, norms, morals, culture, heritage, religion, etc.

As we press deeper into the well of explanation, however, our explanations become more and more amorphous: culture, norms, moral outlooks. What do we formulate as explanandum and what as explanation? Deirdre McCloskey (2016) tells us that culture – honouring commerce – caused the great enrichment. That theory enriches our understanding. But notice that the whiff of economics lies here mainly in the explanandum – the great enrichment – and not the explanation, which seems primarily cultural and historical.

Mittermaier asks us to apprehend 'the hand behind the invisible hand'. He pointed to many of the things we've been juggling since (moral ideals, conventions, institutions, the rule of law, and so on). Such things suggested to him the metaphor of a hand behind the market order. Our South African economist asked whether that hand, too, is invisible? His own answer was that it is not invisible: sustaining and improving the moral and institutional structures require conscious attention. Liberal civilization depends on the liberal intentions of liberals. 'The conditions under which the guidance of the invisible hand may be relied upon have to be deliberately created' (this volume, 21). Moreover, that deliberate creation is not simply uttering *Hands off!*, or *Maximize individual liberty*.

I'm not so sure that culture and so on are usefully seen as a metaphorical hand, to be deemed either visible or invisible. But Mittermaier is right that our talk of a market system presupposes a great deal – including some things perhaps not as readily presupposed in the South African context.

Economics has long had tendencies toward model-bound obsession – a.k.a., scientism. That obsession peaked in the early 1980s. *The Hand Behind the Invisible Hand* was written at the cusp of the McCloskey Experience (McCloskey 1983, 1985). Since that time, the prestige of equilibrium model building has declined substantially. Now, people more readily ask the model builder: Your model is a theory of what? Why should we care? What merit in your explanation?

But was model-bound obsession the principal obstacle to classical liberal wisdom in the Land of Econ? We now find that it was not, just as it has not been in many of the other academic pyramids. Perhaps one of the chief obstacles has been the difficulty in making classical liberalism more coherent.

Mittermaier uses the issue of what lies behind the market's invisible hand to formulate a distinction between types of free-market supporters, a distinction between 'dogmatic' and 'pragmatic'. The dogmatic free-marketeers do not give much attention to the preconditions of the market's invisible hand. To them, 'the simple anti-government prescription is all that is needed' (this volume, 24). Mittermaier associates 'libertarians' with the dogmatic view and quotes Murray Rothbard, 'a truly free market is totally incompatible with the existence of a State' (Rothbard 1970, 1). Rothbard envisions a libertarian order in which, says Mittermaier, 'absolute and all-embracing property rights' (46, 123) would be respected. Mittermaier comments: 'If Rothbard thinks that this institution [that is, of property rights] would also arise spontaneously or naturally … then it appears that he is not aware of the extent to which libertarian values, a vision of the good society, … enter the libertarian order' (47).

Visions of the good society loom large in Mittermaier's thinking. A word he uses abundantly is 'ideal', saying, for example, that 'an ideal or guiding conception of market processes with its attendant criteria must be an indispensable precondition of free-market policy' (this volume, 109).

Mittermaier suggests that we naturally and inevitably carry around with us visions or ideals of the good society or the proper market order, and that such visions and ideals form a glue of social relationships and cohesion. Again he jousts with Rothbard, whom he quotes, '"public interest" is a meaningless term … and is therefore discarded by libertarians' (Rothbard 1970, 196). Rothbard explains that the free market 'breeds harmony, freedom, prosperity, and order'; the State 'produces conflict, coercion, poverty, and chaos' (ibid). Mittermaier says that Rothbard here appeals to a vision of the good society and could have expressed it in terms of 'the public interest'.

'Rothbard's rendition of libertarian order', says Mittermaier, 'is in line with a long tradition of dogmatic views' (this volume, 123). Mittermaier rejects that tradition, which he associates also with John Locke and François Quesnay. The libertarian vein is not the only sort of free-market dogmatism: Mittermaier also presents a sort he associates with 'equilibrium theory' and, while seeing Hayek mainly as pragmatic, a certain reading of Hayek, he suggests, 'the ethics of success' (55ff), might be regarded as a dogmatic view. Rejecting the varieties of dogmatic views, Mittermaier instead embraces the pragmatic free-market view, which recognizes cultural preconditions.

The title of the work evokes Adam Smith ('invisible hand'), and the opening words are 'Adam Smith's *Wealth of Nations*' (this volume, 21). Mittermaier asks whether Smith's view is dogmatic or pragmatic. Some passages in Smith sound dogmatic, but really he was pragmatic, and it is Smith, first and foremost, who represents that view. Mittermaier's work should be understood as a meditation – clearly written and carefully thought out – on how to make a pragmatic classical liberal economic outlook more coherent. Mittermaier himself is not sure how greater coherence is to be achieved: he is meditating aloud. The meditation explores many central questions, such as the distinction between science and policy judgement. Notice the latter words in the title of the work: '… *and the State of Economic Theory*'. Mittermaier is by no means hostile to what he refers to as 'equilibrium theory'. He certainly feels that it plays a central role in giving coherence to classical liberal economic philosophy. Mittermaier conducts his meditation in conversation with Leon Walras, Vilfredo Pareto, Henry C. Simons, Frank Knight, Walter Eucken, Friedrich Hayek, Milton Friedman and James Buchanan, among others.

I share Mittermaier's dissatisfaction with simplistic or niche libertarianism. The impetus to search for a subtler 'pragmatic' approach resonates with me. In drawing a distinction between 'dogmatic' and 'pragmatic' I would multiply the grounds, to go beyond the question of attending to preconditions of market correction mechanisms. I agree with Mittermaier that dogmatic free-market economics offers a coherence that is false; complications accompany our problematics whether we wrestle with them or not; the dogmatist seems coherent only to fellow dogmatists; refining, qualifying and loosening does not reduce our coherence, but, rather, by coping with complications, may enhance our coherence. Like Mittermaier I make Smith central.

Before describing other features of Mittermaier's pursuit of greater classical liberal coherence, I shall say a few things about mine. By doing so I will be able to compare features of mine and his.

In *The Theory of Moral Sentiments*, Smith (1976b) emphasizes the specialness of commutative justice, with its great injunctive duty of not messing with other people's person, property and promises due. The rules of this injunction are grammar-like, 'precise and accurate', at least as compared to the rules of other virtues. Smith flips the duty of commutative justice ('not messing with other people's stuff'): others not messing with one's stuff.

Smith's jural[1] philosophy for the modern world ('commercial society') involves two kinds of jural relationships, equal–equal, like you and your neighbour, and superior–inferior or governor–governed. In the equal–equal relationship, 'others not messing with one's stuff' is *security*, as in home security. In the superior–inferior relationship, it is *liberty*. Liberty is others, particularly the government (jural superior), not messing with one's stuff.

Liberty is used to form a principle of policy reform: in a choice between two reforms, one of which may be no reform at all, the one that rates higher in liberty better serves universal benevolence. But Smith did not maintain the principle as an axiom. Rather, it is defeasible. He held that the principle holds only by and large. Thus, he gives liberty a presumption, which like any presumption can be overturned when the prosecution, so to speak, overcomes the burden of proof.

Notice that Smith's jural dualism implies that our discourse is contextualized to a polity with an integrated and presumably stable jural system with a singular superior. There may be multiple levels of government, but they are integrated. We are accustomed to think of '*the* government' so Smith's presuppositions seem natural to us. But jural integration and the consequent jural dualism is a relatively recent development – and an underlying theme of David Hume's *History of*

England (see Klein and Matson 2019). Such integration is the sort of precondition that concerns Mittermaier.

Critics often point out that details of the parsing of 'not messing with other people's stuff' are historistic, or particular to time and place. The 'grammars' of commutative justice vary with time and place, just as grammars of language do in history. Thus, likewise the flipside, liberty, is historistic, making the purported logic indeterminate. Such reasoning is often used to dismiss or denigrate the classical liberal emphasis on liberty.

It is true that the grammar of commutative justice is somewhat historistic. But that does not subvert the grammar-like reasoning of commutative justice and liberty, or what I call *the jural logic of one's own*. The 'logic' of the jural logic of one's own can nonetheless be pinned down within any modern jural-dualistic society. For all such societies we have a uniformity in applying the following crucial principle: a type of action in the superior–inferior jural relationship is an initiation of coercion if (and only if) such action in equal–equal jural relationships is an initiation of coercion. Yes, what counts as initiation of coercion among equals varies with historical context, but whatever any particular jural-dualistic context recognizes as initiation of coercion among equals will, on the jural logic of one's own, pin down what counts as such when done by the jural superior.

If your neighbour 'taxed' you (that is, extorted wealth from you) or 'regulated' your freedom of association (that is, stalked and assaulted you in private life), we darned-well would regard that as an initiation of coercion, and so we do call it an initiation of coercion when done by government (though we do not call it 'extortion' or 'assault').[2] The jural logic of one's own takes the historistic element on board and domesticates it. Understanding the jural logic of one's own is a necessary condition for wisdom in the modern world, but not a sufficient one.

As I see him, Smith is not seriously concerned to *justify* the superior–inferior relationship. Although he has a sentence here and there about the necessity of government, I think the real message is inevitability. The existence of government is a reality to be managed, and the managing itself involves coordinating with governors, even trying to govern. We usually wish to reduce and curtail its scope and incursions, but government is not something we dream of eliminating.

One *could* make the jural logic of one's own dogmatic. But that's not Smith. He shows sensitivity to many paradoxes, and he hedges and refines accordingly. I list some of the tensions or paradoxes to deal with: (1) Again, sometimes the lesser-liberty option is preferred, and such exceptions to the principle may particularly occur when the greater direct-liberty option has indirect effects and ramifications that over time result in less liberty overall. (2) Another source of exception: liberty enjoys a presumption, but so does something else, the status quo. The two presumptions (of liberty and of the status quo) are in tension for liberty-augmenting reforms. (3) The classical liberal philosophical outlook ('the science of a legislature') is one thing, the art of liberal politics another, and we cannot expect to set about both birds with one discourse stone; discourse is situational and a prime aspect of a discourse situation is the audience; sometimes we bargain instead of challenge; sometimes we write between the lines, or esoterically; sometimes we promote the 17th best because it is salient or practicable; and so on. (4) Ethics-wise, whole trumps part, but we do not have an algorithm for assessing the well-being of the whole, just as we do not have an algorithm for good movies, and thus we confess looseness, vagueness and lack of foundation.

My own survey of classical liberal thought leaves me with the impression that since 1800 that jural logic of one's own has generally been hidden and obscure, as it is in Mittermaier (indeed, sometimes he expresses doubts whether it is so well defined and delineated). It is curious to me that the jural logic of one's own has been so hidden and obscure. Perhaps the embarrassments of limitations and paradoxes, as well as certain taboos, have kept that logic underground. But not all thinkers have obscured it. One major exception is Rothbard, who makes it front and centre. Rothbard, however, claims too much for it, giving it a sort of ethical trump and thereby getting a sort of grammar into his political ethics. Mittermaier rejects Rothbard for claiming too much for the jural logic of one's own.

In my classical liberalism (and I argue Smith's) – whether on the plane of broader generalizations-cum-precepts ('the science of a legislator') or the art of liberal politics – the most important defining aspect concerns the liberal nature of the reforms espoused. That liberal nature, however, neither depends on nor refers to some sort of vision or ideal of a liberal order or a good society. Rather, that liberal nature is directional – that is, it concerns the direction of reform from the status quo. The forswearing of a vision of an ideal possible world is a disavowal of neither possible worlds nor even of the idea of an ideal possible world. It is disavowal only of *a vision*. Such a vision may obtain in the eyes of the being whose hands are invisible, the super-knowledgeable universal beholder, the impartial spectator in the highest sense of the term, God. Such a vision is not for mere mortals. We have breadcrumb visions – bigger and better than those of our ancestors of 12,000 years ago, but breadcrumb nonetheless.

Likewise, our economic expertise, our knowledge of 'the economy' or 'how the world works', is breadcrumb. But if we openly express a breadcrumb attitude about liberal economics it doesn't fly so well in academia, with its keenness for progressive research programmes.

We develop reasons, however, for believing that doing A as opposed to B better serves the whole, even though we do not foresee or, when actualized, even see, that betterment. We see very little, and we project very little. The spirit is to engage the B advocates: 'Actually, there's good reason to believe that B makes for an even worse situation than A does.' It's not about painting a beautiful picture of A or promising that A will be wonderful. It's more about getting people off of B and developing scruples against B-like ideas.

Mittermaier, however, seems to suggest that a vision of the ideal is crucial: 'To guide policy, a theory must be a guiding conception, and to guide the promotion of market economies, a theory must be a guiding conception of market order, an ideal we may analyse and strive towards' (this volume, 108). For such a vision, Mittermaier looks to what he calls 'equilibrium theory'. He writes: 'The implications of equilibrium (market) prices consistent with … equal values passing hands in exchange … are worked out in detail in Walras's general equilibrium … The formal analysis is static, merely showing the interrelationships in an optimal allocation of resources' (185). Mittermaier is highly concerned about ordinary people feeling assured that incomes relate to value produced, and he suggests that visions or ideals help to underwrite whatever such assurances people can be supplied with.

Perhaps Mittermaier does not really stand by the apparent emphasis on a vision of the ideal. Perhaps he is exploring the problems with such an emphasis. At any rate, the small set of economic models that Mittermaier emphasizes does not loom large in my own outlook. (And they played no significant part in the teenage beginnings of my outlook.)

Indeed, Mittermaier's way of referring to that small set of models, using the term 'equilibrium theory', is revealing. For many people like Mittermaier who started in economics in the 1950s and 1960s, 'equilibrium theory' signified a small set of models such as perfect competition and Walrasian general equilibrium. But for later generations, raised on Nash equilibrium, which subsumes Mittermaier's narrow set, 'equilibrium' is a condition in a model and not necessarily anything more than that. If every model were a theory, then equilibrium theories are innumerable, and 'equilibrium theory' is a jumble of disjointed contexts with disparate or even conflicting outcomes. Indeed, any outcome, any pattern of behaviour, can be framed as an equilibrium in a model, so 'equilibrium theory' in my sense would not mean anything because it would not preclude anything. It draws no distinction. McCloskey taught us that equilibrium model building is a genre of creative writing, heavily subsidized by taxpayers, and that a model is not necessarily a theory at all. Equilibrium is a model-specific notion. Sometimes I sigh when I hear people talk 'equilibrium' without reference to any particular model.

Models are a sort of metaphor, and metaphors draw a comparison between two ideas, a target and a figure: Jim (target) was a wreck (figure). In my view, models are useful, not only as descriptions, but also as foils. A model can help us see features of the target of the metaphor either left out of or misrepresented by the model. Models, therefore, are also valuable for *making a list* of pertinent features of the real world[3] not well represented by the figure of the metaphor. The comparison between the real world and the model helps us formulate those features.[4]

If what Mittermaier dubs 'equilibrium theory' plays no important role in classical liberal thought, then what does? The jural logic of one's own is important. It is necessary to define terms such as 'voluntary', 'coercive', 'free market', 'intervention', 'taxation', 'liberty', and so on, and hence is necessary to give meaning to classical liberalism's signal feature, the presumption of liberty. But beyond the jural logic itself, what is the ethical standard that provides the warrant for Smith's presumption of liberty? Likewise, how does Smith decide when to make an exception? Here, I think, we need to learn to not expect anything that will be satisfying to proud scientific economists. Smith's thinking leaves ethical judgment non-grammar-like. Whether brief or lengthy, the account will be like giving an account of what makes for a good movie. It will lack foundations. A self-assured non-foundationalism makes something of a contrast to Mittermaier, who searches for foundations, even if he does not purport to find them.

Again, Mittermaier looks to 'equilibrium theory' for some kind of standard, ideal or vision. He says that any such ideal is merely a guide: 'Ideals do not have to be entirely attainable' (this volume, 101). He is not out to make the world resemble perfect competition. Rather, I think he thinks that such models help people envision certain aspects of what is achieved under liberal policies. He repeatedly expresses concern about 'big business' and 'economic oligarchy' but he does not make clear whether he thinks such problems call for freer markets or intervention.

One of the things that attracts Mittermaier to perfect-market models is the notion that in such equilibria prices are 'consistent with … equal values passing hands in exchange' (this volume, 185). Something that I found striking is the expression Mittermaier uses – and about 30 times – for 'equal values passing hands in exchange', namely 'commutative justice'. On this matter he cites Henry Simons (1948) and William Jaffé (1980). But this 'commutative justice' is not Smith's commutative justice. The Simons-Jaffé-Mittermaier meaning is not idiosyncratic, but I don't think Smith's is, either; and the two meanings may be related. I should like to investigate the semantic history of 'commutative justice' –

which, after all, is an English-language expression said to relate to ideas expressed by Aristotle. The tradition behind the Simons-Jaffé-Mittermaier meaning may indeed help to account for why Smith's own signification of commutative justice, and as but one of several kinds of justice, has not been seized upon – the task of doing so has been made difficult by, among other things, the nebulous polysemy of 'commutative justice'.

As I reflect on Mittermaier's pursuit of classical liberal coherence, I ponder the importance of vision, or ideal, or destination. Mittermaier may be correct when he writes that 'the ideal of market order was presented by Adam Smith and other writers in the classical liberal tradition as a coherent system that would promote material prosperity in conditions of personal freedom' (this volume, 190). Mittermaier suggests that most people will not embrace free enterprise if the idea is unaccompanied by any vision of a good society. That may well be true.

Even if people were to concede that free enterprise best conduces to general prosperity and 'conditions of personal freedom', would that constitute a vision? What is one to do with such freedom? You have plenty of paper to write on and pens to write with; and you must obey grammar. What shall you fill the pages with? What is your purpose? Where shall you find meaning? What is the whole that you belong to and draw meaning from?

Smith urges us to wisdom and virtue, but the life-long bachelor offers little that could count as a shared vision of the good life. In *Moral Sentiments* there are scenes aplenty – young men, old men, soldiers, clergy, gentlemen and savages – and the scenes are attended by many sage tips and pointers. But there is neither a synoptic vision that makes for a goal or shared vision nor a suggested pattern of practices and activities for pursuing wisdom and virtue. The discerning reader sees that Smith is leaving the higher things open, underdetermined. The book's most famous parable – of the poor man's son – leaves the thoughtful reader scratching her head. The underdetermination may help explain why more people do not buy what Smith is selling. And if so, it is likely that that cause of their not buying what Smith is selling will not be clearly or candidly set forth by them. They will give other objections instead.

Mittermaier (1987) ranges further than I have indicated here, and with great insight. The work is rewarding as a perennial discussion of classical liberal coherence and as a document of the mind of a classical liberal economist writing in South Africa in the early to mid 1980s. I recommend the work highly.

Acknowledgements
For feedback I thank Andrew Humphries, Jon Murphy, Dominic Pino and Chris Torr.

Notes

1 For the word *jural*, *Black's Law Dictionary* (1983, 442) begins: 'Pertaining to natural or positive right, or to the doctrines of rights and obligations; as "jural relations."' I use the term – I think not idiosyncratically – to suggest especially the more grammar-like basic rules operative in a community, firstly among neighbours (so to speak), regardless of how those rules are sustained.

2 Note that not seeing taxation and government restrictions as voluntary depends on properly theorizing the configuration of ownership; see Klein 2011.

3 The idiom 'the real world' is here shorthand for: the motley set of beliefs we happen to hold about the universe, particularly about the parts of it we happen to be focusing on.

4 In another work (Mittermaier 1986), Mittermaier remarks at length on models as metaphors, but he does not remark on their value as foils.

References

Black's Law Dictionary. 1983. Abridged 5th edition. St. Paul, MN: West Publishing.

Jaffé, William (1980) 'Walras's Economics as Others See It'. *Journal of Economic Literature* 18 (June) 528–49.

Klein, Daniel B. (2011) 'Against Overlordship'. *The Independent Review* 16:2, 165–71.

Klein, Daniel B. and Matson, Erik W. (2019) 'Mere-Liberty in David Hume' in *A Companion to David Hume*. Edited by Moris Polanco. Guatemala City: Universidad Francisco Marroquin.

McCloskey, Deirdre N. (1983) 'The Rhetoric of Economics'. *Journal of Economic Literature* 21:2, 481–517.

———. (1985/1998) *The Rhetoric of Economics*. Madison, WI: University of Wisconsin Press.

———. (2016) *Bourgeois Equality: How Ideas, Not Capital or Institutions, Enriched the World*. Chicago, IL: University of Chicago Press.

Mittermaier, Karl (1986) 'Mechanomorphism' in *Subjectivism, Intelligibility, and Economic Understanding: Essays in Honor of Ludwig Lachmann on His Eightieth Birthday*, pp 236–51. Edited by I.M. Kirzner. London: Macmillan.

———. (1987) *The Hand Behind the Invisible Hand: Dogmatic and Pragmatic Views on Free Markets and the State of Economic Theory*. PhD thesis, University of Witwatersrand.

———. (2017) 'Menger's Aristotelianism'. *Cambridge Journal of Economics* 42, 577–94.

Rothbard, Murray N. (1970) *Power and Market: Government and the Economy*. Menlo Park, CA: Institute for Humane Studies.

Simons, Henry C. (1948) *Economic Policy for a Free Society*. Chicago, IL: University of Chicago Press.

Smith, Adam (1976a) *An Inquiry Into the Nature and Causes of the Wealth of Nations*. Edited by R.H. Campbell and A.S. Skinner, 2 vols. Oxford: Oxford University Press.

———. (1976b) *The Theory of Moral Sentiments*. Edited by D.D. Raphael and A.L. Macfie. Oxford: Oxford University Press.

Torr, Christopher (2016) 'Karl's Academic Legacy. Remarks at a Service for Karl H. Mittermaier'.

Karl Mittermaier, a Philosopher-Economist with a Penetrating Intellect and Twinkling Eye

Rod O'Donnell

Dr Karl Mittermaier's existence was unknown to me prior to Chris Torr's email in October 2018. But I very much wish we had been acquainted. After reading all his writings then available, I discovered an extensive overlap in our intellectual interests and hence many missed opportunities for thought-provoking conversations.

   This, then, is my tribute to a deep, fearless and brilliant thinker known to me primarily through his writings, but also through the recollections of his devoted wife Isabella, his colleagues and his students.[1] He was a profound and original scholar who deserved far greater recognition than he received.

Economics and philosophy

Karl was one of that small but brave band of economists who insist on being philosopher-economists, people who believe that explorations of the conceptual foundations, methodologies and theoretical manoeuvres in our often contested and argumentative discipline are just as essential as extending the theories that purportedly explain the reality in which we live. Not for him the standard fare of developing more or less recipe-driven, mathematical theories, but the richer intellectual feasts awaiting those seeking deeper appreciations and more critical assessments. As his writings demonstrate, such thinking explores debates, seeks clarity, draws distinctions, pays attention to context, is inter-disciplinary and asks awkward questions. Above all it avoids superficiality. The philosophical cast of his mind was plain in his first paper in 1978 on inflation,[2] and continued to his last, published posthumously in 2018, on Menger's Aristotelianism.

In economics, the schools of thought mostly absorbing his attention were Austrian and Neoclassical economics, the former being highly familiar with internal philosophical debates, the latter somewhat less so. But unlike some, he was never doctrinaire, being always ready to question conventional views and the arguments of eminent thinkers if he saw deficiencies, and to seek counsel elsewhere if that seemed more promising.

His academic output

As a widely read and reflective thinker, Karl wrote a considerable amount.[3] Alongside the central topic of economic order, his writings focused on the nature of economic theorizing and its improvement – doing economics with humans and not 'mechanomorphs';[4] embracing uncertainty, expectations and subjectivity in decision making; exploring the presence of realism and nominalism in the foundations of economic theories; assessing the adequacy of Austrian, Neoclassical and Institutionalist theories; and insisting always on the importance of institutions.

Despite this, only seven papers were pursued to publication. This relative paucity (inconceivable in today's pressured universities) is something of a puzzle. Why did someone with so many valuable things to say, and who committed his reflections to paper, show no interest in maximizing his publication list? No quick answer is forthcoming, even from his colleagues and acquaintances, but some clues may have appeared in 1982. In his published review of Boland's book, *The Foundations of Economic Method*, he noted, after explaining its main propositions, that the author had offered little constructive advice on one of Karl's favourite themes – how to do economics better.

> … the best aspect [here] is the way Boland manages to bring out the *regimented* formats of present-day applied and theory journal articles respectively. One is left with the disturbing impression that the academic who wants to make sure of seeing his name in journals must pick up either one of two standard forms and simply fill in the blanks. (Mittermaier 1982, 257, emphasis added)

Clearly, a mind wanting to probe, criticize and question how things are done would not find clerical or military service congenial.

A further reason may have been his extensive reading of primary and secondary literatures, a feature evident in his writings. As well as being time consuming, this activity is more intellectually pleasurable than the chore of converting manuscripts to papers for publication purposes. Possibly he also preferred not to change his well-crafted typescripts to meet other people's criteria.

Three general features of his writings are notable. First, so much reflection is often packed into his paragraphs that their breadth, depth and insights are not always fully apparent on first readings. Several re-readings, with intervening periods of reflection, may be needed for more complete appreciation. Second, in advancing his viewpoints, arguments and criticisms, his writings are polite, non-dogmatic and generative of reflection in his readers. A favoured practice was to say there *seems* to be a problem here, and then let readers perceive from his remarks that there really *is* a problem here. The relatively few occasions of bluntness or sharpness tend to be expressed through mild sarcasm or subtle humour. Finally, he tried to be as scientifically disinterested and non-ideological as it is possible to be, an attribute not found in every economist's writings.

The doctoral thesis

Its scope, its thoughtful, interrogative probing of texts, and its profound insights took my breath away when I first read it in 2018. But I was also saddened by the loss to the world of its non-publication for over three decades, a loss now happily remedied by Bristol University Press. By way of concluding this most welcome volume, I would like to elaborate on two of its main themes: the issue of market order (and hence disorder) and, within this, Karl's illuminating account of Adam Smith's 'invisible hand' argument.

The topic of market order constitutes the backbone of the thesis – what is it, how is it theorized and what means are available for its achievement? Here Karl organized his thought around the following distinctions, possibly novel at the time. First, two prominent views of market order and associated policies were identified:

(i) The dogmatic laissez-faire/free market view, which sees market order as establishing itself naturally and harmoniously, this being driven by an 'invisible hand' or 'spontaneous process' with no prodding by external agencies. The associated policy prescription is complete economic non-activism by the state.

(ii) The pragmatic laissez-faire/free market view, which sees market order only as an ideal that can be striven after and approximated in reality, this requiring motivated, external, agencies. The policy prescription here is active state guidance so that the economic system moves closer to the ideal while never fully attaining it.

The distinction has multiple opposing dimensions: theoretical/practical, ideal/real, invisible/visible, spontaneity/guidance. On the dogmatic view, with agents left to themselves, reality creates the ideal outcomes expounded by the pure theory. On the pragmatic view, reality can only approximate the ideal outcomes of the pure theory when shaped by deliberate action.

Second, a distinguishing criterion was advanced. Since markets, along with their requisite legal systems and conventions, are institutions, these institutions must exist *prior* to investigating whether the market system produces order or disorder. The issue thus moves to a second level – in a society in which all pursue self-interest, how does this prior framework establish itself? Does it emerge naturally or spontaneously, or does it require deliberate creation by government or others? Metaphorically, there has to be a second hand behind the first hand, a hand establishing the institutional framework within which the hand of the market goes to work. What we now need is an account of the prior framework-building hand and whether it is similar to, or different from, the hand it guides. Hence Karl's title: there must be a hand behind the 'invisible hand', which raises the question of whether this prior hand is itself visible or invisible.

Third, within economic theory, an ambiguity was explored between the *description* of market order *in* actual economies, and the *prescription* of market order *for* actual economies. Dogmatists see the self-regulating theory of market order as a description, so rendering prescription irrelevant. Pragmatists see the same theory as a prescription, an ideal whose attainment requires policy action of the right kind. As Karl perceptively observed, the ambiguity also involves those versions of economic theory that start with a prescription but interpret it as a description.

It is within this overall framework that the meaning of Smith's so-called 'invisible hand' is investigated. Using careful textual exegesis, Karl argues, very persuasively, that no hand with providential or mystical properties exists in *The Wealth of Nations* (Smith 1776 – hereafter *WN*), and that what Smith provides instead is a straightforward logical argument, the conclusion to which only holds if crucial institutional conditions are satisfied.

Finally, Karl notes that while prominent economists may not explicitly espouse allegiance to either type of free market economics, many are nevertheless classifiable in this manner due to the general 'drift of ideas' indicated by careful examination of their writings. Attachment to a group, moreover, does not imply consensus within the group, for major disagreements are possible on other matters. In terms of individuals, the dogmatic group or tendency is seen as including Pareto, Hayek (mostly), and Rothbard (and implicitly other proponents of libertarianism); and the pragmatic group or tendency as encompassing Smith, Walras, (Henry) Simons, Eucken, Buchanan and Hahn. Karl's own sympathies lay strongly with the pragmatists and the idea that market order needs *deliberate* institution building, this doubtless making his views unpopular among dogmatists.[5]

Adam Smith's so-called invisible hand

Karl's detailed analysis of the relevant sections of Smith's texts generates three related propositions:

(i)   While the meaning of the invisible hand in the *History of Astronomy* and the *Theory of Moral Sentiments* is related to divine providence, that in *WN* has a different, non-providential meaning.
(ii) Providential readings of Smith's economic theorizing are misconceptions without actual foundation.[6]
(iii) The phrase is a very inapt and misleading descriptor of the argument in *WN*.[7]

This means Smith's so-called invisible hand differs markedly from its standard representation as the cause of a grand harmony of interests. There is nothing mystical, theistic or providential about it, however, such connotations having shrouded the concept for centuries and turned it into a meaningless slogan. In fact, all that is presented is a simple logical argument. I am no Smith specialist, but it strikes me Karl may have been the first, or at least one of the earliest, to have clearly and fully appreciated the actual nature of the argument in *WN*. Following Karl's line of thought, it may be briefly outlined as follows:

Definitions
1.   The national product is the sum of all individual products.[8]

Premises
1.   It is in the social/national interest to increase the national product.
2.   In a system of natural liberty, all individuals can, and do, pursue their self-interest to make their individual products as large as possible with whatever capital they have at their disposal.

Conclusion

It is in the social/national interest to replace the existing system (say, mercantilism with its state-granted monopolies and privileges) with a system of natural liberty.

The logic is straightforward. With individuals intending only their own benefits, and not those of others or the nation, the unintentional social outcome of all these self-centred efforts is an increase in national product. The conclusion is merely the result of the definitions, premises and arithmetic addition. Plainly, no hand generates the outcome. One might *liken* the outcome to that produced by an unseen providential hand, but this is merely an 'as if' analogy and does not constitute an assertion that such a hand exists and causes the outcome.[9]

Within the institutional framework of a system of natural liberty (this key element being further explained below), output expansion is not caused by an outside invisible agency, but is simply the combined result of the activities of self-interested agents. *Unintentionality* lies at the heart of the outcome. Instead of referring to Smith's 'invisible hand argument', it would be more accurate to refer to his 'unintended outcome argument', one in which the social outcome is not motivational for agents and hence unseen by, or invisible to, them.

Although not deployed by Karl, a useful device for determining whether an idea or remark is essential to an argument is a relevance/necessity test. Remove the idea/remark to see if the reduced argument reaches the same conclusion; if so, the idea/remark can be dispensed with. Consider the first of Smith's two key passages in the relevant *WN* chapter.

> Every individual is continually exerting himself to find out the most advantageous employment for whatever capital he can command. It is his own advantage, indeed, and not that of the society that he has in view. But the study of his own advantage naturally, or rather necessarily leads him to prefer that employment which is most advantageous to the society. (Campbell et al 1976, 454)

What is this naturalness, or even better necessity, of which Smith speaks? It is the naturalness and necessity of two related things: arithmetic addition, as in the definition of the national product, and logic, as in his argument. No invisible hand is needed, so there is here no mention of, or appeal to, such a notion. Had this been the only passage setting forth the argument, we would never have read of an invisible hand in *WN*.

Now take the passage in which the phrase makes its appearance.

> As every individual … endeavours as much as he can both to employ his capital in the support of domestick industry, and so to direct that industry that its produce may be of the greatest value; every individual necessarily labours to render the annual revenue of the society as great as he can. He generally, indeed, neither intends to promote the publick interest, nor knows how much he is promoting it. … [B]y directing that industry in such a manner as its produce may be of the greatest value, he intends only his own gain, and he is in this, as in many other cases, led by an invisible hand to promote an end which was which was no part of his intention. … By pursuing his own interest he frequently promotes that of the society more effectually than when he really intends to promote it. (Campbell et al 1976, 456)

This is the same argument as before, except for the addition of the famous phrase. The irrelevance of the latter can be demonstrated in two ways. Either *omit the remark entirely* and substitute 'he intends only his own gain, and he is in this, as in many other cases, led to promote an end which was no part of his intention'. Or *keep the remark and modify its lead-in* by writing 'he intends only his own gain, and he is in this, as in many other cases, led, as if by an invisible hand, to promote an end which was no part of his intention'. In either case, the hand is irrelevant to the logic. The inapplicability of any divine providence interpretation is also implied by the word 'frequently'. If an omnipotent entity were thought to be invisibly at work, one would write 'always', and not 'frequently', which imposes limits on divine power. In short, the invisible hand concept plays no role in the logic, is irrelevant and merely introduces ideological obfuscations.

Smith's conclusion obviously involves a crucial change in the institutional framework, the replacement of the current mercantilist system with a 'system of natural liberty'. What that involves is clearly an important question. In answering it, Karl begins not with Smith, but with another perceptive economist of a later period.

Frédéric Bastiat

Almost unknown (and hence almost invisible), this tireless French economist presented formidable arguments in 1846–50 that Karl uses to emphasize a key, often neglected, property of Smith's argument. He finds in *WN*, in somewhat different language, components of Bastiat's subsequent analysis.

Bastiat argued that there are only two ways to maintain and improve one's life – production, in which one enjoys the fruits of one's own labour, and plunder or predation, in which one enjoys the fruits of other people's labour (in full or in part). In a neat phrase, he called predation 'the art of living at the expense of others'. He held, as Karl noted, that 'plunder is practised in this world on too vast a scale' for economics to ignore it; and that what keeps the social order from improving is 'the constant endeavour of its members to live and to prosper at one another's expense'.[10] Smith, of course, was also acutely aware of badly motivated self-interested behaviour, especially (but not exclusively) by the monopolistic merchant class.[11]

What Bastiat's argument clarifies is that when Smith's argument is interpreted as being based *solely* on self-interest, it applies just as much to predation as to production. Since this undermines the definition of national product and the validity (and moral acceptability) of the argument, predation-excluding restrictions are necessary for Smith's argument to succeed.

A more explicit form of Smith's syllogism

Smith's solution to the problem, as Karl indicates, was *not* entirely economic, but also extra-economic in being grounded on the moral, legal and political foundations of the concept he labelled 'the system of natural liberty'. Although tempting to interpret this as portraying something like a state of perfect freedom without external authority, as many readers have done, such an understanding is contrary to Smith's definition, quoted below. Although this was presented in Book IV of *WN*, the same book as contains the 'invisible hand' remark, its appearance was delayed until its last chapter. The resulting seven-chapter separation unfortunately works against the recognition that properly understanding Smith's system of natural liberty is essential to his 'invisible hand' argument.

> All systems, either of preference or of restraint, … being thus completely taken away, the obvious and simple system of natural liberty establishes itself of its own accord. Every man, *as long as he does not violate the laws of justice*, is left perfectly free to pursue his own interest his own way, and to bring both his industry and capital into competition with those of any other man, or order of men. … According to the system of natural liberty, the *sovereign* has only three duties to attend to; *three duties of great importance indeed but plain and intelligible to*

> *common understandings: first, the duty of protecting the society from*
> *the violence and invasion of other ... societies; secondly, the duty of*
> *protecting, as far as possible, every member of society from the injustice*
> *or oppression of every other member of it, or the duty of establishing*
> *an exact administration of justice, and thirdly, the duty of erecting*
> *and maintaining certain publick works and certain publick institutions*
> [not profitable for private individuals to undertake]. (Campbell
> et al 1976, 687–8, emphases added)

Contrary to slogans such as 'leave it to the market' or 'markets know best', Smith requires everyone to adhere to 'the laws of justice', which, in Bastiat's terms, would mean an individual receives only what is his or hers, and never takes from others what is theirs. Necessarily, the solution lies outside the domain of economic self-interest because that is the domain that generates the problem. It requires the government to fulfil its three roles of protecting the whole society and hence all individuals; of protecting each individual, as far as possible, from injustice and oppression by other individuals in the same society; and of providing certain public works and institutions. Significant further elaboration of the last duty is then, again unfortunately, postponed until the first chapter of Book V. It notably includes public works and institutions that (i) facilitate commerce, of both society in general and particular branches, (ii) provide education, for both youth and people of all ages, and (iii) sustain both the functions and dignity of the sovereign (or government). The next chapter then outlines the necessary revenue-raising requirements through a taxation system based on justice and utility. Taken in isolation, the first sentence in the above quotation is thus quite wrong. Smith's system of natural liberty does *not* establish itself spontaneously or on its own, but requires the presence of a very significant large government-supplied institutional framework.

While the previous statement of the syllogism is adequate, it can mislead if the meaning of this crucial term is not explicitly included. The remedy is simply augmentation with the definition of Smith's system of natural liberty, this bringing the applicability conditions of the logic fully into view. One concise (but still long-winded) statement of the definition is as follows.

> 2. A system of natural liberty is one in which (a) every person
> is free to pursue his/her own interests provided s/he obeys the
> laws of justice, and (b) the government (i) protects the society
> from violence and invasion by other societies, (ii) provides
> a judicial system protecting every individual from injustice

and oppression by other individuals in the same society, (iii) provides public works and institutions not profitable for individuals to undertake (including the facilitation of commerce, the delivery of widespread education and the requirements of government), and (iv) raises revenue using a well-designed taxation system.

The definition clearly indicates how much institutional structure is a *precondition* of Smith's argument. Other passages in *WN* reinforce the point that multiple regulations of self-interest are essential. Viner (1927, 214–32) is very good on this, devoting more than 40 per cent of his paper to these matters, with Skinner (1991, 370–1) being of like mind.[12] Note also that around 27 per cent of *WN* (its entire last book) focuses extensively on the role of government. The history of the last two centuries reinforces Smith's argument, replete as it is with instances of unjust, predatory self-interested behaviours that have generated public institutions and laws aimed at protecting the interests of both individuals and the public.[13]

Smith's 'simple system of natural liberty' is thus not at all 'simple' but quite complex. And far from being 'natural', its liberty is socially constructed and constrained. As well as individual interests, its author was just as much concerned to protect the social interest. Government is thus not *intrinsically* part of the problem, but *necessarily* part of the solution when engaging in the right way. In short, the hand presented in Smith's argument is not the allegedly smoothly functioning hand of the market left to itself as in free market ideology, but the larger 'double hand' of the market and government combined, the functioning of which is inevitably more complicated and experimental.

In Karl's classificatory scheme, Smith is plainly a pragmatic free market theorist. The *WN* argument is not a depiction of reality (or even of an important part of reality) as dogmatists and many orthodox writers portray it, but a conception guiding attempts to establish an institutional framework allowing self-interest and public interest to coexist in acceptable ways. Similarly, his argument contains no invisible hands at any level, only two visible ones – the collective hand of many self-motivated individuals, and the hand of the state with considerable agency over the kind of institutional system that exists. It is only in Smith's fully specified system that the unintentional but socially beneficial increase in national product will occur.[14]

In terms of Karl's infinite regress argument, if the first-level institution of the market is to increase output and display order, a prior set of institutions is needed at the second level to ensure this. This then takes us to the third level – what institutions exist to make the second institutional framework come into existence? And so on. However, this theoretical regress assumes that determination at each step is an orderly repetition of the same process. Reality, however, is typically very disorderly, involving protracted power struggles between groups with different economic self-interests and moral precepts. What is an infinite regress in abstract theoretical terms is more likely to be a finite regress in reality that is dissipated in power struggles (peaceful or violent), which then determine the relevant institutions or create unstable non-resolutions for extended periods.

Here we encounter the role of the public intellectual, with Smith as an examplar. If sufficient numbers of people, say the sovereign, the clergy and sections of the wealthy, are persuaded by *WN* arguments, the desired change might occur peacefully. But given sufficient opposition, whether for self-interest or intellectual reasons, force might be deployed to protect the status quo or to introduce another system incompatible with Smith's. As he well knew, history, past and present, was full of power struggles.[15] Human-induced climate change further illustrates the insufficiency of pure self-interest and the necessity of collective action to prevent the dramatic diminution, even to zero, of national and global products.

Stigler's claims

Stigler, an indefatigable defender of free market theory, advances two strong claims concerning *WN*. The first presents the obligatory fulsome praise. '[Smith's book] is a stupendous palace erected upon the granite of self-interest. ... The immensely powerful force of self-interest guides resources to their most efficient uses, ... [and] orders and enriches the nation which gives it free rein' (Stigler 1975, 237). The second is strongly critical, postulating that a book by 'the premier scholar of self-interest' contains a fundamental inconsistency concerning self-interest. 'The paradox is [that] if self-interest dominates ... men in all commercial undertakings, why not also in their political undertakings? ... [No] clear distinction can be drawn between commercial and political undertakings: the procuring of favourable legislation *is* a commercial undertaking' (Stigler 1975, 237–8, original emphasis).

Karl's analysis, although not referring to Stigler's paper, shows why both claims are mistaken.

The first is wrong because it neglects the prior institutional framework essential for self-interest to generate the desired result. Smith's 'palace' is not erected on self-interest alone, but equally on the institutions constituting his system of liberty. Stigler neglects these entirely. And the second is wrong because it omits the fact that market institutions can only operate desirably within the right non-market institutional framework. In both cases, Stigler's argument flattens the earth, reducing all matters to the sole factor of self-interest, which is charged with explaining everything because Smith's analysis purportedly rests solely on this foundation. Of course, the procurement of favourable legislation is often driven by self-interest but that does not mean that this self-interest operates in the same sphere, in the same way, and on the same institutional level, as the self-interest of economic ventures producing goods and services. Such differences need to be recognized.

Institutions, order and disorder

While not treated separately in the thesis, institutions run as a continuous thread through its discussion of key theorists, all of whom rely on institutions to varying degrees. Even anti-government libertarians like Rothbard require the pre-existing institutions of 'totally free markets' and enforceable property rights.

Given that well-designed institutions are vital to well-functioning markets, what institutions should be introduced? Karl had solved the theoretical problem of understanding Smith's 'invisible hand' argument and its extensive reliance on institutions, but neither he nor anyone else has succeeded in resolving the practical issue of devising anything approaching an optimal set of institutions for modern capitalist economies (especially if Bastiat is kept in mind).

In this context, Hayek's doctrine of 'spontaneous order' and the idea of institutions arising of their own accord deserves comment. Hayek divides order into two types – a deliberately created or authoritarian order imposed on others, and a spontaneous or non-constructed order arising from within society. The institutions of the former are rejected, those of the latter embraced.[16]

As Karl notes, the doctrine is problematic. If a group which Hayek strongly opposes (social democrats, welfare-statists or socialists allegedly favouring the first kind of order) win power legitimately through properly conducted democratic elections (presumably a spontaneously generated institution) on a platform of reconstructing parts of the existing spontaneous order, and then legislates to change that order (say by limiting current market freedoms and reducing unemployment and inequalities), then Hayek would be obliged to regard this as desirable.

Other problems arise. First, the term has misleading connotations. It is actually shorthand for 'spontaneous *institutional* order', which addition reminds us that institutions can not only facilitate, but also limit, spontaneity. Second, the doctrine is confused and simplistic. In reality, institutional (re)arrangements typically arise from proposals deliberately thought out by individual entities (say monarchs, scholars, practitioners or think tanks) who then seek to persuade others, engage with power, and, if successful, impose their will, directly or indirectly, on other people, many of whom might strongly oppose the changes. Smith again provides an example. His idea of an institution-based system of liberty did not arise spontaneously but only after years of study, travel and reflection. He urged the improvement of society with new institutions that required the purposeful exercise of power by those already in power, so as, quite deliberately, to install a new institutional structure that went against the interests of the significant sections of society enjoying the benefits of the existing (and presumably spontaneously generated) order that served their interests. From start to finish, these orders and processes are hardly captured by the notion of 'spontaneity'.

In the last two sections of the thesis, Karl turns to market disorder, the penultimate section being the longest in his work. Here the bar is set very high by a conception of social order within which market order is but one of many constituent ideals. Social order is said to prevail when all the identifiable ideals of a society are internally consistent and form a coherent whole. Economic or market order is defined similarly as a sub-complex of ideals that needs to be consistent, not only internally, but also externally, with the wider complex of social ideals. Since no actual economy is likely to meet these requirements, economic disorder will be common and the study of how to reduce it (as distinct from its elimination) will be extremely important. Such a study, however, is not well served by a theory that regards the actual state of affairs as the natural outcome of economic forces, invisible hands or spontaneous processes generating market order. Karl also knew that explicitly identifying all economic ideals, checking their internal consistency, and devising institutions that could realize them, were huge and difficult tasks. The entire framework is, however, consistent with his prescriptive pragmatic approach in which institutions and policies can move reality closer to ideal states without ever attaining them.

Overall, the thesis finishes on a pessimistic note. Drawing on various themes such as impersonal market constraints derived from Smith, the production-predation pair of Bastiat, Keynes on unemployment, expectations and distribution, Lachmann's analysis of inflation, the control of capital resting in fewer hands, the use of credit money, the blurring of lines between big business and government, and Marx's class conflict and contradictions, Karl's analysis points to the immense difficulty and likely impossibility of attaining coherence in the sets of ideals constitutive of economic and social order. One only has to reflect on two of his still pertinent questions. Can we obtain a 'wholesome combination' of the following items: coordination by prices, unconcentrated enterprise, growth in material prosperity, full employment, and an equitable distribution of income and wealth? Alternatively, can we find a way to reconcile the ideals of a *free* society and the ideals of a *compassionate* society? It is unclear how dispiriting, as a pragmatist, he would have found this conclusion, but what is clear is that it would have been unwelcome among dogmatists.

Keynes

Keynes was also preoccupied with the problems of market order, disorder, institutions and the fuller acquisition of the benefits of a free enterprise system, alongside other fundamental matters of interest to Karl, such as how to do economics better, decision making under radical uncertainty, theorizing involving human subjectivity and limited knowledge and abilities (as distinct from perfectly endowed robots), and the introduction of institutions aimed at delivering benefits to all citizens in short and long runs, nationally and internationally. Yet references to Keynes's contributions are infrequent in Karl's writings and, when present, tend to be influenced by Shackle's often mistaken interpretations.[17]

Several factors may have led him away from Keynes. One was scope; he had enough big topics and important writers to explore without adding another large literature. Second, as noted below, the mature Keynes falls outside his schematization of free market theorizing. A third factor may have been academic politics. In supporting pragmatic rather than dogmatic free market thinking, Karl was in enough disagreement with major figures such as Hayek, Lachmann[18] and other Austrians who might possibly have played a role in choosing thesis examiners, without opening up further controversy. Nevertheless, it seems unfortunate that, despite Chris Torr's nudging, Karl did not pay Keynes's writings more attention, for they would have added valuable reflections on the themes he explored.

Three matters arise here. First, is Keynes classifiable in terms of Karl's bipartite framework? He was plainly not a dogmatic laissez-faire theorist. But neither was he a pragmatic one (even though he might appear closer to that alternative). Laissez-faire was never a guiding ideal to be pursued, for it was a state of affairs capable of producing extensive market *disorder*.[19] While clearly in favour of the market system as against its main alternative of centrally planned administration, Keynes saw it as producing varying degrees and types of disorder and order (including, of course, suboptimal equilibria). Hence it needed state-related institutions and planning to supplement market forces by practical policies that reinvigorated or restrained these forces on an as-needed basis. The combination of market forces and an economically active state seeking better outcomes introduces elements of pragmatism, but not in the sense of Karl's thesis. Keynes's order was one pursued by an economically engaged state, not an order capable of being approximated or created merely by a combination of self-interest and related institutions and policies.

Second, an important overlap exists between Keynes's and Smith's theorizing concerning output levels, which, to my (incomplete) knowledge, has not been previously noted or at least emphasized. In his *General Theory* (hereafter *GT*) Keynes concluded that a market economy generates varying levels of (equilibrium) output in both the short and long periods, such levels depending on the level of investment and hence on the capital stock. This clashes with orthodox propositions claiming that market economies always deliver maximum resource employment and optimal allocative efficiency in one or both periods, with Smith being celebrated as a founder of this line of thinking (as Stigler's first quotation above illustrates). Smith's actual position on this question, however, is much closer to Keynes's.

The first premise in the syllogism capturing the essence of Smith's argument states that it is in society's interest to *increase* national product; it does not say maximize national product, which is a special case of an increase. This phrasing is important because it is consistent with the parts of *WN* relevant to the 'invisible hand' argument. Prior to the first of his quotations above, Smith states that the 'number of persons employed cannot exceed a certain proportion to the capital of society', which is to say the capital stock determines levels of employment. The quotation itself then says every individual continually exerts himself to find the most advantageous use *for whatever capital he can command*, and that this leads him to deploy this capital so that it is unintentionally *most advantageous* to society, advantageous meaning creating higher output under the relevant conditions. The second quotation adds further content by saying that every individual tries *as much as he can* to employ his capital so that its output has its greatest or maximum value, such attempts again making unintended additions to the annual revenue of society, thus *promoting* the interest of society alongside his own.

When read carefully, important restraints inform both passages. First, the extent of employment in Smith is governed by the amount of *capital*, not the size of the labour force. Obviously, significant sections of the population will *not* have access to, and hence command over, capital, so that the total amount of capital in operation and hence the increases in output and employment will be less than they might be. Second, individuals 'try' and 'endeavour' as much as they can. Again, not all individuals have the same abilities or knowledge, and not all investments will succeed, so that some endeavours will not add as much to output as they might have done. Adding the uncertainty of the future that Keynes emphasized and of which Smith was aware reinforces the point. Likewise, agent deployments of capital *promote* the interest of society without *guaranteeing* maximization.

These considerations constitute grounds for concluding that Smith's argument is focused on the general case of an increase in output of an unspecified amount, and not solely on the special case of the maximum possible increase in output. Orthodox interpretations view him as proclaiming agent self-interest is sufficient cause for full employment, optimal output and complete allocative efficiency, but forget that such conclusions depend on assumptions that he did not make, whether in his own terms as above, or in the terms of modern orthodox theorizing where agents have (or arrive at) perfect knowledge and abilities, everyone has access to capital, full sets of markets exist and the future collapses into the present, such assumptions guaranteeing perfection forever. In Smith's argument, even if every individual with access to capital were to achieve the most advantageous output for himself (few 'herselfs' existed then), adding them up only means that society achieves the total of these individually most advantageous outcomes. It does not mean that society attains the maximum possible output because the previous summation will typically be accompanied by varying levels of unemployment due to insufficient capital to employ all who want to work. It is superficial to think that 'most advantageous' here must mean 'absolute maximum', rather than the highest advantage given non-universal access to capital and successes and failures in enterprise.[20]

Third, institutions play a crucial role in both the *GT* and *WN*, even if overlooked by many writers. Various commentators have indicated the key role of institutions in Keynes's work,[21] while for Smith the institutions underpinning his system of liberty are crucial preconditions for output expansion motivated by self-interest.[22]

The twinkle in the eye

Reading Karl's work can sometimes be heavy going. It is, however, happily leavened from time to time by a delightful sense of humour – subtle, ironic, dry or cheeky, as he saw fit. While occasionally present but appropriately muted in his thesis, it runs more freely in his other writings, usually at the end of intensely academic passages. Here are four unpublished and published instances.

> I come now to the question of how theory relates to what [happens] before our eyes. … It is an enormous and difficult issue. But I have tried to find a shorthand way of giving a vague idea of … the relation … between theories and facts. … Still, you might bear in mind the saying: Fools rush in where angels fear to tread. Except that this particular fool hardly ever rushes … (Mittermaier 1989, 3)

> And even if … we eventually have to give up the process of heuristic reading because of conflicting inferences, we are still left with an ontological inference of a tendency, namely, that the person in question is an idiot. (Mittermaier 1994, 16)

> We have to learn to differentiate between the non–existent and the existent. … If a … pure fiction were immediately presumed to be, and accepted as, some kind of description or model, it would surely make economics even more like economics. (Mittermaier 1994, 22)

> [In relation to] Schumpeter's *perennial gale of creative destruction*, … if an intrepid entrepreneur should launch a creative-destructive attempt on a monopoly owned by the Mafia in Sicily or New York, the perennial gale, one should think, would soon be turned into a deadly calm. (Mittermaier 2000, 243, original emphasis)

Conclusion

Karl's thesis contains much else of importance, including relations between the general and particular, the relevance of the realism–nominalism debate to economic theorizing, and his examination of (general) equilibrium theory. But his examination of the cluster of issues concerning market order and disorder, within which Smith's theorizing has special significance, will, I suggest, be its most important contribution. Like all reflective economists, Karl was aware that, without deeper examination, phrases such as the invisible hand, natural liberty and spontaneous order were misleading slogans. He also knew that an economic system reliant on self-interest alone falls far short of what we want because it possesses serious design flaws that require correction by institutional means. Whether in agreement or disagreement with his arguments, readers will, I hope, come away admiring his search for deeper, non-superficial understandings, his analytic and exegetical powers, and his ability to open up original and illuminating perspectives.

One wonders whether Karl's case was that of a highly intelligent academic who, ahead of his time and seeking to explore, probe and assess foundational matters typically assumed to be beyond serious question, did not receive sufficient intellectual encouragement for his endeavours, or could not be given sufficient support for whatever reason.[23] His depth and originality may not have been fully recognized at the time so that his career suffered due to his pursuit of a fearlessly forensic research programme.[24]

Let us be delighted, however, that the project of making his unpublished writings accessible to wider audiences has begun. His penetrating mind sought greater clarity in theory and methodology, understood that philosophy and not mathematics was the close companion of economics, courageously probed and challenged received views, pursued better ways of doing economics, and wrote with a rare sense of humour. Whether one agrees or disagrees in part or in full, one is always stimulated to think more deeply about the topics under investigation.

Although I never knew this profound, original, stimulating and charming scholar, I certainly wish I had.

Appendix: Smith's more complete syllogism

Definitions
1. The national product is the sum of all individual products.
2. A system of natural liberty is one in which (a) every person is free to pursue his/her own interests provided he/she obeys the laws of justice, and (b) the government (i) protects the society from violence and invasion by other societies, (ii) provides a judicial system protecting every individual from injustice and oppression by other individuals in the same society, (iii) provides public works and institutions not profitable for individuals to undertake (including the facilitation of commerce, the delivery of widespread education and the requirements of government), and (iv) raises revenue using a well-designed taxation system.

Premises
1. It is in the social/national interest to increase the national product.
2. In a system of natural liberty, all individuals can, and do, pursue their self-interest to make their individual products as large as possible with whatever capital they have at their disposal.

Conclusion
It is in the social/national interest to replace the current system (say, mercantilism) with a system of natural liberty.

Note two key points:

(i) The syllogism specifies *three* necessary components – the contents of the individual and public interests, and the conditions required for their simultaneous achievement. These items are defined, and not left open for other non-*WN* meanings to be deployed.

(ii) The previous relevance/necessity test shows that the adjective natural can be dispensed with. A better wording throughout would replace 'a system of natural liberty' with 'a system of institution-based liberty' or 'a system of regulated liberty', the meaning of which is given by the above *WN*-based definition.

Notes
[1] It is a revised, expanded version of my paper to the March 2019 Mittermaier Symposium in Johannesburg. My thanks to Chris Torr and an anonymous referee for helpful comments.
[2] See Mittermaier (1978).
[3] Isabella Mittermaier and Michael Stettler are cataloguing all his writings at the time of writing.
[4] See Mittermaier (1986).
[5] Similar internal debates occur in Neoclassicism in different forms. Note the absence of Keynes, whose different views on market order are discussed below.
[6] For a summary of several providential interpretations, and a defence of a particular one, see Oslington (2012).
[7] Much earlier, Viner (1927, 227) emphasized the same point. Such claims on this particular issue are consistent with Smith's broad remark elsewhere that his various works form parts of an overall plan.
[8] In *WN* and this essay, product is measured in value, not physical, terms.
[9] Missing from this outline is the meaning Smith gave to his 'system of natural liberty'. This concept is explained below, and then added to his syllogism in the Appendix, which provides a more complete and instructive formulation.
[10] See De Guenin (2016, especially 113–38, 473–85). Production and predation both have wide scopes, many forms, and inter-connectivity.
[11] Many remarks in *WN* attest to this.
[12] Viner (1972) is not inconsistent with the argument.

[13] The account in Karl's thesis, and my syllogistic representation thereof, align strongly with Samuels (2011, ch 10) and Samuels and Medema (2005), works that only came to my attention very late.

[14] Mittermaier (1994) revisits the discussion of Smith and relates it to ontological matters.

[15] See also Evensky (2015, 266). This scholarly work is insightful, but sometimes inconsistent in seeking to find something useful in opposing views.

[16] See Hayek (1973, ch 2).

[17] Shackle was heavily influenced by Austrian economics, this making his contributions less than accurate guides to Keynes's mature thought.

[18] Ludwig Lachmann, a student and follower of Hayek and a friend and correspondent of Shackle, was at the University of Witwatersrand as Economics Professor from 1949 to his retirement in 1972, after which he remained associated with it until his death in 1990. Although certainly concerned with methodological matters, much of his energy was devoted to revitalizing and disseminating Austrian theory, and criticizing Neoclassicism and Keynesianism.

[19] In the short period in his earlier works, but in the long and short periods in his final work.

[20] A useful investigation here would be whether most or all statements in *WN* are consistent with this line of thought.

[21] For two contributions to recent debate, see O'Donnell (2019a, 2019b).

[22] Other significant overlaps exist between Smith and Keynes.

[23] Karl was effectively self-supervised in writing his doctoral thesis, no official supervisor being appointed until after its completion.

[24] This comment does not relate to everyone. Chris Torr fully appreciated Karl's abilities and acknowledged the 'impressive research' of his PhD thesis (Torr 1988, 118); Jochen Runde strongly encouraged Karl to publish his reflections and was instrumental in the posthumous appearance of Mittermaier (2018); and Michael Stettler, his student and later colleague, also assisted with his last publication and is now closely involved in the recovery and cataloguing of all Karl's unpublished writings.

References

Bastiat, F. (1846–50) *Sophismes économiques*. English translation in De Guenin, J. (2016).

Campbell, R.H, Skinner, A.S. and Todd, W.B. (eds) (1976) *An Inquiry into the Nature and Causes of the Wealth of Nations*, 2 vols. Oxford: Oxford University Press.

De Guenin, J. (ed) (2016) *The Collected Works of Frederic Bastiat*. Carmel, Indiana: Liberty Fund.

Evensky, J. (2015) *Adam Smith's Wealth of Nations, A Reader's Guide*. Cambridge: Cambridge University Press.

Hayek, F.A. (1973) *Law, Legislation and Liberty*, vol 1. London: Routledge and Kegan Paul.

Mittermaier, K. (1978) 'On the Meaning of "Inflationary": Comment'. *South African Journal of Economics* 46:1 (March) 67–71.

————. (1982) 'Book review of Boland L.A, *The Foundations of Economic Method*, Allen and Unwin'. *South African Journal of Economics* 50:4, 386–93.

————. (1986) 'Mechanomorphism' in *Subjectivism, Intelligibility and Economic Understanding*, ch 17. Edited by I.M. Kirzner. New York: New York University Press.

————. (1989) 'Philosophy and Economics', unpublished manuscript.

————. (1994) 'The Invisible Hand and Some Thoughts on the Non-existent in What we Study'. Invited paper to the Second International Workshop on Methodology of Economics, Selwyn College, Cambridge.

————. (2000) 'On the Delicate Nature of Markets'. *South African Journal of Economics* 68:3, 538–60.

————. (2018) 'Menger's Aristotelianism'. *Cambridge Journal of Economics* 42:2, 577–94.

O'Donnell, R. (2019a) 'General Theorising and Historical Specificity: Hodgson on Keynes'. *Journal of Institutional Economics* 15:4 (August) 741–7.

————. (2019b) 'On the Logical Properties of Keynes's Theorising and Different Approaches to the Keynes–Institutionalism Nexus'. *Journal of Institutional Economics* 15:4 (August) 715–31.

Oslington, P. (2012) 'God and the Market: Adam Smith's Invisible Hand'. *Journal of Business Ethics* 108:4, 429–38.

Samuels, W. (2011) *Erasing the Invisible Hand, Essays on an Elusive and Misused Concept in Economics*. Cambridge: Cambridge University Press.

Samuels, W. and Medema, S. (2005) 'Freeing Smith from the "Free Market": On the Misperception of Adam Smith on the Economic Role of Government'. *History of Political Economy* 37:2, 219–26.

Skinner, A.S. (1991) 'Adam Smith' in *The New Palgrave, A Dictionary of Economics of Economics*. Edited by J. Eatwell, M. Milgate and P. Newman. London: Macmillan.

Smith, A. (1776) *An Inquiry into the Nature and Causes of the Wealth of Nations* in Campbell et al (1976).

Stigler, G.J. (1975) 'Smith's Travels on the Ship of State' in *Essays on Adam Smith*. Edited by S. Skinner and T. Wilson. Oxford: Oxford University Press.

Torr, C. (1988) *Equilibrium, Expectations and Information*. Cambridge: Polity Press.

Viner, J. (1927) 'Adam Smith and Laissez Faire'. *Journal of Political Economy* 2 (April) 198–232.

————. (1972) *The Role of Providence in the Social Order*. Princeton: Princeton University Press.

Index